HISTORY AND RELATED DISCIPLINES
SELECT BIBLIOGRAPHIES
GENERAL EDITOR: R. C. RICHARDSON

THE STUDY OF HISTORY

MANCHESTER
UNIVERSITY PRESS

HISTORY AND RELATED DISCIPLINES
SELECT BIBLIOGRAPHIES
GENERAL EDITOR: R. C. RICHARDSON

Bibliographical guides designed to meet the needs of under-graduates, postgraduates and their teachers in universities and colleges of higher education. All volumes in the series share a number of common characteristics. They are selective, manageable in size, and include those books and articles which are most important and useful. All volumes are edited by practising teachers of the subject and are based on their experiences of the needs of students. The arrangement combines chronological with thematic divisions. Most of the items listed receive some descriptive comment.

Published volumes:

ANCIENT GREECE AND ROME

AFRICA, ASIA AND SOUTH AMERICA SINCE 1800

BRITISH AND IRISH ARCHAEOLOGY

BRITISH ECONOMIC AND SOCIAL HISTORY

EUROPEAN ECONOMIC AND SOCIAL HISTORY 1450–1789

JAPANESE STUDIES

RUSSIA AND EASTERN EUROPE 1789–1985

UNITED STATES HISTORY

WESTERN POLITICAL THOUGHT

WOMEN'S HISTORY IN BRITAIN

THE STUDY OF HISTORY
A BIBLIOGRAPHICAL GUIDE

SECOND EDITION

COMPILED BY
R. C. RICHARDSON
Head of Research and the Graduate Centre
King Alfred's College, Winchester

MANCHESTER UNIVERSITY PRESS
Manchester and New York

Distributed Exclusively in the USA by St. Martin's Press

First edition published 1988 by Manchester University Press

This edition published 2000 by
Manchester University Press
Oxford Road, Manchester M13 9NR, UK
and Room 400, 175 Fifth Avenue, New York, NY 10010, USA
http://www.man.ac.uk/mup

Distributed exclusively in the USA by
St. Martin's Press, Inc., 175 Fifth Avenue, New York,
NY 10010, USA

Distributed exclusively in Canada by
UBC Press, University of British Columbia, 2029 West Mall,
Vancouver, BC, Canada V6T 1Z2

British Library Cataloguing-in-Publication Data
A catalogue record for this book is available from the British Library

Library of Congress Cataloging-in-Publication Data applied for

ISBN 0 7190 5899 6 *hardback*

This edition first published 2000

09 08 07 06 05 04 03 02 01 00   10 9 8 7 6 5 4 3 2 1

Typeset in 9.5 on 10 Plantin
by Best-set Typesetter Ltd., Hong Kong
Printed in Great Britain
by Bookcraft (Bath) Ltd, Midsomer Norton

CONTENTS

General editor's preface—ix
Preface—xi
Abbreviations—xiii

GENERAL EDITOR'S PREFACE

History, to an even greater extent than most other academic disciplines, has developed at prodigious pace in the twentieth century. Its scope has extended and diversified, its methodologies have been revolutionized, its philosophy has changed, and its relations with other disciplines have been transformed. The number of students and teachers of the subject in the different branches of higher education has vastly increased, and there is an ever-growing army of amateurs, many of them taking adult education courses. Academic and commercial publishers have produced a swelling stream of publications – both specialist and general – to cater for this large and expanding audience. Scholarly journals have proliferated. It is no easy matter even for the specialist to keep abreast of the flow of publications in his particular field. For those with more general academic interests the task of finding what has been written on different subject areas can be time-consuming, perplexing, and often frustrating.

It is primarily to meet the needs of undergraduates, postgraduates and their teachers in universities and colleges of higher education, that this series of bibliographies is designed. It will be a no less valuable resource, however, to the reference collection of any public library, school or college.

Though common sense demands that each volume will be structured in the way which is most appropriate for the particular field in question, nonetheless all volumes in the series share a number of important common characteristics. First – quite deliberately – all are *select* bibliographies, manageable in size, and include those books and articles which in the editor's judgement are most important and useful. To attempt an uncritically comprehensive listing would needlessly dictate the inclusion of items which were frankly ephemeral, antiquarian, or discredited and result only in the production of a bulky and unwieldy volume. Like any select bibliography, however, this series will direct the reader where appropriate to other, more specialised and detailed sources of bibliographical information. That would be one of its functions. Second, all the volumes are edited not simply by specialists in the different fields but by practising teachers of the subject, and are based on their experience of the needs of students in higher education. Third, there are common features of arrangement and presentation. All volumes begin with listings of general works of a methodological or historiographical nature, and proceed within broad chronological divisions to arrange their material thematically. Most items will receive some descriptive comment. Each volume, for ease of reference, has an index of authors and editors.

R. C. RICHARDSON

PREFACE

The professionalisation of history since the nineteenth century has necessarily involved a growing interest in historiography, philosophy of history and historical method. All engaged in the discipline of history would now recognise that as a subject history is an intellectual as well as a practical activity and that it has a past of its own that is worth exploring. Accordingly it is now commonplace to find that in degree courses in the subject explicit attention is given to the theory and methodology of history. The Open University makes much of these aspects and there are now a number of taught master's courses in which the study of historiography figures prominently. Historiography has also found a place for itself in A Level syllabuses in schools and colleges.

A large body of literature on historiography and philosophy of history has come into being. Within the last two years three enormous reference books on the subject have appeared (see pp. 1–2). In 1998 Manchester University Press launched Issues in Historiography, a major new series of case studies whose subjects stretch from the Norman Conquest to the Holocaust. There are now a number of specialist periodicals devoted to these facets of history – *History and Theory*, the *Journal of the History of Ideas* and the invaluable *Storia della Storiografia*.

The first edition of this book in 1988 was a response to the perception that a compact, easily accessible bibliographical guide to historiography was needed. In the intervening years the need has increased rather than diminished. As a subject history never stands still but is always changing its philosophies, its contours, its leading questions, its politics, its subdivisions, its conceptual apparatus and its methodologies. 'All flesh is grass,' said R. H. Tawney, 'but historians, poor things, wither more quickly than most.' The cast list of the subject's practitioners can change significantly even in a short space of time. Since the first edition of this book appeared famous figures like G. R. Elton, J. R. Hale, J. H. Hexter, J. P. Kenyon, A. D. Momigliano, Lawrence Stone, and E. P. Thompson have all died. New men and women are taking the subject in other directions. The first edition contained 2,100 items. This second edition contains well over 3,000. Enlarged or new sections on social history, gender studies, the historian and film, and more generally on history's changing relations with other academic disciplines and on the impact of theory, are symptomatic of the changing dimensions of historical studies at the end of the twentieth century.

The book retains the broad structure of the first edition. It begins with a much lengthened general section and then proceeds chronologically from studies of the ancient world up to histories of our own recent past. The chronological structure embraces both past historians and the historiography of past events and processes in each time band. Thus, for example, in the section on the eighteenth century will be found listings dealing with individual writers like Gibbon and Voltaire and with the historiography of the Enlightenment and the French Revolution, two of the greatest upheavals of the age. The book deals predominantly with Western historiography and there is more on historical writing in Britain than in any other country. But the volume is not designed to be a celebration of national insularity; substantial listings of material dealing with the historiography of other European countries, with the United States, and with the wider world testify to broader parameters. The conceptualisation and practice of history in all kinds of ways transcend national boundaries.

The principles underlying the book are clear. The volume is selective and makes no pretence to be comprehensive. Most of the items included are in English. Most of them have been published in the last fifty years. Most books included in the selection receive some descriptive comment. Attention is drawn to items containing helpful bibliographies of their own. Places of publication are given where these were outside the British Isles. Each of the nine sections into which the book is divided is consecutively numbered. An index of authors, editors and compilers is provided.

Many friends and colleagues have helped me in preparing the book; for a few months Joseph Pirillo acted as my part-time research assistant. The dedication affectionately recalls an old friend and collaborator and walking bibliography in his own right.

R. C. R.

ABBREVIATIONS

A.H.R. *American Historical Review*
Am. J. Ec. and Sociol. *American Journal of Economics and Sociology*
Am. J. Legal Hist. *American Journal of Legal History*
Am. Q. *American Quarterly*
Arch. J. *Archaeological Journal*
Aust. Ec. H.R. *Australian Economic History Review*
Aust. J. Pol. and Hist. *Australian Journal of Politics and History*
B.I.H.R. *Bulletin of the Institute of Historical Research*
Brit. J. Sociol. *British Journal of Sociology*
Bull. Bd. Celt. Studs. *Bulletin of the Board of Celtic Studies*
Bull. Brit. Ass. Am. Studs. *Bulletin of the British Association of American Studies*
Bull. J. Ryl. Lib. *Bulletin of the John Rylands Library*
Bus. H.R. *Business History Review*
Cal. Hist. Soc. Q. *California Historical Society Quarterly*
Camb. H.J. *Cambridge Historical Journal*
Cath. H.R. *Catholic Historical Review*
Cen. European Hist. *Central European History*
Comp. Studs. Soc. and Hist. *Comparative Studies in Society and History*
Durham U.J. *Durham University Journal*
Ec.H.R. *Economic History Review*
Econ. and Soc. *Economy and Society*
E. European Q. *East European Quarterly*
E.H.R. *English Historical Review*
Eng. Studs. *English Studies*
Ex. Entrep. Hist. *Explorations in Entrepreneurial History*
Hisp. Am. Hist. *Hispanic American History*

Hist. *History*
Hist. J. *Historical Journal*
Hist. Methods *Historical Methods*
Hist. Pol. Econ. *History of Political Economy*
Hist. Studs. *Historical Studies*
Hist. Studs. Aust. and N.Z. *Historical Studies, Australia and New Zealand*
Hist. Today *History Today*
Hist. Workshop J. *History Workshop Journal*
Internat. Soc. Sci. J. *International Social Science Journal*
J.A.H. *Journal of American History*
J. African Hist. *Journal of African History*
J. Am. Studs. *Journal of American Studies*
J. Asian Studs. *Journal of Asian Studies*
J. Brit. Studs. *Journal of British Studies*
J. Contemp. Hist. *Journal of Contemporary History*
J. Ecc. Hist. *Journal of Ecclesiastical History*
J. Ec. Hist. *Journal of Economic History*
J. Ec. Lit. *Journal of Economic Literature*
J. Europ. Ec. H. *Journal of European Economic History*
J. Hist. Geog. *Journal of Historical Geography*
J. Hist. Ideas *Journal of the History of Ideas*
J. Hist. Philos. *Journal of the History of Philosophy*
J. Hist. Studs. *Journal of Historical Studies*
J. Imp. and Comm. Hist. *Journal of Imperial and Commonwealth History*
J. Interdis. Hist. *Journal of Interdisciplinary History*
J. Legal Hist. *Journal of Legal History*
J.M.H. *Journal of Modern History*
J. Med. and Renaiss. Studs. *Journal of Medieval and Renaissance Studies*
J. Negro Hist. *Journal of Negro History*

J. Philos. *Journal of Philosophy*
J. Pol. *Journal of Politics*
J. Rel. Hist. *Journal of Religious History*
J. Soc. Archivists *Journal of the Society of Archivists*
J. Soc. Hist. *Journal of Social History*
J. Southern Hist. *Journal of Southern History*
J. World Hist. *Journal of World History*
Lit. and Hist. *Literature and History*
London J. *London Journal*
Med. and Hum. *Medievalia and Humanistica*
Med. Studs. *Medieval Studies*
Nat. Lib. Wales J. *National Library of Wales Journal*
New England Q. *New England Quarterly*
New Left R. *New Left Review*
N.Z. J. Hist. *New Zealand Journal of History*
Nottingham Med. Studs. *Nottingham Medieval Studies*
Pacific H.R. *Pacific Historical Review*
Parl. Hist. *Parliamentary History*
P.P. *Past and Present*
Philos. *Philosophy*
Philos. Q. *Philosophical Quarterly*
Philos. Soc. Sci. *Philosophy of Social Science*
Pol. Sci. Q. *Political Science Quarterly*
Proc. Am. Phil. Soc. *Proceedings of the American Philosophical Society*
Proc. Brit. Acad. *Proceedings of the British Academy*

Pub. Mod. Lang. Ass. America *Publications of the Modern Language Association of America*
Renaissance Q. *Renaissance Quarterly*
Rev. Hist. *Revue Historique*
Scand. J. Hist. *Scandinavian Journal of History*
Science and Soc. *Science and Society*
Scot. H.R. *Scottish Historical Review*
Slav. R. *Slavonic Review*
Soc. Hist. *Social History*
Soc. Research *Social Research*
Soc. Sci. *Social Science*
Sociological R. *Sociological Review*
Sov. Studs. *Soviet Studs.*
S. Atlantic Q. *South Atlantic Quarterly*
Storia de Storiog. *Storia della Storiografia*
Studs. Higher Ed. *Studies in Higher Education*
Studs. Renaiss. *Studies in the Renaissance*
Theol. Studs. *Theological Studies*
T.R.H.S. *Transactions of the Royal Historical Society*
Tran. I.B.G. *Transactions of the Institute of British Geographers*
U. Birm. J. *University of Birmingham Journal*
Urb. Hist. Year. *Urban History Yearbook*
Vict. Studs. *Victorian Studies*
Welsh H.R. *Welsh History Review*
Wm and Mary Q. *William and Mary Quarterly*

1

GENERAL WORKS

BIBLIOGRAPHIES AND REFERENCE WORKS

1.1 **Bentley**, M. (ed.), *Companion to Historiography*, 1997. Thirty-nine chapters divided into five main sections offering an eclectic treatment of the development of historical consciousness and writing from ancient times to the late twentieth century. Broad period coverage and international scope are combined with case studies of particular themes and contentious issues. Separate chapters are included on history's interface with philosophy, anthropology and archaeology. Art history receives extended treatment. The *Annales* experiment, Marxist historiography and women's history each have chapters devoted to them. Good bibliographies.

1.2 **Berghahn**, V. and **Schissler**, Hanna (eds), *Perceptions of History. International Textbook Research on Britain, Germany, and the United States*, 1987. A general introduction assesses the importance of school textbooks and their mediation of the past. Individual chapters follow on depictions of phases of British, German and American history.

1.3 **Birkos**, A. S. and **Tambs**, L. A. (comps.), *Historiography, Method and History Teaching. A Bibliography of Books and Articles in English, 1965–73*, Hamden, CT, 1975.

1.4 **Bowman**, F. J., *A Handbook of Historians and History Writing*, Dubuque, IA, 1951.

1.5 **Boyd**, K. (ed.), *Encyclopaedia of Historians and Historical Writing*, 2 vols, 1999. Extensive 1,500 page multi-authored compendium of biographies, period surveys and articles on trends, philosophical movements and methodologies. Coverage is most extensive on Europe and North America, but China, Japan, South East Asia, Australia, Africa and the Middle East are given space. Useful brief bibliographies are appended to all articles. See also Woolf (1.22).

1.6 **Burston**, W. H. and **Thompson**, D. (eds), *Studies in the Nature and Teaching of History*, 1967.

1.7 **Cannon**, J. (ed.), *The Blackwell Dictionary of Historians*, 1988. Provides biographies of about 500 historians. Bibliography.

1.8 **Cook**, C., *Dictionary of Historical Terms*, 1983.

1.9 **Day**, A. E., *History. A Reference Handbook*, 1977. 787 items which blend biographical and bibliographical information. Concentrates chiefly on British political and imperial history.

1.10 **Donaldson**, G. and **Morpeth**, R. S. (eds), *Who's Who in Scottish History*, 1973.

1.11 **Elton**, G. R., *Modern Historians on British History, 1485–1945. A Critical Bibliography, 1945–69*, 1970. Deals with

1

1,350 items. Though principally orientated towards content and period section 11 (pp. 176–97) is devoted to history of ideas.

1.12 **Frey**, Linda, **Frey**, Marsha, and **Schneider**, Joanne (comps), *Women in Western European History. A Select Chronological, Geographical and Topical Bibliography from Antiquity to the French Revolution*, 1982.

1.13 **Iggers**, G. C. and **Parker**, H. T. (eds), *International Handbook of Historical Studies. Contemporary Research and Theory*, 1980. Part One explores methodological reorientations (demographic history, social history, psychohistory, historiography and linguistics). Part Two looks at the historiography of individual countries and regions.

1.14 *International Bibliography of the Historical Sciences*, I, 1926–date. Each annual volume includes sections on historiography and philosophy of history.

1.15 **Kinnell**, Susan K. (ed.), *Historiography. An Annotated Bibliography of Journal Articles, Books and Dissertations*, Santa Barbara, CA, 1987.

1.16 **Marius**, R., *A Short Guide to Writing about History*, 2nd ed., New York, 1995.

1.17 **Norton**, Mary B. and **Gerardi**, Pamela (eds), *The American Historical Association's Guide to Historical Literature*, 3rd ed., 2 vols, New York, 1995.

1.18 **Rodger**, R., (ed.), *A Consolidated Bibliography of Urban History*, 1996. A massive – but unannotated – compilation.

1.19 **Storey**, W. K., *Writing History. A Guide for Students*, New York, 1996. A down-to-earth, concise manual.

1.20 **Tobey**, J. L., *The History of Ideas. A Bibliographical Introduction*, 2 vols, Santa Barbara, CA, 1975–77.

1.21 **Watson**, C. A., *The Writing of History in Britain. A Bibliography*, New York, 1982. Deals with post-1945 writings.

1.22 **Woolf**, D. R. (ed.), *A Global Encyclopaedia of Historical Writing*, New York, 1998. Similar in scope to Boyd (1.5) but two-thirds its length. Generally the articles on individuals, topics, periods, concepts and themes

are shorter. Brief guides to sources and further reading are provided in each case.

PHILOSOPHY OF HISTORY

1.23 **Althusser**, L., *Politics and History. Montesquieu, Rousseau, Hegel and Marx*, 1977. See also Gordy (1.124) and Thompson (1.264).

1.24 **Anchor**, R., 'Realism and ideology', *Hist. and Theory, XXII*, 1983, 107–19.

1.25 **Ankersmit**, F. R., 'Historical representation', *Hist. and Theory, XXVII*, 1988, 205–28.

1.26 ——'On historiographical progress', *Storia de Storiog., XXII*, 1992, 103–8.

1.27 ——*History and Tropology. The Rise and Fall of Metaphor*, Berkeley, CA, 1994.

1.28 ——*The Reality Effect in the Writing of History*, Amsterdam, 1989.

1.29 ——and **Kellner**, H., *A New Philosophy of History*, Chicago, IL, 1995.

1.30 **Aron**, R, *Introduction to the Philosophy of History*, 1961. Divided into sections dealing with 'The past and the concepts of history', 'Human development and historical understanding', 'Historical determinism and causal thought' and 'History and truth'.

1.31 ——*History, Truth, Liberty. Selected Writings*, Chicago, IL, 1986.

1.32 **Atkinson**, R. F., *Knowledge and Explanation in History. An Introduction to the Philosophy of History*, 1978. Has sections on 'Knowledge of the past', 'Objectivity', 'Explanation', 'Causation' and 'Values'.

1.33 **Baillie**, J., *The Belief in Progress*, 1950. Originally given as a series of lectures in theology.

1.34 **Bann**, S., 'Towards a critical historiography; recent work in philosophy of history', *Philos., LVI*, 1981, 365–85.

1.35 **Barker**, P., *Michael Foucault. Subversions of the Subject*, 1993. See also Goldstein (1.118).

1.36 **Beards**, A., 'Reversing historical skepticism; Bernard Longeran on the writing of history', *Hist. and Theory*, XXXIII, 1994, 198–219.

1.37 **Bellah**, R. N., 'Durkheim and history' in R. A. Nisbet (ed.), *Emile Durkheim*, Englewood Cliffs, NJ, 1965, 153–76.

1.38 **Berdyaev**, N., *The Meaning of History*, 1936. Eschatology rather than progress figures prominently.

1.39 **Berlin**, I., *The Hedgehog and the Fox. An Essay on Tolstoy's View of History*, 1953.

1.40 ——'History and theory; the concept of scientific history', *Hist. and Theory*, I, 1960, 1–31.

1.41 ——*Four Essays on Liberty*, 1969. Includes Berlin's well known discussion of historical inevitability.

1.42 ——*Historical Inevitability*, 1954. A compact but wide-ranging exploration of the inevitability concept and its advocates.

1.43 **Bradley**, F. H., *The Presuppositions of Critical History* 1877.

1.44 **Brandon**, S. G. F., *History, Time and Deity. A Historical and Comparative Study of the Conception of Time in Religious Thought and Practice*, 1965.

1.45 **Brown**, D., *Hierarchy, History and Human Nature. The Social Origins of Historical Consciousness*, Tucson, AZ, 1988.

1.46 **Burns**, T. (ed.), *After History? Francis Fukuyama and his Critics*, Lanham, MD, 1994.

1.47 **Butterfield**, H., *Christianity and History*, 1949. Originally given as lectures. The topics include 'Providence and the historical process', 'Christianity as an historical religion', 'History, religion and the present day'.

1.48 **Cairns**, Grace E., *Philosophies of History. Meeting of East and West in Cycle Pattern Theories of History*, 1962. Deals with recurrent cosmic cycles, one-grand-scale patterns and culture cycles. Bibliography.

1.49 **Calincos**, A., *Theories and Narratives. Reflections on the Philosophy of History*, Durham, NC, 1995.

1.50 **Carr**, D. *et al.* (eds), *Philosophy of History and Contemporary Historiography*, Ottawa, 1982.

1.51 **Carr**, E. H., *What is History?*, 1961, 2nd ed. 1986, with supplementary material ed. R. W. Davies. Bold in its time and still provocative in the issues it

raises about the nature of history. See Jenkins (9.62).

1.52 **Case**, Shirley, J., *The Christian Philosophy of History*, Chicago, IL, 1943.

1.53 **Casement**, W., 'Husserl and the philosophy of history', *Hist. and Theory*, XXVII, 1988, 229–40.

1.54 **Casserley**, J. V. L., *Toward a Theology of History*, 1965. Originally a series of lectures. Has chapters on 'The concept of revelation', 'The Bible and the historians', 'The epistemology of history' and 'The ontology of history'.

1.55 **Collingwood**, R. G., *The Idea of History*, 1946. A classic by a unique figure in twentieth-century historiography.

R. G. Collingwood

1.56 **Bates**, D., 'Rediscovering Collingwood's spiritual history (in and out of context)', *Hist. and Theory*, XXXV, 1996, 29–55.

1.57 **Cebik**, L. B., 'Collingwood; action, re-enactment and evidence', *Philos. Forum*, II, 1970, 68–90.

1.58 **Donagan**, A. H., *The Later Philosophy of R. G. Collingwood*, 1962. Chapters 8 and 9 (pp. 173–250) deal with scientific history and the philosophy of history.

1.59 **Dray**, W. H., *History as Re-enactment. R. G. Collingwood's Idea of History*, 1995.

1.60 **Goldstein**, L. J., 'Collingwood's theory of historical knowing', *Hist. and Theory*, IX, 1970, 3–36.

1.61 **Harris**, E. E., 'Collingwood's theory of history', *Philos. Q.*, VII, 1957, 35–49.

1.62 **Kanachi**, C., *R. G. Collingwood's Philosophy of History*, Alwaye, India, 1981.

1.63 **Krausz**, M. (ed.), *Critical Essays on the Philosophy of R. G. Collingwood*, 1972. A collection including essays on 'Collingwood and philosophical method', 'Collingwood's historicism' and 'Collingwood and the constitution of the historical past'. Bibliography of Collingwood's writings, 327–48.

1.64 **Martin**, R., *Historical Explanation. Re-enactment and Practical Inference*, 1977. Defends Collingwood's concept of re-enactment of past thought from the objections commonly made against it. The book proceeds to appraise the more recent work of Gardiner, Dray,

Danto, Walsh and others, offering in the process 'a philosophical history of contemporary philosophy of history'.

1.65 **Mink**, L. O., 'Collingwood's dialectic of history', *Hist. and Theory*, VII, 1968, 3–37.

1.66 **Patrick**, J., 'Is "The theory of history" Collingwood's first essay on the philosophy of history?', *Hist. and Theory*, XXIX, 1990, 1-13.

1.67 **Rubinoff**, L., 'Collingwood's theory of the relation between philosophy and history; a new interpretation', *J. Hist. Philos.*, VI, 1968, 363–80.

1.68 **Saari**, H., *Re-enactment. A Study in R. G. Collingwood's Philosophy of History*, Abo, Finland, 1984.

1.69 **Skagestad**, P., *Making Sense of History. The Philosophies of Popper and Collingwood*, Oslo, 1975. Focuses on the two leading rationalists and finds Collingwood the more convincing and consistent.

1.70 **Taylor**, D. S., 'A bibliography of the publications and manuscripts of R. G. Collingwood', *Hist. and Theory*, supplement 24, 1985, 1–89.

1.71 **Tomlin**, E. W. F., *R. G. Collingwood*, 1953, 2nd ed. 1961. One of the Writers and their Work pamphlet series.

1.72 **van der Dussen**, W. J., 'Collingwood's "lost" manuscript of *The Principles of History*', *Hist. and Theory*, XXXVI, 1997, 32–62.

1.73 —— *History as a Science. The Philosophy of R. G. Collingwood*, The Hague, 1981.

1.74 **White**, D. A., 'Imagination and description; Collingwood and the historical consciousness', *Clio*, I, 1972, 14–28.

1.75 **Colquhoun**, R., *Raymond Aron*, I: *The Philosopher in History, 1905–55*; II: *The Sociologist in Society, 1955–83*, 1986.

1.76 **Conkin**, P., 'Causation revisited', *Hist. and Theory*, XIII, 1974, 1–20.

1.77 **Croce**, B., *History as the Story of Liberty*, 1941. Has major sections on the nature of history, on historicism and its history, on historiography and politics, historiography and morals, and on the prospects for historiography.

1.78 —— *Theory and History of Historiography*, 1921. A classic by one of the great twentieth-century liberal historians.

Benedetto Croce

1.79 **Caponigri**, A. R., *History and Liberty. The Historical Writings of Benedetto Croce*, 1955.

1.80 **Carr**, H. W., *The Philosophy of Benedetto Croce. The Problem of Art and History*, 1917. Chapter 1, 'Philosophy of mind', strikes the keynote; chapter 11 deals explicitly with the concept of history.

1.81 **Pois**, R. A., 'Two poles within historicism: Croce and Meinecke', *J. Hist. Ideas*, XXXI, 1970, 253–72.

1.82 **Roberts**, D. D., *Benedetto Croce and the Uses of Historicism*, Berkeley, CA, 1987. Argues that Croce's historicism was innovative, open-ended and radical in its humanism. Extensive bibliography, 413–40.

1.83 **White**, H. V., 'The abiding relevance of Croce's idea of history', *J.M.H.*, XXXV, 1963, 109–24.

1.84 **Cullman**, O., *Christ and Time. The Primitive Christian Conception of Time and History*, Philadelphia, PA, 1950.

1.85 **Danto**, A. C., *Analytical Philosophy of History*, 1965. Deals with chronicle and narrative, relativism and explanation.

1.86 —— 'On historical questioning', *J. Philos.*, LI, 1954, 89–99.

1.87 **D'Arcy**, M. C., *The Meaning and Matter of History. A Christian View*, New York, 1959. Considers the ways in which Christianity assists a deeper understanding of history.

1.88 **Devries**, W. A., 'Meaning and interpretation in history', *Hist. and Theory*, XXII, 1983, 253–63.

1.89 **Dietl**, P. J., 'Deduction and historical explanation', *Hist. and Theory*, VII, 1968, 167–88.

1.90 **Donagan**, A., 'The verification of historical theses', *Philos, Q.*, VI, 1956, 193–209.

1.91 —— and Barbara (eds), *Philosophy of History*, New York, 1965. An anthology which ranges from St Augustine via Descartes, Vico, Hegel and Marx to Collingwood and Dray.

1.92 **Downing**, F. G., 'Philosophy of history and historical research', *Philos.*, XLIV, 1969, 33–45.

1.93 **Dray**, W. H., *Laws and Explanation in History*, 1957. Considers covering law, implicit law, causal laws and causal analysis, the rationale of actions and their bearing on historians' explanations of how and why.

1.94 —— *On History and Philosophers of History*, Leiden and New York, 1989. Reprints ten significant essays. Collingwood and Oakeshott receive individual chapters. The issues surrounding narrative, hypothesis, value judgements and presentism are rehearsed.

1.95 —— *Perspectives on History*, 1980. Case studies of Collingwood, Beard, Watkins, A. J. P. Taylor and Spengler.

1.96 —— *Philosophical Analysis and History*, New York, 1966. A collection of reprinted essays which includes 'The concept of scientific history', 'The objectivity of history', 'The autonomy of historical understanding'. The authors include Isaiah Berlin, J. A. Passmore and L. O. Mink.

1.97 —— *Philosophy of History*, Englewood Cliffs, NJ, 1964. An introductory text in the Foundations of Philosophy series. Includes brief chapters on the nature of historical understanding, on historical objectivity, on causal judgment in history, on metaphysical, empirical and religious approaches.

1.98 **du Toit**, A., 'Legitimate anachronism as a problem for intellectual history and for philosophy', *S. African J. Phil.*, X, 1991, 87–95.

1.99 **English**, J. C., 'Existentialism and the study of history', *Soc. Sci.*, XLI, 1966, 153–60.

1.100 **Esposito**, J. L., *The Transcendance of History*, Athens, OH, 1984.

1.101 **Fain**, H., *Between Philosophy and History. The Resurrection of Speculative Philosophy of History within the Analytic Tradition*, Princeton, NJ, 1970. Bibliography, 319–26.

1.102 **Fay**, B., **Pomper**, P., and **Vann**, R. T. (eds), *History and Theory. Contemporary Readings*, 1998. Nineteen readings chiefly from the journal *History and Theory*, divided into seven sections dealing with narrativity, writing and reading history, realism, constructivism and beyond, postmodernism, representation and trauma, gender, sexuality and objectivity.

1.103 **Fever**, L. S., 'What is philosophy of history?', *J. Philos.*, XLIX, 1952, 329–39.

1.104 **Field**, G. C., 'Some problems in the philosophy of history', *Proc. Brit. Acad.* XXIV, 1938, 55–83.

1.105 **Foster**, M., *Critical Theory and Poststructuralism. In Search of a Context*, Ithaca, NY, 1989.

1.106 **Frye**, N., 'Towards a theory of cultural history', *Toronto Q.*, XXII, 1952, 325–41.

1.107 **Fukuyama**, F., *The End of History and the Last Man*, New York, 1992. Explores the direction of history, emphasising two powerful forces – 'the logic of modern science' and 'the struggle for recognition'.

1.108 —— 'The End of History, five years later', *Hist. and Theory*, XXXIV, 1995, 27–43. See Burns (1.46).

1.109 **Gadamer**, H. G. (ed.), *Truth and Historicity*, The Hague, 1972. Explores the distinction between historical and extra-historical knowing.

1.110 **Gallie**, W. B., *Philosophy and the Historical Understanding*, 1964. Attempts to bridge the unfortunate divide that has come between history and philosophy.

1.111 **Gardiner**, P., *The Nature of Historical Explanation*, 1952. Examines the distinctiveness of the historian's procedures.

1.112 —— (ed.), *The Philosophy of History*, 1974. A collection of essays which includes Collingwood, Dray, Skinner, Walsh and Berlin.

1.113 —— (ed.), *Theories of History*, Glencoe, IL, 1959. An anthology which extends from Vico to the present day. Croce, Berlin, Collingwood and Mandelbaum are among those included.

1.114 **Geyl**, P., *The Use and Abuse of History*, 1955. Briefly outlines the author's own personal philosophy of history. Originally a lecture series.

1.115 **Gillespie**, N. C., 'George Frederick Holmes and the philosophy of history', *S. Atlantic Q.*, LXVII, 1968, 436–98.

1.116 **Gilliam**, Harriet, 'The dialectics of realism and idealism in modern historiographic theory', *Hist. and Theory*, XV, 1976, 231–56.

1.117 **Goldstein**, Doris S., 'J. B. Bury's philosophy of history; a reappraisal', *A.H.R.*, LXXXII, 1977, 896–919.

1.118 **Goldstein**, J. (ed.), *Foucault and the Writing of History*, 1994. See Barker (1.35).

1.119 **Goldstein**, L. J., *Historical Knowing*, Austin, TX, 1976.

1.120 —— '*The Idea of History* as a scale of forms', *Hist. and Theory*, XXIX, 1990, 42–50.

1.121 —— 'Theory in history', *Philos. of Sci.*, XXXIV, 1967, 23–40.

1.122 **Gombrich**, E. H., *In Search of Cultural History*, 1969. Lecture.

1.123 —— *Ideals and Idols. Essays on Values in History and in Art*, 1979. Collects together some of the author's essays, including 'Art history and the social sciences'.

1.124 **Gordy**, M., 'Time and the social whole; reading Althusser', *Hist. and Theory*, XXII, 1983, 1–21.

1.125 **Gorman**, J. L., *The Expression of Historical Knowledge*, 1982. Includes chapters on the principles of knowledge, evidence, scepticism, truth and relevance. Bibliography.

1.126 **Gray**, J., *Isaiah Berlin*, Princeton, NJ, 1996.

1.127 **Gruner**, R., *Philosophies of History. A Critical Essay*, 1985. Discusses ideas of perfectibility, millenarianism, progressivism and historicism.

1.128 —— 'The substantiation of historical statements', *Durham U.J.*, LVIII, 1966, 75–85.

1.129 **Haddock**, B. A., *An Introduction to Historical Thought*, 1980. The sequence is chiefly chronological. Bibliography.

1.130 **Hamilton**, P., *Historicism*, 1996. A compact guide to the rise of historicism and its applications.

1.131 **Harbison**, E. H., *Christianity and History. Essays*, Princeton, NJ, 1964. There is an extremely long essay on 'The Christian understanding of history', 3–146.

1.132 **Hawthorn**, G., *Plausible Worlds. Possibility and Understanding in History and the Social Sciences*, 1991.

1.133 **Heehs**, P., 'Myth, history and theory', *Hist. and Theory*, XXXIII, 1994, 1–19.

1.134 **Helde**, T. T., 'Historians and historical knowledge', *Maryland Hist. Mag.*, XIX, 1964, 243–61.

1.135 **Hempel**, C. G., 'Explanation in science and in history' in Dray (1.96), 95–126.

1.136 **Hobart**, M. E., 'The paradox of historical constructionism', *Hist. and Theory*, XXVIII, 1989, 43–58.

1.137 **Holborn**, H., 'The history of ideas', *A.H.R.*, LXXIII, 1968, 683–95. Looks briefly at changing concepts from Voltaire onwards and assesses the present potential.

1.138 **Holscher**, L., 'The new Annalistic; a sketch of a theory of history', *Hist. and Theory*, XXXVI, 1997, 317–35.

1.139 **Hook**, S. (ed.), *Philosophy and History*, New York, 1963. An invaluable collection. Has sections on 'The logic of historical narration', 'The problems of the working historian', 'Patterns in history'. There are seventeen other essays, including 'History as enquiry' and 'Essentials in history'.

1.140 **Hughes**, H. S., *Oswald Spengler. A Critical Estimate*, New York, 1952. A critique of the author of *The Decline of the West*, his context and his influence.

1.141 **Hutton**, P., *History as an Art of Memory*, Hanover, NH, 1993.

1.142 **Huizinga**, J. H., *Dutch Civilisation in the Secventeenth Century and other Essays*, 1968. Section Two is historiographical and includes a chapter on 'Two wrestlers with the angel' (Spengler and Wells), and another on 'The aesthetic element in historical thought'.

1.143 **Ingram**, D., 'Blumenburg and the philosophical grounds of Historiography', *Hist. and Theory*, XXIX, 1990, 1–15.

1.144 **Isenberg**, M. T., *Puzzles of the Past. An Introduction to Thinking about History*, College Station, TX, 1985. General reflections on the processing of the past by historians. Determinism, the role of the individual, history and morality are among the subjects dealt with.

1.145 **Jacoby**, R., 'A new intellectual history', *A.H.R.*, XCVII, 1992, 405–24.

1.146 **Jaeger**, H., 'Generations in history; reflections on a controversial concept', *Hist. and Theory*, XXIV, 1985, 273–92.

1.147 **Jenkins**, K., *Rethinking History*, 1991. A

primer which emphasises the value of a methodological rather than a skills-based approach to history.

1.148 **Kellner**, H., *Language and Historical Representation. Getting the Story Crooked*, Madison, WI, 1989.

1.149 **Kemp**, A., *The Estrangement of the Past. A Study in the Origins of Modern Historical Consciousness*, New York, 1991.

1.150 **Kiefer**, H. E. and **Munz**, M. H. (eds), *Mind, Science and History*, Albany, NY, 1970. Includes essays on 'Is there a philosophy of history?' and 'Can philosophy learn from historians?'.

1.151 **King**, P. and **Parekh**, B. C. (eds), *Politics and Experience. Essays presented to Michael Oakeshott*, 1968. Includes 'The practical and the historical past' and 'Michael Oakeshott's theory of history'.

1.152 **Kitangawa**, J. M. (ed.), *The History of Religions. Retrospect and Prospect*, New York, 1985.

1.153 **Klibansky**, R. and **Paton**, H. J. (eds), *Philosophy and History. Essays presented to Ernst Cassirer*, 1936. A miscellaneous collection which includes discussions of historical objectivity, the philosophical character of history and history as a system.

1.154 **Kosso**, P., 'Observing the past', *Hist. and Theory*, XXI, 1992, 21–36.

1.155 **Kracauer**, S., *History*, New York, 1969.

1.155a ——'Time and history', *Hist. and Theory*, supplement 6, 1966, 65–78.

1.156 **Krieger**, L., 'The autonomy of intellectual history', *J. Hist. Ideas*, XXXIV, 1973, 499–516.

1.157 ——*Ideas and Events. Professing History*, Chicago, IL, 1992.

1.158 ——*Time's Reasons. Philosophies of History Old and New*, Chicago, IL, 1989.

1.159 **Kristeller**, P. O., 'History of philosophy and history of ideas', *J. Hist. Philos.*, II, 1964, 1–14.

1.160 **Kuhn**, H., 'Dialectic in history', *J. Hist. Ideas*, X, 1949, 14–29.

1.161 **Kuzminski**, A., 'Archetypes and paradigms; history, politics and persons', *Hist. and Theory*, XXV, 1986, 225–47.

1.162 ——'Defending historical realism', *Hist. and Theory*, XVIII, 1979, 316–49.

1.163 ——'The problem of historical knowledge', *Hist. and Theory*, XII, 1973, 269–89.

1.164 **La Capra**, D., 'Is everyone a *mentalité* case? Transference and the "culture" concept', *Hist. and Theory*, XXIII, 1984, 296–311.

1.165 ——'Intellectual history and its ways', *A.H.R.*, XCVII, 1992, 425–39.

1.166 ——*Rethinking Intellectual History. Texts, Contexts and Language*, Ithaca, NY, 1983. Includes a discussion of Hayden White, Wittgenstein and Ricoeur, and has chapters on Marx's *18th Brumaire* and on 'Marxism and intellectual history'.

1.167 **Lawrence**, J. and **Taylor**, M., 'The poverty of protest', *Soc. Hist.*, XVIII, 1993, 1–15.

1.168 **Le Goff**, J., *History and Memory*, New York, 1992.

1.169 **Lemon**, M. C., *The Discipline of History and the History of Thought*, 1995.

1.170 **Lerner**, Gerda, *Why History Matters. Life and Thought*, 1997.

1.171 **Levich**, M., 'Interpretation in history; or, What historians do and philosophers say', *Hist. and Theory*, XXIV, 1985, 44–61.

1.172 **Lewis**, S. M., 'Unity and continuity; J. B. Bury's philosophy of history in the development of Byzantine studies', *Orientalia Christiana Periodica*, LIX, 1993, 483–506.

1.173 **Lichtheim**, G., *The Concept of Ideology and other Essays*, New York, 1967.

1.174 **Lindenfeld**, D., 'On systems and embodiments as categories for intellectual history', *Hist. and Theory*, XXVII, 1988, 30–50.

1.175 **Lloyd**, C., *The Structures of History*, 1993.

1.176 **Lorenz**, C., 'Historical knowledge and historical reality; a plea for "internal realism"', *Hist. and Theory*, XXXIII, 1994, 297–327.

1.177 **Lovejoy**, A. O., *Essays on the History of Ideas*, Baltimore, MD, 1948. Includes a general essay on 'The historiography of ideas'. Bibliography, 339–54.

1.178 ——'Present standpoints and past history', *J. Philos.*, XXXVI, 1939, 477–89.

1.179 **Löwith**, K., *Meaning in History*, Chicago, IL, 1949. A wide-ranging study – running chronologically backwards – from Burckhardt and Marx, through Voltaire to St Augustine and the Biblical view of history.

1.180 ——Nature, History and Existentialism, and other Essays in the Philosophy of History, Evanston, IL, 1966.

1.181 ——Permanence and Change. Lectures on the Philosophy of History, Cape Town, 1969.

1.182 **Lukács**, J. A., Historical Consciousness or the Remembered Past, New York, 1968.

1.183 **Lyman**, E. W., 'Ernst Troeltsch's philosophy of history', Philos. R., XLI, 1932, 443–65.

1.184 **McCullagh**, C. B., Justifying Historical Descriptions, 1984. Considers the importance of particularisation and generalisation in history and the search for causes.

1.185 **McDougall**, W., 'Mais ce n'est pas l'histoire! Some thoughts on Toynbee, McNeill, and the rest of us', J.M.H., LVIII, 1986, 19–42.

1.186 **McIntyre**, C. T. (ed.), God, History and Historiography. An Anthology of Modern Christian Views of History, New York, 1977. Gives pride of place to Butterfield's Christianity and History and Niebuhr's Faith and History (both published in 1949).

1.187 **McKeon**, R., Freedom and History. The Semantics of Philosophical Controversies and Ideological Conflicts, New York, 1952.

1.188 **McNeill**, W. H., Mythistory and other Essays, Chicago, IL, 1986.

1.189 **Mairet**, C., Le Discours et l'historique. Essai sur la représentation historienne du temps, Tours, 1974.

1.190 **Mandelbaum**, M., The Anatomy of Historical Knowledge, 1977. Attempts to establish the grounds and limits of historical objectivity.

1.191 ——'A. O. Lovejoy and the theory of historiography', J. Hist. Ideas, IX, 1948, 412–23.

1.192 ——The Problem of Historical Knowledge. An Answer to Relativism, New York, 1938. In its assault on relativism this has sections on judgements of fact and judgements of value, and on relevance and causation in history.

1.193 ——'Some neglected problems regarding history', J. Philos., XLIX, 1952, 317–62.

1.194 **Manuel**, F. E., Shapes of Philosophical History, 1965. Originally lectures. Moves chronologically from the early Christians to the twentieth century.

1.195 ——'Two styles of philosophical history', Daedalus, XCI, 1962, 400–17.

1.196 **Marcus**, J. T., Heaven, Hell and History. A Survey of Man's Faith in History from Antiquity to the Present, New York, 1967.

1.197 **Maritain**, J., On the Philosophy of History, 1957. Originally lectures. Deals with the nature of the philosophy of history, with functional and vectorial laws and with God and history.

1.198 **Marrou**, H. I., De la connaissance historique, Paris, 1955.

1.199 **Marsak**, L. M. (ed.), The Nature of Historical Inquiry, New York, 1970. An anthology.

1.200 **Martin**, R., The Past within Us. An Empirical Approach to Philosophy of History, Princeton, NJ, 1989.

1.201 **Mayr**, E., 'When is historiography Whiggish?', J. Hist. Ideas, LI, 1990, 301–7.

1.202 **Mazlish**, B. and **Buultjens**, R., Conceptualising Global History, Boulder, CO, 1993.

1.203 **Mazzeo**, J. A., 'Some interpretations of the history of ideas', J. Hist. Ideas, XXXIII, 1972, 379–94.

1.204 **Mead**, S. E., History and Identity, Missoula, MT, 1979. Four general essays on the nature of history by an American historian of religion.

1.205 **Megill**, A., 'Recounting the past; description, explanation, and narrative in historiography', A.H.R., XCIV, 1989, 627–53.

1.206 ——'Why was there a crisis of historicism?', Hist. and Theory, XXXIV, 1997, 416–29.

1.207 **Meiland**, J. W., Scepticism and Historical Knowledge, New York, 1965. A critique of Croce, Oakeshott and Collingwood which moves towards a constructionist view of history.

1.208 **Meyerhoff**, H. (ed.), The Philosophy of History in our Time, New York, 1959. An anthology arranged under four heads: 'The heritage of historicism', 'Clio: science or muse?' 'History and morality', The meaning of history'.

1.209 **Mikeshin**, N. P., History v. Anti-history, 1977.

1.210 **Mink**, L. O., 'The autonomy of historical understanding', *Hist. and Theory*, V, 1965, 24–47.

1.211 **Mises**, L. von, *Theory and History*, 1958. Considers the problems of value, determinism and materialism, and epistemology.

1.212 **Mohan**, R. P., *Philosophy of History. An Introduction*, New York, 1970.

1.213 **Munz**, P. 'From Max Weber to Joachim of Floris: the philosophy of religious history', *J. Rel. Hist.*, XI, 1980, 167–200.

1.214 —— *The Shapes of Time. A New Look at the Philosophy of History*, Middletown, CT, 1977.

1.215 **Murphy**, M. G., *Philosophical Foundations of Historical Knowledge*, Albany, NY, 1994.

1.216 **Murray**, M. E., *Modern Philosophy of History. Its Origin and Destination*, The Hague, 1970. Explores the significance of philosophy of history in Joachim, Hegel and Heidegger. Bibliography, 130–4.

1.217 **Nadel**, G. H. (ed.), *Studies in the Philosophy of History*, New York, 1960. A collection of essays from *History and Theory* divided into three groups: 'History and philosophical theory', 'History of historical theory', 'History and social theory'.

1.218 **Nash**, R. (ed.), *Ideas of History*, 2 vols, New York, 1969.

1.219 **Niethammer**, L. and **Laak**, D. V., *Posthistoire. Has History come to an End?*, 1992.

1.220 **Nisbet**, R. A., *Social Change and History. Aspects of the Western Theory of Development*, New York, 1969. Looks at the theory and metaphor of growth from ancient to modern times.

1.221 **Nota**, J. H., *Phenomenology and History*, Chicago, IL, 1967.

1.222 **Nowak**, L., *Dimensions of the Historical Process*, Amsterdam, 1988.

1.223 **Nowell-Smith**, P. H., 'Are historical facts unique?', *Proc. Aristotelian Soc.*, LVII, 1956, 107–60.

1.224 ——'The constructionist theory of history', *Hist. and Theory*, XVI, 1977, 1–28.

1.225 **Oakeshott**, M., *On History and other Essays*, 1983. Includes essays on 'Present, future and past', 'Historical events' and 'Historical change'.

1.226 **Olafson**, F. A., *The Dialectic of Action. A Philosophical Interpretation of History and the Humanities*, Chicago, IL, 1979. Deals with the logic of historical analysis, with narrative and with the nature of historical understanding.

1.227 **Ollman**, B., *Dialectical Investigations*, New York, 1993.

1.228 **Osborne**, P., *The Politics of Time. Modernity and Avant Garde*, 1995.

1.229 **Ostrowski**, D., 'The historian and the virtual past', *Historian*, LI, 1989, 201–20.

1.230 **Patrides**, C. A., *The Grand Design of God. The Literary Form of the Christian View of History*, 1972. Discusses the evolution of the Christian view of history from biblical times to the twentieth century. An expanded version of (1.231).

1.231 —— *The Phoenix and the Ladder. The Rise and Decline of the Christian View of History*, Berkeley, CA., 1964.

1.232 **Pippen**, R. B., *Modernism as a Philosophical Problem. On the Dissatisfactions of European High Culture*, 1991.

1.233 **Plumb**, J. H., *The Death of the Past*, 1969. Has three sections: 'The sanction of the past', 'The past as destiny' and 'The role of history'.

1.234 **Pompa**, L. and **Dray**, W. H. (eds), *Substance and Form in History*, 1981. A *festschrift* for W. H. Walsh. Includes essays on Collingwood, Kant and Hegel, on 'History as patterns of thought and action' and on 'Truth and fact in history.

1.235 **Popper**, K. R., 'A pluralist approach to the philosophy of history' in E. Streissler (ed.), *Roads to Freedom. Essays in Honour of F. A. von Hayek*, New York, 1969, 181–200.

1.236 —— *The Poverty of Historicism*, 1957, 2nd ed. 1960. A forceful attack on beliefs in historical laws.

1.237 **Pork**, A., 'Assessing relative causal importance in history', *Hist. and Theory*, XXIV, 1985, 62–9.

1.238 **Porter**, D. H., *The Emergence of the Past. A Theory of Historical Explanation*, Chicago, IL, 1981. Provides a philosophical framework for the tasks and judgements of the historian.

1.239 **Richardson**, A., *History Sacred and Profane*, Philadelphia, PA, 1964. Originally a series of lectures. Considers the ways in which history has variously reinforced or challenged religious faith.

1.240 **Rickert**, H., *Science and History. A Critique of Positivist Epistemology*, New York, 1962. English translation of a book first published in German in 1926. Emphasises the substantial differences between history and the natural sciences.

1.241 **Ricoeur**, P., *History and Truth*, Evanston, IL, 1965. In two parts, dealing with 'Truth in the knowledge of history' and 'Truth in historical action'.

1.242 **Rigney**, Ann, 'Time for visions and revisions; interpretive conflict from a communicative perspective', *Storia de Storiog.*, XXII, 1992, 85–92.

1.243 **Roberts**, G., 'Postmodernism versus the standpoint of action', *Hist. and Theory*, XXXIV, 1997, 249–60.

1.244 **Rosenthal**, Abigail L., 'The intelligibility of history'. *J. Hist. Philos.* XV, 1977, 55–70.

1.245 **Roth**, M. S., *Knowing and History. Appropriations of Hegel in Twentieth-Century France*, Ithaca, NY, 1988.

1.246 **Roth**, P. A., 'Narrative explanations: the case of history', *Hist. and Theory*, XXVII, 1988, 1–13.

1.247 —— and **Ryckman**, T. A., 'Chaos, Clio and scientist illusions of understanding', *Hist. and Theory*, XXXIV, 1995, 30–44.

1.248 **Rozov**, N. S., 'An apologia for theoretical history', *Hist. and Theory*, XXXVI, 1997, 336–52.

1.249 **Rusen**, J., 'Some theoretical approaches to intercultural comparative historiography', *Hist. and Theory*, XXXV, 1994, 5–22.

1.250 —— and **Duvenage**, P., *Studies in Metahistory*, Pretoria, South Africa, 1993.

1.251 **Rushdoony**, R. J., *The Biblical Philosophy of History*, 1969.

1.252 **Russell**, B., *History as an Art*, 1954. Lecture.

1.253 —— *Understanding History and other Essays*, New York, 1957. Three essays on 'How to read and understand history', 'The value of free thought', 'Mentalism v. materialism'.

1.254 **Schmidt**, A., *History and Structure. An Essay on Hegelian–Marxist and Structuralist Theories of History*, Cambridge, MA, 1982.

1.255 **Shankel**, G. E., *God and Man in History. A Study in the Christian Understanding of History*, Nashville, TN, 1967.

1.256 **Shiner**, L., 'A phenomenonological approach to historical knowledge', *Hist. and Theory*, VIII, 1969, 260–74.

1.257 **Simmel**, G., *The Problems of the Philosophy of History. An Epistemological Essay*, 1977. English translation of a major work first published in Germany in 1895 which attacked the naiveties of historical realism.

1.258 **Sorokin**, P. A. (ed.), *Modern Historical and Social Philosophies*, New York, 1963.

1.259 **Starr**, C., 'Historical and philosophical time', *Hist. and Theory*, supplement 6, 1967, 24–35.

1.260 **Stern**, A., *Philosophy of History and the Problem of Values*, The Hague, 1962. Includes chapters on the new historical sense, historical reality, philosophy of history – origins and aims, historical knowledge and values, historicism, historical projects and values.

1.261 **Stromberg**, R. N., 'Some models used by intellectual historians', *A.H.R.* LXXX, 1975, 563–73.

1.262 **Sullivan**, J. E., *Prophets of the West. An Introduction to the Philosophy of History*, New York, 1970. Four sections, 'The metamorphoses of Augustine's City of God', 'Historicism, complete and incomplete', 'The rhythms of history' and 'The ascent of history'. Augustine, Vico, Herder, Hegel, Marx, Ranke, Collingwood and Toynbee are among the writers addressed.

1.263 **Teggart**, F. J., *Theory and Processes of History*, Gloucester, MA, 1972. Reprint of two books first published in 1925 and 1918. Deals with the study of events, change and the present.

1.264 **Thompson**, E. P., *The Poverty of Theory*, 1978. Four essays. 'The peculiarities of the English' is a general essay on the tendencies of modern British historiography. The longest and most substantial on 'The poverty of theory' is an assault on Althusserian Marxism which reinstates the values of historicism, empiricism, moralism and socialist humanism. See also Gordy (1.124) and Wardle (1.291).

1.265 **Toews**, J. E., 'A new philosophy of history? Reflections on postmodern historicizing', *Hist. and Theory*, XXXVI, 1997, 235–48.

1.266 **Topolski**, J., 'The concept of theory in historical research: theory versus myth', *Storia de Storiog.*, XIII, 1988, 67–79.

1.267 **Toynbee**, A. J., *A Study of History*, 12 vols, 1934–61. A 2 vol. abridgment was published in 1946 and 1956. Speculative history on the grand scale. The whole of history comes within its schematisation.

1.268 ——*An Historian's Approach to Religion*, 1956, 2nd ed. 1979.

A. J. Toynbee

1.269 **Burn**, A. R., 'The comparative study of civilisations: Toynbee's *Study of History*', *Hist.*, n.s. XLI, 1956, 1–15.

1.270 **Dray**, W. H., 'Toynbee's search for historical laws', *Hist. and Theory*, I, 1960–61, 32–54.

1.271 **Gargan**, E. T. (ed.), *The Intent of Toynbee's History. A Co-operative Appraisal*, Chicago, IL, 1961. A collection of nine conference papers.

1.272 **Montagu**, M. F. A. (ed.), *Toynbee's History. Critical Essays and Reviews*, Boston, MA, 1956. Collects together a variety of specialist and general critiques of Toynbee's work.

1.273 **Perry**, M., *Arnold Toynbee and the Crisis of the West*, Washington, DC, 1982.

1.274 **Rule**, J. C. and **Crosby**, Barbara, 'Bibliography of works on Arnold J. Toynbee, 1946–60', *Hist. and Theory*, IV, 1965, 212–33.

1.275 **Stromberg**, R. N., *Arnold J. Toynbee, Historian for an Age of Crisis*, Carbondale, IL, 1972.

1.276 **Thompson**, K. W., *Toynbee's Philosophy of World History and Politics*, Baton Rouge, LA, 1985.

1.277 **Tholfsen**, T. R., *Historical Thinking. An Introduction*, New York, 1967. A broadly based collection of essays extending from Thucydides to Fustel de Coulanges. There are general essays on

'Theories of historical knowledge', 'Historical approach' and 'Historical analysis'.

1.278 **Tillinghast**, P. E., *The Specious Past. Historians and Others*, Reading, MA, 1972. The essays are arranged in three sections, 'History and its audience', 'Insiders and outsiders' and 'Attempts to come to terms'. Bibliography, 179–84.

1.279 **Trompf**, G. W., *The Idea of Historical Recurrence in Western Thought from Antiquity to the Reformation*, 1980. Discriminatingly explores cyclical thinking and recurrence paradigms.

1.280 **Trouillot**, M. R., *Silencing the Past. Power and the Production of History*, Boston, MA, 1995.

1.281 **Tully**, J. (ed.), *Meaning and Context. Quentin Skinner and his Critics*, Princeton, NJ, 1988.

1.282 **Turne**, B. S., *Theories of Modernity and Postmodernity*, 1990.

1.283 **van der Dussen**, W. J. and **Rubinoff**, L., *Objectivity, Method and Point of View. Essays in the Philosophy of History*, Leiden, 1991.

1.284 **Vann**, R. T., 'Louis Mink's linguistic turn', *Hist. and Theory*, XXVI, 1987, 1–14.

1.285 **Van Til**, C., *A Christian Theory of Knowledge*, 1969.

1.286 **Vedrine**, Hélène, *Les Philosophes de l'histoire. Déclin ou crise?*, Paris, 1974.

1.287 **Veit-Brause**, Irmline, 'Historicism revisited', *Storia de Storiog.*, XXIX, 1996, 99–126.

1.288 **Veyne**, P., *Writing History. Essay on Epistemology*, 1984. Divided into three principal parts covering the aims of history, understanding, and the progress of history.

1.289 **Vovelle**, M., *Ideologies and Mentalities*, Chicago, IL, 1990.

1.290 **Walsh**, W. H., *An Introduction to the Philosophy of History*, 1951, 3rd ed. 1967. A well known guide to the definition of philosophy of history and to the relations between history and the sciences. Truth and fact in history are considered, as is the possibility of objectivity. Kant, Herder and Hegel are taken as exemplars of speculative philosophy of history. Bibliography, 207–10.

1.291 **Wardle**, A., 'E. P. Thompson and "poor theory"'. *Brit. J. Sociol.*, XXXIII, 1982, 224–37. See Gordy (1.124) and Thompson (1.264).

1.292 **Waters**, B., 'The past and the historical past', *J. Philos.*, LII, 1955, 253–69.

1.293 **Watkins**, J. W. N., 'Ideal types and historical explanation' in H. Feigl and Mary Brodbeck (eds), *Readings in the Philosophy of Science*, 1953, 732–43.

1.294 **Weingartner**, R. H., 'Some philosophical comments on cultural history', *Hist. and Theory*, VII, 1968, 38–59.

1.295 **Weinstein**, F., *History and Theory after the Fall*, Chicago, IL, 1990.

1.296 **White**, H. V., 'The politics of contemporary philosophy of history', *Clio*, III, 1973, 35–53.

1.297 —— 'Response to Arthur Marwick', *J. Contemp. Hist.*, XXX, 1995, 233–46.

1.298 —— 'A response to Professor Chartier's four questions', *Storia de Storiog.*, XXVII, 1995, 63–72.

1.299 —— 'The rhetoric of interpretation', *Poetics Today*, IX, 1988, 253–79.

1.300 —— *Tropics of Discourse. Essays in Cultural Criticism*, Baltimore, MD, 1978. A continuation of *Metahistory* (8.213), no less wide-ranging in its assessment of the interface between history, literary criticism and historicism. Vico, Croce and Foucault receive special treatment.

1.301 —— (ed.), *The Uses of History. Essays in Intellectual and Social History presented to William J. Bossenbrook*, Detroit, MI, 1968. Includes essays on romanticism, Hintze, and Löwith.
On White see special issues of *Storia de Storiog.*, XXIV–XXV, 1993–94, devoted to *Metahistory* twenty years after.

1.302 **Widgery**, A. G., *Interpretations of History. Confucius to Toynbee*, 1961. A philosopher's introduction to historical theorising on the grand scale.

1.303 **Wiener**, P. P. and **Noland**, A. (eds), *Ideas in Cultural Perspective*, New Brunswick, NJ, 1962. A collection of articles originally published in the *Journal of the History of Ideas*. It includes Lovejoy on 'Reflections on the history of ideas' and Mandelbaum on 'Recent trends in the theory of historiography'.

1.304 **Wickens**, B. T., *Has History any Meaning? A Critique of Popper's Philosophy of History*, 1978.

1.305 **Wolfson**, H. A., *Studies in the History of Philosophy and Religion*, Cambridge, MA, 1973.

1.306 **Wood**, H. G., *Freedom and Necessity in History*, 1957. Lecture.

1.307 **Wright**, G., 'History as a moral science', *A.H.R.*, LXXXI, 1976, 1–11.

1.308 **Yolton**, J. W., 'History and metahistory', *Philos. and Phenomenological R.*, XV, 1955, 477–92.

PURPOSES AND METHODS IN HISTORY

1.309 **Abbot**, A., 'Conceptions of time and events in social science methods; causal and narrative approaches', *Hist. Methods*, XXIII, 1990, 140–50.

1.310 **Abbott**, Mary (ed.), *History Skills. A Student's Handbook*, 1996. A helpful survey of basics for undergraduates.

1.311 **Alstyne**, R. W. van, 'History and the imagination', *Pacific H.R.*, XXXIII, 1964, 1–24.

1.312 **Anderle**, O. F., 'A plea for theoretical history', *Hist. and Theory*, IV, 1964, 27–56.

1.313 **Ankersmit**, F. R., *Narrative Logic. A Semantic Analysis of the Historian's Language*, The Hague, 1983.

1.314 **Appleby**, Joyce, **Hunt**, Lynn, and **Jacob**, Margaret, *Telling the Truth about History*, New York, 1994. Deals with the legitimacy of the historian's search for truth and with the stabilities and instabilities of the American past.

1.315 **Bailyn**, B., *On the Teaching and Writing of History*, Hanover, NH, 1991. Reflections by a master historian on his craft.

1.316 **Baker**, A. R. H., *Place, Practice and Structure*, 1988.

1.317 —— and **Billinge**, M. (eds), *Period and Place. Research Methods in Historical Geography*, 1982. Includes sections on the development of historical geography, on behavioural approaches to the study of geographical change and on theoretical perspectives in historical geography. Bibliography.

1.318 **Barros**, C., 'The history ahead', *Storia de Storiog.*, XXX, 1996, 77–106.

1.319 **Barthes**, R., *The Rustle of Language*, New York, 1986. Contains Barthes's essays 'The discourse of history' (1967) and 'The reality effect' (1968).

1.320 **Barzun**, J. and **Graff**, H. F., *The Modern Researcher*, 1957, 2nd ed., New York, 1970. A manual of scholarly practice.

1.321 **Baumer**, F. L. van, 'Intellectual history and its problems', *J.M.H.*, XXI, 1949, 191–203.

1.322 **Beale**, H. K., 'The professional historian: his theory and his practice', *Pacific H.R.*, XXII, 1953, 227–55.

1.323 **Bendix**, R., 'The comparative analysis of historical change' in R. Bendix and G. Roth (eds), *Scholarship and Partisanship*, Berkeley, CA, 1971, 207–41.

1.324 **Benson**, Susan P. *et al.* (eds), *Presenting the Past. Essays on History and the Public*, Philadelphia, PA, 1986. Eighteen essays exploring aspects of the methodologies of the 'new' history in America and divided into three sections – 'Packaging the past', 'Professionalizing the past' and 'Politicizing the past'.

1.325 **Beringer**, R. E., *Historical Analysis. Contemporary Approaches to Clio's Craft*, 1978. A basic introduction to various modes of analysis, including collective biography, 'role theory' and cliometrics.

1.326 **Bermejo-Barrera**, J. C., 'Exploring the past: in praise of history', *Hist. and Theory*, XXXII, 1993, 14–24.

1.327 **Bevir**, M., 'Mind and method in the history of ideas', *Hist. and Theory*, XXXVI, 1997, 167–89.

1.328 —— 'Objectivity in history', *Hist. and Theory*, XXXIII, 1994, 328–44.

1.329 **Black**, J., 'Historical atlases', *Hist. J.*, XXXVII, 1994, 643–68.

1.330 —— and **Macraild**, D. M., *Studying History*, 1997. A beginner's book offering reflections on the scope and development of history and on theorising about researching and writing. Bibliography, 213–18.

1.331 **Blake**, C., 'Can history be objective?', *Mind*, LXIV, 1955, 61–78.

1.332 **Blatti**, J. (ed.), *Past Meets Present. Essays about Historic Interpretation and Public Audiences*, Washington, DC, 1987.

1.333 **Blaut**, J. M., 1492. *The Debate on Colonialism, Eurocentrism and History*, Trenton, NJ, 1992.

1.334 —— *The Colonizer's Model of the World. Geographical Diffusion and Eurocentric History*, New York, 1993.

1.335 **Block**, M., *The Historian's Craft*, 1954. Posthumously published reflections by one of the greatest modern masters of the discipline and co-founder of *Annales*.

1.336 **Bottomore**, T., 'Structure and history' in P. Blau (ed.), *Approaches to the Study of Social Structure*, 1976, 159–71.

1.337 **Boucher**, D., *Texts in Context. Revisionist Methods for Studying the History of Ideas*, The Hague, 1985.

1.338 **Boulding**, K. E., *A Primer on Social Dynamics. History as Dialectics and Development*, New York, 1970. A study of dialectical and developmental processes, with some reflections on how history may be written.

1.339 **Burns**, A. L., 'Ascertainment, probability and evidence in history', *Hist. Studs. Aust. and N.Z.*, IV, 1951, 327–39.

1.340 **Butterfield**, H., *History and Human Relations*, 1951. A collection of essays which includes discussions of 'Marxist history', 'Moral judgments in history' and 'History as a branch of literature'.

1.341 —— 'Narrative history and the spadework behind it', *Hist.*, LIII, 1968, 165–80.

1.342 **Campbell**, R., *Truth and Historicity*, 1992.

1.343 **Canary**, R. H. and **Kozicki**, H. (eds), *The Writing of History. Literary Form and Historical Understanding*, Madison, WI, 1978. Includes essays on history and on the purposes of narrative.

1.344 **Cannadine**, D., *The Pleasures of the Past*, 1990. A miscellaneous collection of essays. Reflections on urban history, economic history, London history, welfare state history, socialist history and elite history are included. Other essays deal with the historiography of time, sex, food, poverty, secrets and nostalgia, and with the *D.N.B.*

1.345 **Cannon**, J. (ed.), *The Historian at Work*, 1980. Extends from the Enlightenment to the present day. There are essays on Gibbon, Ranke, Macaulay, Marx, Maitland, Bloch, Namier, Butterfield and Braudel.

1.346 **Cantor**, N. F. and **Schneider**, R. L., *How to Study History*, New York, 1967.

1.347 **Cappon**, L. J., 'A rationale for historical editing: past and present', *Wm and Mary Q.*, XXIII, 1966, 56–75.

1.348 **Carpenter**, R. H., *History as Rhetoric. Style, Narrative and Persuasion*, 1995.

1.349 **Carrier**, D., *Principles of Art History Writing*, 1991.

1.350 **Carroll**, R. N., *Memory, Nostalgia, and the Art of History*, Athens, GA, 1990. Blends autobiography and historiography.

1.351 **Chamberlain**, Mary and **Thompson**, P. (eds), *Narrative and Genre*, 1998. Dedicated to the memory of Raphael Samuel, a collection of essays on the methodologies of oral history by social historians and cultural anthropologists.

1.352 **Chatman**, S., *Story and Discourse*, Ithaca, NY, 1978.

1.353 **Chatterjee**, P., *The Nation and its Fragments. Colonial and Postcolonial Histories*, Princeton, NJ, 1993.

1.354 **Chesnaux**, J., *Pasts and Futures, or, What is History for?*, 1978. A controversial reappraisal of the study of history and its purposes, arguing that it should be kept in rather than out of the battleground of current politics.

1.355 **Chrimes**, S. B., *Some Reflections upon the Study of History*, 1954. Inaugural lecture.

1.356 **Church**, C. H., 'Disciplinary dynamics', *Studs. Higher Ed.*, I, 1976, 101–18.

1.357 **Clark**, G. K., *The Critical Historian*, 1967. Wise counsel on matters relating to the power and methods of history. Part Three addresses the methodological and interpretative problems involved in the handling of historical facts. Part Four is concerned with groups in history and generic statements about them.

1.358 **Clive**, J., *Not by Fact Alone. Essays on the Writing and Reading of History*, Boston, MA, 1989. A collection of stimulating short essays and reviews which takes in Gibbon, Macaulay, Carlyle, Michelet, Trevelyan and Butterfield. Essays on 'Why read the great nineteenth-century historians?' and 'The great historians in the age of cliometrics' make a convincing case for the study of historiography.

1.359 **Cohen**, D. W., *The Combing of History*, Chicago, IL, 1994. Deals with how knowledge of the past is gained and historians and others confront gaps and silences in the evidence.

1.360 **Cohen**, S., *Historical Culture. On the Recoding of an Academic Discipline*, Berkeley, CA, 1986. A radical assault on the autonomy and necessity of history. Conventional historical thinking, it is argued, is an obstacle to proper criticism.

1.361 **Collini**, S., *English Pasts. Essays in History and Culture*, 1999. Sixteen essays clustered in three groups – 'Histories', 'Minds' and 'Arguments'. Includes 'Writing the national history; Trevelyan and after', 'Idealizing England; Elie Halévy and Lewis Namier' and essays on J. S. Mill, R. H. Tawney, Isaiah Berlin and Raymond Williams.

1.362 **Commager**, H. S., *The Nature and Study of History*, Columbus, OH, 1965. A primer – aimed chiefly at American schoolteachers – on the nature, variety, study, philosophy and problems of history.

1.363 **Conkin**, P. K. and **Stromberg**, R. N. (eds), *Heritage and Challenge. The History and Theory of History*, 1989. Part One provides a succinct survey of the development of historiography. Part Two looks at history's relations with the generalising sciences and at the problems connected with objectivity and causation.

1.364 **Connell-Smith**, G. and **Lloyd**, H. A., *The Relevance of History*, 1972. A vigorous attack on the inadequacies of academic history and a plea for greater relevance to current issues and concerns.

1.365 **Costello**, P., *World Historians and their Goals*, DeKalb, IL, 1993.

1.366 **Crump**, C. G., *History and Historical Research*, 1928. A practical handbook.

1.367 **Curti**, M., *Probing our Past*, Gloucester,

MA, 1962. Includes essays on democracy as a theme in American historical literature, on Turner, and on the influence of John Locke on the growth of ideas in America.

1.368 **D'Amico**, R., *Historicism and Knowledge*, New York, 1988.

1.369 **Daniels**, R. V., *Studying History. How and Why?*, Englewood Cliffs, NJ, 1966, 3rd ed. 1981. A basic primer. Sections on the uses of history, fields of history, history as social science, how to study, writing about history, historical research and interpretation. Bibliography, 119–121.

1.370 **Davis**, R. H. C., 'The content of history', *Hist.*, LXVI, 1981, 361–74.

1.371 —— *Good History and Bad*, 1971. Inaugural lecture.

1.372 **de Certeau**, M., *The Writing of History*, 1988. Written by a member of the French Freudian school, this is an attempt to rethink the categories of history and the approach to historiography.

1.373 **Deininger**, W. T., 'Some reflections on epistemology and historical enquiry', *J. Philos.*, LIII, 1956, 429–42.

1.374 **Dening**, G. M., 'History as a social system', *Hist. Studs.*, XV, 1971–73, 673–85.

1.375 **Denley**, P., 'Models, sources and users: historical database design in the 1990s', *Hist. and Computing*, VI, 1994, 33–43.

1.376 **Duby**, G., *History Continues*, Chicago, IL, 1994. Collected essays by a leading medievalist.

1.377 **Dumoulin**, J. and **Moisi**, D. (eds), *The Historian between the Ethnologist and the Futurologist*, The Hague, 1973.

1.378 **Dunn**, J., 'The identity of the history of ideas', *Philos.*, XLIII, 1967, 85–104.

1.379 **Dunning**, W. A., *Truth in History and other Essays*, New York, 1937. The collection includes 'Truth in history' and 'A generation of American historiography'.

1.380 **East**, W. G., *The Geography behind History*, 1938. A general discussion, illustrated chiefly from prehistory. Has chapters on 'Geography as a historical document' and 'Climate and history'.

1.381 **Easthope**, G., *A History of Social Research Methods*, 1974. Deals with the origins and development of sociology and with survey, comparative and life-history methods, and with measurement and analysis. Bibliography, 150–64.

1.382 **Elliott**, J. H., *National and Comparative History. An Inaugural Lecture delivered before the University of Oxford on 10 May 1991*, 1991.

1.383 **Elton**, G. R., *The Future of the Past*, 1968. Inaugural lecture.

1.384 —— 'The historian's social function', *T.R.H.S.*, 5th ser., XXVII, 1977, 197–211.

1.385 —— *The Practice of History*, 1967. Commonsense approach by one of the leading traditionalists in the field.

1.386 —— *Return to Essentials. Some Reflections on the Present State of Historical Study*, 1991. Brings together Elton's Cook Lectures of 1990, dealing with the 'The claims of theory', 'The burden of philosophy' and 'Some prescriptions', with his Cambridge inaugural lectures of 1968 ('The future of the past') and 1984 ('The history of England').

1.387 **Evans**, R. J., *In Defence of History*, 1997. Asserts the traditional values in history in the face of the debilitating effects of postmodernism. Bibliography, 284–301.

1.388 **Ferguson**, N. (ed.), *Virtual History. Alternatives and Counterfactuals*, 1997. Nine case studies, together with an introduction and overview, in cliometrics which attempt to escape the tyranny of facts by exploring alternative trajectories of the past.

1.389 **Ferro**, M., *The Use and Abuse of History, or, How the Past is Taught*, 1984. Enormously wide-ranging study of the varied purposes of history in countries as different as South Africa, India, China, Japan and Australia.

1.390 **Fisher**, D. H., *Historians' Fallacies. Towards a Logic of Historical Thought*, 1971. Eleven chapters concerned with fallacies of enquiry, explanation and argument.

1.391 **Fitch**, Nancy, 'Statistical fantasies and historical facts; history in crisis and its methodological implications', *Hist. Methods*, XVII, 1984, 239–54.

1.392 **Foucault**, M., *The Archaeology of*

Knowledge, 1972. Attempts a marriage of the methods and concerns of the historian with those of the structuralist critic.

1.393 **Frank**, A. G., 'A theoretical plea for world system history', *J. World Hist.*, II, 1991, 1–28.

1.394 **Fry**, R., *Art History as an Academic Study*, 1933. Inaugural lecture.

1.395 **Furet**, F., *In the Workshop of History*, Chicago, IL, 1984. A miscellaneous collection which links the study of history with the preoccupations of the present and attempts to enlarge the methodology of history through links with the social sciences.

1.396 **Gadamer**, H. G., *Truth and Method*. New York, 1975.

1.397 **Galbraith**, V. H., *An Introduction to the Study of History*, 1964. Has two general chapters on 'The historian at work' and on 'Historical research and the preservation of the past'.

1.398 **Gardiner**, Juliet (ed.), *The History Debate*, 1990. Sixteen leading historians, including Asa Briggs, Jonathan Clark, G. R. Elton, Roy Porter and Raphael Samuel, briefly air their views on history and its place in the national curriculum.

1.399 **Garraghan**, G. J., *A Guide to Historical Method*, New York, 1946.

1.400 **Genette**, G., *Narrative Discourse*, Ithaca, NY, 1980.

1.401 **Gershenkron**, A., *Continuity in History and Other Essays*, Cambridge, MA, 1968. Includes a long discussion of methodology, 11–76.

1.402 —— 'The discipline and I', *J.Ec.H.*, XXVII, 1967, 443–59.

1.403 **Ginzburg**, C., 'Checking the evidence: the judge and the historian', *Critical Inquiry*, XVIII, 1991, 79–98.

1.404 **Gottschalk**, L., *Understanding History. A Primer of Historical Method*, New York, 1950, 2nd ed. 1969. Divided into three general sections on historians' objectives, on historical methods, and on the theory of history.

1.405 **Graham**, G., *The Shape of the Past*, 1997.

1.406 **Green**, W. A., *History, Historians and the Dynamics of Change*, Westport, CT, 1993.

1.407 **Grew**, R., 'The case for comparing histories', *A.H.R.*, LXXXV, 1980, 763–79.

1.408 **Guinsberg**, T. N. (ed.), *The Dimensions of History. Readings on the Nature of History and the Problems of Historical Interpretation*, Chicago, IL, 1971. An anthology which includes extracts from Becker, Bury, Hexter, Kitson Clark and Thernstrom.

1.409 **Hampson**, N., *History as an Art*, 1968. Inaugural lecture.

1.410 **Hannagan**, M. *et al.* (eds), *Challenging Authority. The Historical Study of Contentious Politics*, Minneapolis, MN, 1997.

1.411 **Hanham**, H. J., 'Clio's weapons', *Daedalus*, C, 1971, 509–19.

1.412 **Harlan**, D., 'Intellectual history and the return of literature', *A.H.R.*, XCIV, 1987, 581–609.

1.413 **Hartman**, G., 'Toward literary history', *Daedalus*, XCVIII, 1970, 355–83.

1.414 **Harvey**, V. A., *The Historian and the Believer. The Morality of Historical Knowledge and Christian Belief*, 1967. Explores the ways in which the historian's knowledge and methods can be applied to and reconciled with faith and theology.

1.415 **Hay**, Cynthia, 'Historical theory and historical confirmation', *Hist. and Theory*, XIX, 1980, 39–57.

1.416 **Heller**, L. G., *Communicative Analysis and Methodology for Historians*, New York, 1972.

1.417 **Herrick**, F. H., 'The profession of history', *Pacific H.R.*, XXXI, 1962, 1–19.

1.418 **Hexter**, J. H., *Doing History*, 1971. Its inelegant title notwithstanding, this collection of essays has valuable discussions of the rhetoric of history and of history and the social sciences.

1.419 —— *The History Primer*, 1971. Despite its offputting chapter headings this is a valuable exploration of purpose, method and explanation in history.

1.420 **Hobsbawm**, E. J., 'The revival of narrative: some comments', *P.P.*, 86, 1980, 3–8. See Stone (9.249).

1.421 —— *On History*, 1997. Twenty-one of the author's essays, originally published between 1969 and 1993.

1.422 **Hodder**, I., *Reading the Past. Current*

Approaches to Interpretation in Archaeology, 1991.

1.423 **Horne**, D., *The Great Museum. The Representation of History*, 1984. A seminal text in the emergence of 'public history'.

1.424 **Humphreys**, R. S., 'The historian, his documents, and the elementary modes of historical thought', *Hist. and Theory*, XIX, 1980, 1–20.

1.425 **Johnson**, A., *The Historian and Historical Evidence*, New York, 1926. Discusses the need for scepticism, criticism, assessment, hypothesis and proof in the historian's handling of his sources.

1.426 **Jones**, H. M., *History and Relevance*, Latrobe, PA, 1969.

1.427 —— 'The nature of literary history', *J. Hist. Ideas*, XXVIII, 1967, 147–60.

1.428 **Joyce**, D. D., *History and Historians*, Washington, DC, 1983. A basic introduction.

1.429 **Karsten**, P. and **Modell**, J. (eds), *Theory, Method, and Practice in Social and Cultural History*, New York, 1992.

1.430 **Kaye**, H. J., *The Powers of the Past. Reflections on the Crisis and the Promise of History*, Minneapolis, MN, 1991.

1.431 —— '*Why do Ruling Classes fear History?' and other Questions*, New York, 1996. Essays on radical themes from a radical American historian. Includes a tribute to E. P. Thompson.

1.432 **Kent**, S., *Writing History*, revised ed., New York, 1967.

1.433 **Koenig**, D. (ed.), *Historians and History. Essays in Honour of Charlton W. Tebeau*, Coral Gables, FL, 1966. Includes brief essays on 'The historian and community service', 'Clio: muse or minion?', 'Who were the great historians of the West? An invitation to a game'.

1.434 **Kress**, G. and **Hodge**, C., *Language as Ideology*, 1979. Included are discussions of 'classification and control', 'classification as process' and 'reality, power and time'. Bibliography, 152–58.

1.435 **Kuklick**, B., 'History as way of learning', *Am. Q.*, XXII, 1970, 609–28.

1.436 —— 'The mind of the historian', *Hist. and Theory*, VIII, 1969, 313–31.

1.437 **La Capra**, D. and **Kaplan**, S. L. (eds), *Modern European Intellectual History.*

Reappraisals and New Perspectives, Ithaca, NY, 1982.

1.438 **Lamont**, W. (ed.), *Historical Controversies and Historians*, 1998. The product of a long-running introductory course at the University of Sussex. Eighteen chapters address a wide range of controversies – including those surrounding Oliver Cromwell, German society and the Nazis, race in South African history – and individual historians (Burckhardt, Tawney, Stone, Bailyn, E. P. Thompson, among others).

1.439 **Laue**, T. H. von, 'Is there a crisis in the writing of history?', *Bucknell R.*, XLV, 1966, 1–15.

1.440 **Leff**, G., *History and Social Theory*, 1969. A development of some of the themes in the same author's *The Tyranny of Concepts* (9.341). The first part of the book explores different aspects of history as a branch of knowledge. Part Two considers the place of ideology in knowledge.

1.441 **Lloyd**, C., 'Realism and structurism in historical theory: a discussion of the thought of Maurice Mandelbaum', *Hist. and Theory*, XXVIII, 1989, 296–325.

1.442 **Lord**, D. C., 'The historian as villain: the historian's role in the training of teachers', *Historian*, XXXIV, 1972, 407–20.

1.443 **Louch**, A. R., 'History as narrative', *Hist. and Theory*, VIII, 1969, 54–70.

1.444 **Lowenthal**, D., *The Heritage Crusade and the Spoils of History*, New York, 1996. Shows the sometimes uneasy relations between the competing claims of history and heritage. Bibliography, 293–314.

1.445 **Luthy**, H., 'What's the point of history?', *J. Contemp. Hist.*, III, 1968, 3–22.

1.446 **McCloskey**, D. N., 'History, differential equations and the problems of narration', *Hist. and Theory*, XXX, 1991, 21–36.

1.447 **McCullagh**, C. B., 'Can our understanding of old texts be objective?', *Hist. and Theory*, XXX, 1991, 302–23.

1.448 —— *The Truth of History*, 1998.

1.449 **MacHardy**, Karin J., 'Crises in history,

or, Hermes unbounded', *Storia de Storiog.*, XVII, 1990, 5–27.

1.450 **McNeill**, W. H., 'The changing shape of world history', *Hist. and Theory*, XXXIV, 1995, 8–26.

1.451 **Magnusson**, C., 'History and social theory of today: an introduction', *Storia de Storiog.*, XVIII, 1990, 61–72.

1.452 **Mali**, J., 'Real narratives: myth, history and mythhistory', *Storia de Storiog.*, XXX, 1996, 3–18.

1.453 **Margolis**, J., *The Flux of History and the Flux of Science*, Los Angeles, CA, 1993.

1.454 **Martin**, R., 'The essential difference between history and science', *Hist. and Theory*, XXXVI, 1997, 1–14.

1.455 ——'Objectivity and meaning in historical studies: towards a post-analytic view', *Hist. and Theory*, XXII, 1993, 25–50.

1.456 **Marwick**, A., *The Nature of History*, 1970, 2nd ed. 1982. A useful primer which places the present practice of history in its historiographical context and considers the relations between history and the humanities and the social sciences. Bibliography, 289–96.

1.457 **Mitchison**, Rosalind (ed.), *Why Scottish History Matters*, 1991.

1.458 **Morris**, W., *Toward a New Historicism*, Princeton, NJ, 1972. Written from the standpoint of the post-new criticism literary scene. Argues for a new, less uncompromising and autonomous historicism to be applied to literature.

1.459 **Morton**, L., 'The historian and the study of war', *Miss. Vall. H.R.*, XLVIII, 1962, 599–613.

1.460 **Myers**, D. N., *Reinventing the Jewish Past. European Jewish Intellectuals and the Zionist Return to History*, New York, 1995.

1.461 **Nevins**, A., *The Art of History. Two Lectures*, Washington, DC, 1967.

1.462 **Newman**, F. D., *Explanation by Description. An Essay on Historical Methodology*, The Hague, 1968. Starting from the covering law analysis of explanation and prediction, the author moves to the specific practice of historians in handling actualities and possibilities.

1.463 **Norman**, A. P., 'Telling it like it was: historical narratives on their own terms', *Hist. and Theory*, XXX, 1991, 119–35.

1.464 **Nugent**, W. T. K., *Creative History. An Introduction to Historical Study*, Philadelphia, PA, 1967.

1.465 **Olafson**, F. A., 'Narrative history and the concept of action', *Hist. and Theory*, IX, 1970, 265–89.

1.466 **Oldfield**, A., 'Moral judgements in history', *Hist. and Theory*, XX, 1981, 260–77.

1.467 **Oman**, C., *On the Writing of History*, 1939. By one of the 'old guard' professionals.

1.468 **Pares**, R., *The Historian's Business*, 1961. Pares's inaugural lecture, included here, gives the book its title. The other historiographical essays deal with Toynbee's *Study of History* and with Bernard Pares.

1.469 **Pencak**, W., *History Signing In. Essay in History and Semiotics*, New York, 1993.

1.470 **Perkins**, D., *Is Literary History Possible?*, Baltimore, MD, 1992. Examines the tasks of narrative literary history and the problems of classifying and contextualising authors and books.

1.471 **Pomper**, P., 'World history and its critics', *Hist. and Theory*, XXXIV, 1995, 1–7.

1.472 ——'Historians and individual agency', *Hist. and Theory*, XXXV, 1996, 281–308.

1.473 **Porphyrios**, D. (ed.), *On the Methodology of Architectural History*, 1981.

1.474 **Preziosi**, M., *Rethinking Art History. Meditations on a Coy Science*, New Haven, CT, 1989.

1.475 **Redlich**, F., 'Toward comparative historiography', *Kyklos*, XI, 1958, 362–89.

1.476 **Reisch**, G. A., 'Chaos, history and narrative', *Hist. and Theory*, XXX, 1991, 1–20.

1.477 **Renier**, G. J., *History. Its Purpose and Method*, 1950. A general overview of the nature of history and of historians' methods in defining and reconstructing it.

1.478 **Richardson**, R. C., 'Methodologies of history', *Lit. and Hist.*, 5:2, 1979, 220–4.

1.479 **Rigby**, S. H., 'Historical causation: is

one thing more important than another?', *Hist.*, LXXX, 1995, 227–42.

1.480 **Ringer**, F. K., 'Causal analysis in historical reasoning', *Hist. and Theory*, XXVIII, 1989, 154–72.

1.481 **Roberts**, C., *The Logic of Historical Explanation*, Philadelphia, PA, 1996.

1.482 **Roberts**, G., 'Narrative history as a way of life', *J. Contemp. Hist.*, XXXI, 1996, 221–8.

1.483 **Robin**, Régine, *Histoire et linguistique*, Paris, 1973.

1.484 **Roskill**, M., *What is Art History?*, New York, 1976.

1.485 **Roth**, M. S., *Rediscovering History. Culture, Politics and the Psyche*, Stanford, CA, 1994.

1.486 **Roth**, S., 'Is history a process?', *Soc. Sci. Hist.*, XVI, 1992, 197–243.

1.487 **Rowse**, A. L., *The Use of History*, 1946. A straightforward justification for studying the subject.

1.488 **Runciman**, S., 'On the Writing of History', *Historical Ass. Jubilee Addresses*, 1956.

1.489 **Rusen**, J., 'The development of narrative competence in historical learning: an ontogenetic hypothesis concerning moral consciousness', *Hist. and Memory*, 1, 1989, 35–59.

1.490 **Salmi**, H., 'On the nature and structure of historical narration', *Storia de Storiog.*, XXIII, 1993, 123–34.

1.491 **Samuel**, R., *Theatres of Memory*, 1994. A stimulating collection of essays, including 'Unofficial knowledge', 'Living history' and 'Heritage history'. Whole sections are devoted to 'Old photographs' and 'Costume drama'.

1.492 —— *Theatres of Memory* II, *Island Stories. Unravelling Britain*, 1998. Posthumously published, this is a sequel to (1.491). Twenty-one essays divided into four main sections – 'Nations, states, empires'; 'English journeys'; 'History, the nation and the schools'; 'The war of ghosts'. Some of the longest and most provocative essays are 'Unravelling Britain', 'Religion and politics: the legacy of R. H. Tawney', 'The discovery of Puritanism, 1820–1914', 'Mrs Thatcher and Victorian values' and 'Reading the runes'.

1.493 —— and Thompson, P. (eds), *The Myths we Live by*, 1990. The proceedings of an international conference on oral history. Seventeen chapters are divided into four sections, 'The making of myth', 'Nationhood and minorities', 'Manhood and the images of women' and 'Family stories'. Bibliography, 252–4.

1.494 **Sanderson**, S. K., *Civilisations and World Systems. Studying World Historical Change*, Walnut Creek, CA, 1995.

1.495 **Sato**, M., 'Comparative ideas of chronology', *Hist. and Theory*, XXX, 1991, 275–301.

1.496 **Schottler**, P., 'Historians and discourse analysis', *Hist. Workshop J.*, XXVII, 1989, 37–65.

1.497 **Scott**, Joan W., 'History in crisis? The others' side of the story', *A.H.R.*, XCIV, 1989, 680–92. Defends the 'new' history in the face of criticism from the conservatives, especially from Gertrude Himmelfarb (9.54).

1.498 **Shafer**, R. J., *A Guide to Historical Method*, Homewood, IL, 1969.

1.499 **Shaw**, C. and **Chase**, M. (eds), *The Imagined Past. History and Nostalgia*, 1989. A mixed bag of essays. Those on 'Rider Haggard and rural England', on historical fabrications about the 1930s and on the rise of the heritage industry are particularly successful.

1.500 **Sjodell**, U., 'The structure of a historian's reasoning: historical explanation in practice', *Scand. J. Hist.*, VI, 1981, 91–115.

1.501 **Skinner**, Q., 'The limits of historical explanations', *Philos.*, LXI, 1966, 199–215.

1.502 —— 'Meaning and understanding in the history of ideas', *Hist. and Theory*, VIII, 1969, 3–53.

1.503 **Smith**, P. (ed.), *The Historian and Film*, 1976. Divided into sections on film as raw material, historical evidence, as historical factor, and on film in the interpretation and teaching of history. Bibliography, 186–200.

1.504 **Smith**, Page, *The Historian and History*, New York, 1964. Follows a three-part division, dealing with the development of the concept of history, with modern thought on the nature of history, and with contemporary American academic history. Bibliography, 251–60.

1.505 **Southgate**, B., *History. What and Why? Ancient, Modern and Postmodern Perspectives*, 1996. Divided into six sections which deal with the relations between history, philosophy and historiography; the recovery of the past; reasons for studying the past; external challenges to scientific history; internal challenges; the future of history. Bibliography, 154–61.

1.506 **Spiller**, R. E., *The Third Dimension. Studies in Literary History*, New York, 1965. Concerned chiefly with American studies but has some general discussion of 'The province of literary history' and of 'The province of literary history' and of 'The alchemy of literature'.

1.507 **Sprinzak**, E., 'Thesis as an historical explanation', *Hist. and Theory*, XI, 1972, 294–320.

1.508 **Stalnaker**, R. C., 'Events, periods and institutions in historians' language', *Hist. and Theory*, VI, 1967, 159–79.

1.509 **Stambovsky**, P., 'Metaphor and historical understanding', *Hist. and Theory*, XXVII, 1988, 125–34.

1.510 **Stanford**, M., *The Nature of Historical Knowledge*, 1986. Deals with the concept of history, with evidence, the construction of historical interpretations, historiography, the reception of history and the making of history.

1.511 ——*A Companion to the Study of History*, 1994. A guide to concepts and methods in history. Ten main sections, including 'History as outlook', 'History as discourse', 'History as relic' and 'History as sequence'. Bibliography, 287–99.

1.512 **Stearns**, P. N. 'History advances; recasting a historical reference classic', *Historian*, LVII, 1994, 113–20.

1.513 **Steedman**, Carolyn, 'Why Clio doesn't care', *Hist. and Theory*, XXXI, 1992, 33–50.

1.514 **Stover**, R., *The Nature of Historical Thinking*, Chapel Hill, NC, 1967. Includes chapters on 'The historian's commitment to determinism', 'Evaluation', rational action and on historical thinking and present concerns.

1.515 **Strayer**, J. R. (ed.), *The Interpretation of History*, Princeton, NJ, 1943. A collection of essays by well known practitioners Jacques Barzun, Hajo Holborn and Herbert Heaton.

1.516 **Sturley**, D. M., *The Study of History*, 1969. A basic introduction to the nature, philosophy and writing of history.

1.517 **Taylor**, A. J. P., *Politicians, Socialism and Historians*, 1982. Includes short essays on Acton and Geyl, and more extended treatments of accidents as a factor in history and of the historian as biographer.

1.518 **Teute**, Fredrika J., 'A historiographical perspective in historical editing', *Am. Archivist*, XLIII, 1980, 43–56.

1.519 **Thomas**, M., 'Applying the social accounting matrix to historical problems', *Hist. Methods*, XVIII, 1985, 85–95.

1.520 **Thompson**, M. P., 'Reception theory and the interpretation of historical meaning', *Hist. and Theory*, XXXII, 1993, 248–72.

1.521 **Thomson**, D., *The Aims of History. Values of the Historical Attitude*, 1969. A brief introduction to and justification of the study of history.

1.522 **Todorova**, A., 'Historical sources and methodology; principles of sources analysis', *Bulgarian H. R.*, VIII, 1980, 89–100.

1.523 **Topolski**, J., 'Conditions of truth in historical narratives', *Hist. and Theory*, XX, 1981, 47–60.

1.524 ——*Methodology of History*, The Hague, 1977. A large-scale, clearly structured survey of changing practices of history. Makes a plea for placing historiography and methodology higher on the historian's agenda.

1.525 ——'Towards an integrated model of historical explanation', *Hist. and Theory*, XXX, 1991, 324–38.

1.526 **Tosh**, J., *The Pursuit of History. Aims, Methods and New Directions in the Study of Modern History*, 1984 3rd ed. 1999. An invaluable primer which discusses the raw materials, preoccupations and applications of history. There are sections on the limits of historical knowledge and on quantitative and oral history.

1.527 **Trevelyan**, G. M., *History and the Reader*, 1945. Lecture.

1.528 **Trevor-Roper**, H. R., 'History; professional and lay' (1957 inaugural lecture); 'History and the imagination; a valedictory lecture' (1980) in H. Lloyd-Jones *et al.* (eds), *History and the Imagination. Essays in Honour of H. R. Trevor-Roper*, 1981, 1–14, 356–70.

1.529 **van de Braembussche**, A. A., 'Historical explanation and comparative method; towards a theory of the history of society', *Hist. and Theory*, XXVIII, 1989, 1–24.

1.530 **Vaughn**, S. (ed.), *The Vital Past. Writings on the Uses of History*, Athens, GA, 1985. Thirty-five essays considering the nature and relevance of history and its applications in the present.

1.531 **Veit-Brause**, Irmline, 'Paradigms, schools, traditions – conceptualizing shifts and changes in the history of historiography', *Storia de Storiog.*, XVII, 1990, 51–66.

1.532 **Verhaegen**, B., *Introduction à l'histoire immédiate. Essai de méthodologie qualitative*, Paris, 1974.

1.533 **Veyne**, P., 'L'histoire conceptualisante' in J. le Goff and P. Nora (eds) *Faire de l'histoire*, Paris, 1974, I, 62–92. ——'A contestation of sociology', *Diogenes*, 75, 1971, 1–23.

1.534 **Walker**, J. A., *Design History and the History of Design*, 1989.

1.535 **Ward**, R. B., *Uses of History*, Armidale, NSW, 1968.

1.536 **Ware**, V., 'Moments of danger; race, gender and memoirs of empire', *Hist. and Theory*, XXXI, 1992, 116–37.

1.537 **Warren**, J., *The Past and its Presenters. An Introduction to Issues in Historiography*, 1998. A brief survey concluding with interviews with two of today's historians and with reflections on the value and relevance of historical studies at the end of the twentieth century.

1.538 **Warren**, W. L., *Undergraduate History*, 1974. Inaugural lecture.

1.539 **Wear**, A. and **Pittock**, J. (eds), *Interpretation and Cultural History*, New York, 1991.

1.540 **Wehler**, H. U., 'What is the history of society?', *Storia de Storiog.*, XVIII, 1990, 5–20.

1.541 **Whalley**, P., *An Essay on the Manner of Writing History*, New York, 1970.

1.542 **White**, H. V., *The Content of the Form. Narrative Discourse and Historical Representation*, Baltimore, MD, 1987.

1.543 ——'Historical employment and the problem of truth', in S. Friedlander (ed.), *Probling the Limits of Representation. Nazism and the Final Solution*, Cambridge, MA, 1992, 37–53.

1.544 ——'The politics of historical interpretation; discipline and desublimation', *Crit. Inquiry*, IX, 1982, 113–38.

1.545 ——'The question of narrative in contemporary historical theory', *Hist. and Theory*, XXIII, 1984, 1–33.

1.546 ——'The structure of historical narrative', *Clio*, I, 1972, 5–20.

1.547 **White**, M. G., *Foundations of Historical Knowledge*, New York, 1965. Based on a lecture series. Has chapters on 'Fact, law and value in history', 'Explanatory arguments', Explanatory statements', 'Causal interpretation', 'Reasons and causes', 'Historical narration', 'History, ethics and free will'.

1.548 **Willis**, K., 'In defence of true Whiggism; Bertrand Russell and the Whig interpretation of history', *Storia de Storiog.*, XI, 1987, 17–43.

1.549 **Winks**, R. W. (ed.), *The Historian as Detective. Essays on Evidence*, 1969.

1.550 **Worster**, D., 'Transformations of the earth; toward an agroecological perspective in history', *J.A.H.*, LXXVI, 1990, 1087–106.

1.551 **Young**, R., *White Mythologies. Writing History and the West*, 1990.

1.552 **Zammito**, J., 'Are we being theoretical yet? The new historicism, the new philosophy and "practising historians"', *J.M.H.*, LXV, 1993, 783–814.

QUANTIFICATION

1.553 **Aydelotte**, W. O., *Quantification in History*, Reading, MA, 1971. Essays, partly of a general methodological kind and partly concerned with case studies in modern British political history.

1.554 ——(ed.), *The Dimensions of Quantitative Research in History*, 1972. Case studies drawn from modern British and American history showing the application of quantitative methods.

1.555 **Bogue**, A. G., *Clio and the Bitch Goddess. Quantification in American Political History*, Beverly Hills, CA, 1983.

1.556 **Clubb**, J. M. and **Allen**, H., 'Computers and historical studies', '*J.A.H.*, LIV, 1967, 599–607. A pioneering article.

1.557 **Denley**, P. and **Hopkin**, D. (eds), *History and Computing*, 1987. Papers from a 1986 conference which illustrate virtually all types of historical computing activities. The chapters are arranged thematically and chronologically. Bibliography.

1.558 **Dollar**, C. M. and **Jensen**, R. J., *Historian's Guide to Statistics. Quantitative Analysis and Historical Research*, New York, 1971. A practical handbook on quantitative methods.

1.559 **Edington**, S., *Micro History. Local History and Computing Projects*, 1985.

1.560 **Erickson**, Charlotte, 'Quantitative history', *A.H.R.*, LXXX, 1975, 351–65.

1.561 **Fitch**, Nancy., 'Statistical fantasies and historical facts; history in crisis and its methodological implications', *Hist. Methods*, XVII, 1984, 239–54.

1.562 **Floud**, R., 'Disk history', *Hist. Today*, XXXV, 1985, 39–40.

1.563 ——*An Introduction to Quantitative Method for Historians*, 1973, 2nd ed. 1980.

1.564 **Fogel**, R. W., 'The limits of quantitative methods in history', *A.H.R.*, LXXX, 1975, 329–50.

1.565 **Greenstein**, D., *A Historian's Guide to Computing*, 1994.

1.566 **Hall**, J. R., 'Temporality, social action and the problem of quantification in historical analysis', *Hist. Methods*, XVII, 1984, 206–18.

1.567 **Haskins**, L. and **Kirk**, J., *Understanding Quantitative History*, Cambridge, MA, 1990.

1.568 **Herlihy**, D., 'Quantification in the 1980s; numerical and formal analysis in European history', *J. Interdis. H.*, XII, 1981, 114–35.

1.569 **Jaravsch**, K., 'The role of quantitative methods in history; decline or reawakening?' *Storia de Storiog.*, XVIII, 1990, 43–60.

1.570 **Jensen**, R., 'The microcomputer revolution for historians', *J. Interdis. H.*, XIV, 1983, 91–111.

1.571 **Langholm**, S., 'On the scope of micro history', *Scand. J. Hist.*, I, 1976, 3–24.

1.572 **Lewis**, M. J. and **Lloyd Jones**, R., *Using Computers in History. A Practical Guide*, 1996.

1.573 **Lorwin**, V. R. and **Price**, J. M. (eds), *The Dimension of the Past. Materials, Problems and Opportunities for Quantitative Work in History*, New Haven, CT, 1972. Wide-ranging chronologically and geographically. Includes chapters on 'Quantification and the Middle Ages' and 'A data archive for modern British political history'.

1.574 **Lynch**, K. A., 'The use of quantitative data in the historical analysis of social classes', *Hist. Methods*, XVII, 1984, 230–7.

1.575 **McCloskey**, D., *Econometric History*, 1987.

1.576 **Marczewski**, J., 'Quantitative history', *J. Contemp. Hist.*, III, 1968, 179–91.

1.577 **Marsh**, Catherine, 'Historians and the computer', *Soc. Hist.*, V, 1980, 283–90.

1.578 **Mawdsley**, E. and **Munck**, T., *Computing for Historians. An Introductory Guide*, 1993.

1.579 **Middleton**, R. and **Wardley**, P., 'Information technology in economic and social history; the computer as philosopher's stone or Pandora's box?', *Ec.H.R.*, XLIII, 1990, 667–96.

1.580 **Morris**, R. J., 'Computers and the subversion of British history', *J. Brit. Studs.*, XXXIV, 1995, 503–28.

1.581 **Reiff**, Janice L., *Structuring the Past. The Use of Computers in History*, Washington, DC, 1991.

1.582 ——'Numeracy, computer literacy and history; a view from both sides', *Hist. Methods*, XVII, 1984, 265–9.

1.583 **Rowney**, D. K. and **Graham**, J. Q. (eds), *Quantitative History. Selected Readings in the Quantitative Analysis of*

Historical Data, Homewood, IL, 1969. Includes sections on 'Social history and social change', 'Historical demography' and 'Cliometrics'. Bibliography.

1.584 **Shapiro**, G. *et al.* 'Quantitative studies on the French Revolution', *Hist. and Theory*, XII, 1973, 163–91.

1.585 **Shorter**, E., *The Historian and the Computer. A Practical Guide*, Englewood Cliffs, NJ, 1971. Deals with existing (1971) uses of computers and with programming and processing. Descriptive and correlative analyses are considered. The conclusion provides some warnings.

1.586 **Swierenga**, R. P., 'Computers and American history; the impact of the "new" generation', *J.A.H.*, LX, 1974, 1045–70.

1.587 ——'Clio and the computers; a survey of computerized research in history', *Computers and the Humanities*, V, 1970, 1–21.

HISTORIOGRAPHICAL SURVEYS

1.588 **Acheson**, D., *History as Literature*, New York, 1966.

1.589 **Albright**, W. F., *History, Archaeology and Christian Humanism*, New York, 1964. See esp. 'The expansion of historical horizons', 16–46.

1.590 **Alexander**, H. G., *Time as Dimension and History*, Albuquerque, NM, 1945.

1.591 **Allen**, H. C., *American History in Britain*, 1955. Inaugural lecture.

1.592 **Angus-Butterworth**, L. M., *Ten Master Historians*, 1961. Includes Hume, Gibbon, Southey, Macaulay and Green.

1.593 **Apter**, D. E., 'Radicalization and embourgeoisement; some hypotheses for a comparative study of history', *J. Interdis. H.*, I, 1971, 511–76.

1.594 **Barnes**, H. E., *A History of Historical Writing*, 1937, 2nd ed., Dover, NH, 1963. A basic survey.

1.595 ——*History and Social Intelligence*, New York, 1926. Divided into four parts:

'Aspects of the newer history', 'History and some problems of nationalism', 'creation tales' and 'The rise and fall of democracy'.

1.596 **Barraclough**, G., *History and the Common Man*, 1966. Lecture.

1.597 **Baron**, S. W., *History and Jewish Historians. Essays and Addresses*, Philadelphia, PA, 1964.

1.598 **Beard**, C. and **Vagts**, A., 'Currents of thought in historiography', *A.H.R.*, XLII, 1937, 460–83.

1.599 **Bebbington**, D., *Patterns in History*, 1979. Thematically divided into chapters dealing with cyclical history, Christian history, the idea of progress, historicism, Marxist history and the philosophy of history. Good bibliography, 189–202.

1.600 **Bentley**, M., *Modern Historiography. An Introduction*, 1999. Largely reprints Bentley's contribution to (1.1). A brief survey covering the period from the Enlightenment to the present. Further reading, 176–7.

1.601 **Best**, G., *History, Politics and Universities*, 1969. Inaugural lecture.

1.602 **Billington**, R. A. *et al.* (eds), *The Historian's Contribution to Anglo-American Misunderstanding*, 1966. A study of the different educational systems and of history textbooks in England and America. Compares the ways in which the American Revolution, the War of 1812 and the First World War are presented in the two countries.

1.603 **Block**, J., *Understanding Historical Research. A Search for Truth*, Glen Rock, NJ, 1971.

1.604 **Bowditch**, J., 'War and the historian' in Hughes (1.665), 320–40.

1.605 **Breisach**, E., *Historiography. Ancient, Medieval and Modern*, Chicago, IL, 1983 2nd ed. 1994. An ambitious, though unavoidably breathless, survey of the development of the discipline of history. Extensive bibliography.

1.606 **Bridbury**, A. R., *Historians and the Open Society*, 1972. A kind of continuation of Butterfield's *Whig Interpretation of History*. It examines the ways in which – consciously and unconsciously – the historian reinforces social divisions, authoritarianism and economic success in his own society.

1.607 **Brooke**, C. N. L., *The Dullness of the Past*, 1957. Inaugural lecture.

1.608 **Bury**, J. B., *The Idea of Progress. An Inquiry into its Origin and Growth*, 1920. Looks at the changing concepts of progress from the sixteenth century to the 1850s. See also Ginsberg (1.649) and Pollard (1.698).

1.609 ——*Selected Essays*, ed. H. Temperley, 1930. Includes Bury's inaugural lecture 'The science of history' together with others on 'Darwinism and history', 'The place of modern history in the perspective of knowledge' and 'Cleopatra's nose'.

1.610 **Butterfield**, H., 'Delays and paradoxes in the development of historiography' in K. Bourne and D. C. Watt (eds), *Studies in International History. Essays presented to W. Norton Medlicott*, 1967, 1–15.

1.611 ——*The Englishman and his History*, 1944. A wartime diagnosis of the development and appropriateness of the Whig interpretation of English history.

1.612 ——'The role of the individual in history', *Hist.*, XL, 1955, 1–17.

1.613 ——*The Study of Modern History*, 1944. Inaugural lecture.

1.614 ——*The Whig Interpretation of History*, 1931. A classic account many times reprinted. In its day considered a veiled attack on G. M. Trevelyan.

1.615 **Calvert**, P., *The Concept of Class. An Historical Introduction*, 1982. Offers sensible guidance on Turgot, Ferguson, Marx and Weber.

1.616 **Chadwick**, O., *Freedom and the Historian. An Inaugural Lecture*, 1969. Considers the ways in which the history of freedom figured in the work of Acton, Bury and Trevelyan.

1.617 **Child**, A., 'Moral judgement in history', *Ethics*, LXI, 1951, 297–308.

1.618 **Christenson**, A. L. (ed.), *Tracing Archaeology's Past. The Historiography of Archaeology*, Carbondale, IL, 1989.

1.619 **Clark**, J. C. D., 'The strange death of British history? Reflections on Anglo-American scholarship', *Hist. J.*, XL, 1997, 787–810.

1.620 **Clubb**, J. M. and **Scheuch**, E. M. (eds), *Historical Social Research*, Stuttgart, 1980.

1.621 **Cochrane**, E., 'What is Catholic historiography?' *Cath. H.R.*, LXI, 1975, 169–90.

1.622 **Conant**, Miriam B. (ed.), *Politics and History. Selected Essays by Raymond Aron*, New York, 1978. Part One has four essays on the nature and limits of historical and sociological knowledge. Part Two includes essays on Machiavelli, Marx, and history and politics.

1.623 **Conkin**, P. K. and **Stromberg**, R. N., *The Heritage and Challenge of History*, New York, 1971.

1.624 **Crowe**, C., 'The emergence of progressive history', *J. Hist. Ideas*, XXVII, 1966, 109–24.

1.625 **Dance**, E. H., *History for a United World*, 1971. A plea for the teaching of 'relevant' history. Chapter 12 is specifically historiographical.

1.626 ——*History the Betrayer. A Study in Bias*, 1960. A study of bias and national perspectives in history textbooks.

1.627 **Davis**, H. E., *History and Power. The Social Relevance of History*, Lanham, MD, 1983. Has chapters on the definition of history, on the reality of historical knowledge, historical logic, the social relevance of history, Marxist and neo-Marxist history, religious reactions, and on history and social power.

1.628 **Donnachie**, I. and **Whatley**, C. (eds), *The Manufacture of Scottish History*, 1992. Nine essays with an introduction that show how different periods, themes and landmarks in Scottish history have been constructed according to different historical fashions and needs.

1.629 **Douglas**, D. C., *Time and the Hour*, 1977. Includes five historiographical essays ranging from the development of medieval studies between 1660 and 1730 to an assessment of Marc Bloch.

1.630 **Dubnow**, S., *Nationalism and History. Essays on Old and New Judaism*, Philadelphia, PA, 1958. Contains essays on Jewish history and the philosophy of history and on the sociological view of Jewish history.

1.631 **Eisenstein**, Elizabeth L., 'Clio and Chronos; an essay on the making and breaking of history book time', *Hist. and Theory*, V, 1966, 36–64. Explores the ways in which views of history have been shaped by record keeping, transmission and retrieval.

1.632 **Erdman**, K. D., 'A history of the International Historical Congresses. Work in Progress', *Storia de Storiog.*, VIII, 1985, 3–22.

1.633 **Fawcett**, J. (ed.), *The Future of the Past. Attitudes to Conservation, 1174–1974*, 1976.

1.634 **Febvre**, L., *A Geographical Introduction to History*, 1932. A challenging early publication by one of the founders of *Annales*.

1.635 **Fell**, A. P. (ed.), *Histories and Historians*, 1968. A selection of brief historiographical essays from *History Today*, extending from Herodotus to Burckhardt.

1.636 **Finley**, M. I., 'Myth, memory and history', *Hist. and Theory*, IV, 1964–65. 281–302.

1.637 **Fitzsimons**, M. A. *et al.* (eds), *The Development of Historiography*, New York, 1954.

1.638 ——*The Past Recaptured. Great Historians and the History of History*, Notre Dame, IN, 1983. Ten rather sketchy essays on historians extending from Herodotus to Lord Acton.

1.639 **Francois**, M. *et al.*, *Historical Study in the West*, New York, 1968.

1.640 **Frankel**, J. (ed.), *Reshaping the Past. Jewish History and the Historians*, New York, 1994.

1.641 **Gagnon**, S., *Man on his Past. The Nature and Role of Historiography*, Montreal, 1982. Surveys the views of French, British and American historians, sociologists and philosophers on the relatavist nature of historiography.

1.642 **Gardiner**, Juliet (ed.), *What is History Today?*, 1988. Thirteen sections dealing with different branches of history, including women's history, history of art, intellectual history, popular culture and Third World history. Characteristically each section contains five or six contributions from specialists in the field with individual, differing, viewpoints expressed.

1.643 **Gay**, P., *Style in History*, 1975. After a general chapter on the importance of style as a subject for the historian there

are case studies of Gibbon, Ranke, Macaulay and Burckhardt. Bibliography, 219–38.

1.644 ——*et al.* (eds), *Historians at Work*, 4 vols, New York, 1972–75. Readings with editorial commentary.

1.645 **Geyl**, P., *Debates with Historians*, 1962. Includes chapters on Ranke, Macaulay's *Essays*, Carlyle, Michelet, Toynbee and Isaiah Berlin.

1.646 ——*Encounters in History*, 1963. A collection of case studies and reflections.

1.647 ——*From Ranke to Toynbee. Five Lectures on Historians and Historiographical Problems*, Northampton, MA, 1952.

1.648 **Gilderhus**, M. T., *History and Historians. A Historiographical Introduction*, 1987, 3rd ed., Englewood Cliffs, NJ, 1996. A concise primer.

1.649 **Ginsberg**, M., *The Idea of Progress. A revaluation*, 1953. See also Bury (1.608) and Pollard (1.698).

1.650 **Gottschalk**, L. (ed.), *Generalization in the Writing of History*, Chicago, IL, 1963. Has chapters on the use of generalisation in the study of ancient history, social roles, national character and revolution. Very good bibliography, 213–48.

1.651 **Grant**, A. J. (ed.), *English Historians*, 1906. A long introduction prepares the way for an anthology which illustrates changing aims, methods and styles of history.

1.652 **Hale**, J. R., *The Evolution of British Historiography from Bacon to Namier*, 1967. Extracts with substantial introduction and linking commentary.

1.653 **Halperin**, S. W. (ed.), *Essays in Modern European Historiography*, Chicago, IL, 1970. A collection of sixteen reprinted essays. The historians studied include Lavisse, Lefebvre, Schmoller and Seignobos.

1.654 **Handlin**, O., *Truth in History*, 1979. Seventeen essays offering historiographical case studies and general reflections on the state of the discipline.

1.655 **Harbison**, E. H., 'The "meaning of history" and the writing of history', *Church Hist.*, XXI, 1952, 97–106.

1.656 **Hay**, D., *Annalists and Historians. Western Historiography from the Eighth to the Eighteenth Century*, 1977. Well researched, clearly presented account.

1.657 **Hearder**, H., *Ideological Commitment and Historical Interpretation*, 1969. Inaugural lecture.

1.658 **Henderson**, J. L., *A Bridge across Time. The Role of Myths in History*, 1975. Chapters on the 'The advent of the psychohistorian' and on 'Fiction as the third dimension of history'.

1.659 **Higham**, J., 'Beyond consensus; the historian as moral critic', *A.H.R.*, LXVII, 1962, 609–25.

1.660 ——**Krieger**, L., and **Gilbert**, F., *History*, Englewood Cliffs, NJ, 1965. Sections on the historical profession, on theories of history, on American history, European history in America, and on European and American historiography.

1.661 **Hobsbawm**, E. J., 'The social function of the past', *P.P.*, 55, 1972, 3–17.

1.662 ——and **Ranger**, T. (eds), *The Invention of Tradition*, 1983. Ranging from nineteenth-century Scotland to imperial India and Africa, this lively collection of essays illustrates the political and social uses of history in securing the advantages and guarantees of tradition.

1.663 **Holdsworth**, W. S., *The Historians of Anglo-American Law*, New York, 1928. Includes chapters on the historians of the seventeenth and eighteenth centuries and on Maitland.

1.664 **Howard**, M., *The Lessons of History*, 1981. Inaugural lecture.

1.665 **Hughes**, H. S. (ed.), *Teachers of History. Essays in Honor of Lawrence Bradford Packard*, Ithaca, NY, 1954. A collection which ranges widely both geographically and chronologically. Includes chapters on Erasmus, Henry Adams and Huizinga, and on 'War and the historian'.

1.666 **James**, R. R., 'Thoughts on writing military history', *J. Roy. United Service Institution*, III, 1966, 99–109.

1.667 **Jelenski**, K. A., *History and Hope. Tradition, Scepticism and Fanaticism in Modern Society*, 1962. Includes essays on 'A rehabilitation of nationalism?' and 'Beyond nihilism'.

1.668 **Kelley**, D. R., *Versions of History from Antiquity to the Enlightenment*, New Haven, CT, 1991. A collection of readings.

1.669 ——*Faces of History. From Herodotus to Herder*, New Haven, CT, 1998. An insightful general survey which forms a companion piece to the anthology by the same author (1.668).

1.670 **Kent**, G. O., 'Clio the tyrant; historical analogies and the meaning of history', *Historian*, XXXII, 1969, 99–106.

1.671 **Kenyon**, J. P., *The History Men. The Historical Profession in England since the Renaissance*, 1983. Gives most weight to the century after 1840. Upholds the traditional values in its treatment, and in some cases, dismissal of modern trends.

1.672 **Kiernan**, V. G., *Intellectuals in History*, 1979. Pamphlet.

1.673 **Kohn**, H., *Reflections on Modern History. The Historian and Human Responsibility*, Princeton, NJ, 1963. Chapters on Bagehot, Acton, Bryce and Toynbee, and a general discussion of academic freedom and history's place in a liberal education.

1.674 **Kozicki**, H. (ed.), *Developments in Modern Historiography*, 1993. A wide-ranging collection of essays by a distinguished team of contributors. Georg G. Iggers writes on 'Rationality and history', T. K. Rabb on historians and scientists, Arthur Marwick on source-based history and R. T. Vann on Marxism and the history of the family.

1.675 ——*Western and Russian Historiography. Recent Views*, 1993. Essays by historians and philosophers generated by changing international politics. Hard-liners are predominant and air their convictions.

1.676 **Krey**, A. G., *History and the Social Web. A Collection of Essays*, Minneapolis, MN, 1955.

1.677 **Krieger**, L., 'The horizons of history', *A.H.R.*, LXIII, 1957, 62–74.

1.678 **Langmuir**, G. I., 'Tradition, history and prejudice', *Jewish Soc. Studs.*, XXX, 1968, 147–68.

1.679 **Lefebvre**, G., *La Naissance de l'historiographie moderne*, Paris, 1971.

1.680 **Lenman**, B. P., 'The teaching of Scottish history in the Scottish universities', *Scot. H.R.*, LII, 1973, 165–90.

1.681 **Lewis**, B., *History. Remembered, Recovered, Invented*, 1975. Originally lectures. The book is rich in anecdote and illustration but weak on theory.

1.682 **Loewenberg**, R. J., ' "Value free" v. "value laden" history; a distinction without a difference', *Historian*, XXXIX, 1976, 439–54.

1.683 **Lowe**, D. M., *History of Bourgeois Perception*, Chicago, IL, 1982.

1.684 **Lowenthal**, D., *The Past is a Foreign Country*, 1985. A wide-ranging study – drawing on the author's varied background in geography, landscape design and political science as well as history – of social attitudes to the past and the social uses of history.

1.685 **MacDougall**, H. A., *Racial Myth in English History. Trojans, Teutons and Anglo Saxons*, Montreal, 1982. A brief survey from early medieval to modern times of the rise and disintegration of racial myths.

1.686 **McIntire**, C. T. (ed.), *God, History and Historians. An Anthology of Modern Christian Views of History*, 1977.

1.687 **Meyer**, M. A. (ed.), *Ideas of Jewish History*, New York, 1974.

1.688 **Momigliano**, A., *Essays in Ancient and Modern Historiography*, 1977. Twenty-one essays. Polybius, Ammianus, Marcellinus, Niebuhr, Vico, Burckhardt Droysen, de Coulanges and Croce are among the authors discussed.

1.689 **Morgan**, P. T. J., 'The clouds of witnesses; the Welsh historical tradition', in R. B. Jones (ed.), *Anatomy of Wales*, 1972, 18–42.

1.690 **Nisbet**, R., *History of the Idea of Progress*, 1980. Complements Bury's classic of 1920 by taking stock of classical and medieval ideas on the subject.

1.691 **Offer**, A., 'Using the past in Britain; retrospect and prospect', *Public Historian*, VI, 1984, 17–36.

1.692 **Paret**, P., 'The history of war', *Daedalus*, C., 1971, 376–96.

1.693 **Parker**, C., *The English Historical Tradition since 1850*, 1990. Stresses many of the continuities in historical writing and the resilience of Whig

assumptions. Acton, Maitland, Gardiner and Bury are reassessed. The creative impact of mavericks such as R. H. Tawney and E. H. Carr is underlined.

1.694 **Phillips**, R., *History Teaching, Nationhood and the State. A Study of Educational Politics*, 1998. Deals with the evolution of policy making and practice in connection with the national curriculum.

1.695 **Plumb**, J. H., *Men and Places*, 1963. A collection of essays which includes studies of 'History and biography', Trevelyan and Macaulay.

1.696 **Pocock**, J. G. A., 'The origins of the study of the past; a comparative approach', *Comp. Studs. Soc. and Hist.*, IV, 1961–62, 209–46.

1.697 **Pollock**, R. C., 'Freedom and history', *Thought*, XXVII, 1952, 400–20.

1.698 **Pollard**, S., *The Idea of Progress. History and Society*, 1968. See also Ginsberg (1.649) and Bury (1.608).

1.699 **Potter**, D. M., 'The historian's use of nationalism and vice versa', *A.H.R.*, LXVII, 1962, 924–50.

1.700 **Randall**, J. G., 'Historianship', *A.H.R.*, LVIII, 1953, 249–64.

1.701 **Read**, C., 'The social responsibilities of the historian', *A.H.R.*, LV, 1950, 275–85.

1.702 **Roller**, D. H. D. (ed.), *Perspectives in the History of Science and Technology*, Norman, OK, 1971.

1.703 **Rotenstreich**, N., 'The idea of historical progress and its assumptions', *Hist. and Theory*, X, 1971, 197–227.

1.704 **Schevill**, F., *Six Historians*, Chicago, IL, 1956. Succinct case studies which extend from Thucydides to Henry Adams.

1.705 **Schlesinger**, A. J., 'The historian as participant', *Daedalus*, C, 1971, 323–39.

1.706 **Schmitt**, B., *The Fashion and the Future of History. Historical Studies and Addresses*, Cleveland, OH, 1960. Besides the essay which gives the book its title there are chapters on 'Fifty years of exploring history' and on 'Modern European history in the USA'.

1.707 **Sinor**, D. (ed.), *Orientalism and History*, 1954. Surveys of broad fields of oriental research; ancient and Near East, Islam, India, China, central

Eurasia. Each chapter contains a bibliographical note.

1.708 **Smith**, P. H., 'Time as a historical construct', *Hist. Methods*, XVII, 1984, 182–91.

1.709 **Stern**, F. (ed.), *The Varieties of History. From Voltaire to the Present*, 1956, 2nd ed. 1970. A collection of readings with introduction and linking commentary.

1.710 **Taylor**, A. J. P., *Essays in English History*, 1976. Includes short pieces on 'Fiction in history', 'Tory history', 'Cromwell and the historians', Macaulay and Carlyle.

1.711 **Thompson**, J. W. and **Holm**, B. J., *History of Historical Writing*, 2 vols, New York, 1958. Encyclopaedic survey.

1.712 **Trevor-Roper**, H. R., *Historical Essays*, 1957. Includes some essays which are primarily historiographical in character – on Clarendon, Macaulay, Strachey and Marx.

1.713 **Watkin**, D., *The Rise of Architectural History*, 1980. A wide-ranging survey of developments – chiefly in England – from the seventeenth century to the present day. European and American contexts are kept in view.

1.714 **Wedgwood**, C. V., *History and Hope. Collected Essays*, 1987.

1.715 **Weintraub**, K. J., *Visions of Culture. Voltaire, Guizot, Burckhardt, Lamprecht, Huizinga, Ortega y Gasset*, Chicago, IL, 1966. Considers the different ways in which these writers assembled their interpretations of culture.

1.716 **Weiss**, P., *History, written and lived*, Carbondale, IL, 1962. Divided into two general sections: the recovery of the past, and the reality and dimensions of the historical world. There are chapters on history and science, on the historian's objectives, historical narrative, historical time, historical causation, and on the exteriority of the past.

1.717 **Williams**, C. H. (ed.), *The Modern Historian*, 1938. An anthology.

1.718 **Williams**, E., *British Historians and the West Indies*, 1966. A survey of changing views from 1830 to *c.* 1960.

1.719 **Wilson**, E., *To the Finland Station. A Study in the Writing and Acting of History*, 1942, rev. 1972. A classic, three-part study centring on Michelet,

Marx and Engels, and on Lenin and Trotsky.

1.720 **Winks**, R. W. (ed.), *The Historiography of the British Empire–Commonwealth. Trends, Interpretations, and Resources*, Durham, NC, 1966. Twenty-one essays on recent historiography.

1.721 **Wollheim**, R., 'Historicism reconsidered', *Sociological R.*, XI, 1954, 76–97.

1.722 **Woodward**, E. L., *British Historians*, 1943. Very brief overview from medieval to modern times. Illustrated.

1.723 **Zinn**, H., *The Politics of History*, Boston, MA, 1970.

COUNTRIES AND REGIONS

Africa

1.724 **Alagoa**, E. J., 'Communicating African history', *Storia de Storiog.*, XV, 1989, 75–88.

1.725 ——'Oral tradition and cultural history in Nigeria', *Storia de Storiog.*, V, 1984, 66–76.

1.726 **Brooks**, G. E., 'A schema for integrating Africa into world history', *Hist. Teacher*, III, 1970, 5–19.

1.727 **Falola**, T. (ed.), *African Historiography. Essays in Honour of J. F. Ade Ajayi*, 1993.

1.728 **Foner**, E., '"We must forget the past"; history in the new South Africa', *S. African H.J.*, XXXII, 1995, 163–76.

1.729 **Gabel**, C. and **Bennet**, N. R. (ed.), *Reconstructing African Cultural History*, Boston, MA, 1967. Papers deriving from a 1962 symposium. Included are essays on ethnology, language, oral tradition, music, art and a general consideration of interdisciplinary methodology in African cultural history.

1.730 **Gordon**, D. C., *Self-determination and History in the Third World*, Princeton, NJ, 1971. Examines the uses and misuses of history for political ends in the Third World. There are case studies of Morocco and Algiers. Bibliography, 195–208.

1.731 **Harms**, R. W. *et al.* (eds), *Paths to the African Past. African Historical Essays in Honor of Jan Vansina*, Atlanta, GA, 1994.

1.732 **Hooker**, J. R., 'African history in general education; can Africans rejoin world history?', *J. Human Relations*, XV, 1967, 44–52.

1.733 **Jewsiewicki**, B. and **Newbury**, D. (eds), *African Historiographies. What History for which Africa?*, Beverly Hills, CA, 1986.

1.734 **Linne Eriksson**, T., 'Modern African history; some historiographical observations', *Scand. J. Hist.*, IV, 1979, 75–97.

1.735 **McCall**, D. F., *Africa in Time Perspective. A Discussion of Historical Reconstruction from Unwritten Sources*, New York, 1969.

1.736 **Marcus**, H. G., 'The greening of African history', *Historian*, LI, 1989, 467–74.

1.737 **Marks**, S., 'African and Afrikaner history', *J. African Hist.*, XI, 1970, 435–47.

1.738 **Saunders**, C., *The Making of the South African Past. Major Historians on Race and Class*, Cape Town, 1988.

1.739 **Smith**, K., *The Changing Past. Trends in South African Historical Writing*, Johannesburg, 1988.

1.740 **van Jaarsveld**, F. A., *The Afrikaners' Interpretation of South African History*, Cape Town, 1964.

1.741 **Wansborough**, J., The decolonization of North African history', *J. African Hist.*, IX, 1968, 643–50.

1.742 **Wright**, H. M., *The Burden of the Present. Liberal–Radical Controversy over South African History*, Cape Town, 1977.

Australia

1.743 **Lechte**, J., *Politics and the Writing of Australian History. An Introduction to a Structural Study*, Melbourne, 1975.

1.744 **Osborne**, G. and **Nandle**, W. F. (eds), *New History. Studying Australia Today*, Sydney and Boston, MA, 1982.

1.745 **Pascoe**, R., *The Manufacture of Australian History*, Melbourne, 1979.

Canada

1.746 **Berger**, C., *The Writing of Canadian History. Aspects of English–Canadian Historical Writing since 1900*, 2nd ed., Toronto, 1986.

1.747 **Gagnon**, S., *Quebec and its Historians. The Twentieth Century*, Montreal, 1985. See also Gagnon (8.359).

1.748 **Granatstein**, J. L., *Who Killed Canadian History?*, 1998. Seeks to explain why Canadians have allowed the study of the history of their own country to come near to extinction.

China

1.749 **Barme**, G., ' "History for the masses" in using the past to serve the present; historiography and politics', in J. Unger (ed.), *Contemporary China*, 1993, 260–86.

1.750 **Beasley**, W. G. and **Pulleyblank**, E. G. (eds), *Historians of China and Japan*, 1961.

1.751 **Chang**, C., 'The periodisation of Chinese history; a survey of major schemes and hypotheses', *Bull. Inst. Hist. and Philology Academia Sinica*, XLV, 1973, 157–79.

1.752 **Dirlik**, A., 'Chinese history and the question of orientalism', *Hist and Theory*, XXV, 1996, 96–118.

1.753 **Duara**, P., *Rescuing History from the Nation. Questioning Narratives of Modern China*, Chicago, IL, 1995.

1.754 **Feuerwerker**, A. (ed.), *History in Communist China*, Cambridge, MA, 1968. Seventeen essays which explore different facets of the ideologically charged historiography of communist China. There are chapters on the reinterpretation of the Middle Ages, attitudes to Buddism and Confucianism, on China's modern economic history and on Mao Tse Tung as historian.

1.755 **Franke**, W., 'Historical writing during the Ming' in F. W. Mote and D. Twitchett (eds), *Cambridge History of China* VII *The Ming Dynasty*, 1988, 736–60.

1.756 **Gardner**, C. S., *Chinese Traditional*

Historiography, Cambridge, MA, 1938, 2nd ed., 1961.

1.757 **Schwartz**, B., 'History in Chinese culture; some comparative reflections', *Hist. and Theory*, XXV, 1996, 23–33.

1.758 **Wang**, Q., 'Western historiography in the People's Republic of China (1949 to the present)', *Storia de Storiog.*, XIX, 1991, 23–46.

1.759 **Weigelin-Schweidrzik**, Susanne, 'On Shi and Lun; towards a typology of historiography in the People's Republic of China', *Hist. and Theory*, XXV, 1996, 74–95.

1.760 **Wright**, A. F. and **Hall**, J. W., 'Chinese and Japanese historiography; some trends, 1961–66', *Annals Am. Acad. Pol. and Soc. Sci.*, 371, 1967, 178–93.

Eastern Europe

1.761 **Banal**, I., 'Historiography of the countries of eastern Europe: Yugoslavia', *A.H.R.*, XCVII, 1992, 1084–104.

1.762 **Bartosek**, K., 'Czechoslovakia: the state of historiography', *J. Contemp. Hist.*, II, 1967, 143–55.

1.763 **Deak**, I., 'Historiography of the countries of eastern Europe: Hungary', *A.H.R.*, XCVII, 1992, 1041–63.

1.764 **Glatz**, F., 'Historiography, cultural policy and the organisation of scholarship in Hungary in the 1920s', *Acta Hist. Acad. Sci. Hungaricae*, XVII, 1971, 273–93.

1.765 **Hanak**, P., 'Problems of East European history in recent Hungarian historiography', *E. European Q.*, I, 1967, 123–42.

1.766 **Hitchins**, K., 'Historiography of the countries of eastern Europe: Romania', *A.H.R.*, XCVII, 1992, 1064–83.

1.767 **Horak**, S. M., 'Ukrainian historiography 1953–63', *Slav. R.*, XXIV, 1965, 258–72.

1.768 **Jablonski**, H., 'Etat actuel et perspectives des sciences historiques en Pologne', *R. Acad. Polon. Sci.*, II, 1965, 12–22.

1.769 **Jankovic**, D. (ed.), *The Historiography of Yugoslavia, 1965–75*, Belgrade, 1975.

1.770 **Kellogg**, F., *A History of Romanian Historical Writing*, Bakersfield, CA, 1990.

1.771 **Koralka**, V., 'Historiography of the countries of eastern Europe: Czechoslovakia', *A.H.R.*, XCVII, 1992, 1026–40.

1.772 **Maciu**, V., *Introduction à l'historiographie roumaine jusq'en 1918*, Bucharest, 1964.

1.773 **Tapié**, V. L., 'Les études historiques en Tchécoslovaquie', *Rev. Hist.*, 228, 1962, 119–28.

1.774 **Todorova**, Maria, 'Historiography of the countries of eastern Europe: Bulgaria', *A.H.R.*, XCVII, 1992, 1105–17.

1.775 **Velychenko**, S., *Shaping Identity in Eastern Europe and Russia. Soviet Russian and Polish Accounts of Ukrainian History, 1914–91*, New York, 1993.

1.776 ——*National History as Cultural Process. A Survey of the Interpretations of Ukraine's Past in Polish, Russian, and Ukrainian Historical Writing from the earliest Times to 1914*, Edmonton, Alta., 1992.

1.777 **Wandyca**, P., 'Historiography of the countries of eastern Europe: Poland', *A.H.R.*, XCVII, 1992, 1011–25.

France

1.778 **Gildea**, R., *The Past in French History*, 1994.

1.779 **Nora**, P. (ed.), *Realms of Memory. The Reconstruction of the French Past*, 3 vols, New York, 1996–98. A rewarding treatment of the roots of social, political and cultural differences in French society and of symbols of French identity.

1.780 **Revel**, J. and **Hunt**, Lynn (eds), *Histories. French Reconstructions of the Past*, New York, 1995.

Germany

1.781 **Antoni**, C., *From History to Sociology. The Transition in German Historical Thinking*, 1959. Dilthey, Troeltsch, Meinecke, Weber and Huizinga are included in the case studies.

1.782 **Castellan**, G., 'Remarques sur l'historiographie de la République démocratique allemande', *Rev. Hist.*, 228, 1962, 409–26.

1.783 **Dorpalen**, A., 'Historiography as history; the work of Gerhard Ritter', *J.M.H.*, XXXIV, 1962, 1–18.

1.784 ——*German History in Marxist Perspective. The East German Approach*, 1986.

1.785 **Duke**, F., 'Historiography as *Kulturkampf*; the Fischer thesis, German democracy, and the authoritarian state', *Lit. and Hist.*, 6:1, 1980, 94–110.

1.786 **Fletcher**, R., 'History from below comes to Germany; the new history movement in the Federal Republic of Germany', *J.M.H.*, LX, 1988, 557–68.

1.787 **Heuser**, Beatrice, 'Museums, identity and warring historians; observations on history in Germany', *Hist. J.*, XXXIII, 1990, 417–40.

1.788 **Iggers**, G. G. (ed.), *The Social History of Politics. Critical Perspectives on West German Historical Writing since 1945*, 1985.

1.789 **Kohn**, H. (ed.), *German History. Some New German Views*, 1954.

1.790 **Maier**, C., *The Unmasterable Past. History, Holocaust and the German National Identity*, Cambridge, MA, 1988.

1.791 **Mommsen**, H., 'Historical scholarship in transition; the situation in the Federal Republic of Germany', *Daedalus*, C, 1971, 485–508.

1.792 ——'Between revisionism and neohistoricism; recent trends in West Germany historiography', *Storia de Storiog.*, XI, 1987, 104–21.

1.793 **Moses**, J. A., 'The crisis of West German historiography; origins and trends', *Hist. Studs.*, XIII, 1969, 445–59.

1.794 **Pflanze**, O., 'Another crisis among German historians? Helmut Böhme's *Deutschlands Weg zur Grossmacht*', *J.M.H.*, XL, 1968, 118–29.

1.795 **Ringer**, F., '*Bildung*; the social and ideological context of the German historical tradition' *Hist. European Ideas*, X, 1989, 193–202.

1.796 **Werner**, K. F., 'On some examples of the National Socialist view of history', *J. Contemp. Hist.*, III, 1968, 193–206.

The Iberian Peninsula

1.797 **Hillgarth**, J. N., 'Spanish historiography and Iberian reality',

Hist. and Theory, XXIV, 1985, 23–43.

1.798 **Mauro**, F. 'L'histoire au Portugal', *Rev. Hist.*, 229, 1963, 433–42.

India

1.799 **Ahmad**, A., 'Approaches to history in late nineteenth-century and early twentieth-century Muslim India', *J. World Hist.*, IX, 1966, 987–1008.

1.800 **Chakrabarty**, D., 'Postcoloniality and the artifice of history; who speaks for the "Indian" pasts?', *Representations*, XXXVII, 1992, 1–26.

1.801 **Evans**, H., 'Recent Soviet writing on India', *Central Asian Rev.*, XVI, 1968, 110–21, 229–43.

1.802 **Philips**, C. H. (ed.) *Historians of India, Pakistan, and Ceylon*, 1961.

1.803 **Ray**, S., 'India after independence (contemporary Indian historiography)', *J. Contemp. Hist.*, II, 1967, 125–40.

1.804 **Sarkar**, S., 'Many worlds; the construction of history in modern India', *Storia de Storiog.*, XIX, 1991, 61–72.

1.805 **Spodek**, H., 'Pluralist politics in modern India; the Cambridge cluster of historians of modern India', *A.H.R.*, LXXXIV, 1979, 688–707.

1.806 **Warder**, A. K., *An Introduction to Indian Historiography*, Bombay, 1972.

Ireland

1.807 **Barnard**, T. C., 'Farewell to Old Ireland', *Hist. J.*, XXXVI, 1993, 909–28.

1.808 **Boyce**, D. G., and **O'Day**, A. (eds), *The Making of Modern Irish History. Revisionism and the Revisionist Controversy*, 1996.

1.809 **Brady**, C. (ed.), *Interpreting Irish History. The Debate on Historical Revisionism, 1938–94*, Dublin, 1994.

1.810 **Daly**, Mary E., 'Recent writings on modern Irish history; the interaction between past and present', *J.M.H.*, LXIX, 1997, 512–33.

1.811 **Foster**, R., 'The problems of writing Irish history', *Hist. Today*, XXXIV, 1984, 27–30.

1.812 **Lee**, J. (ed.), *Irish Historiography, 1970–1979*, Cork, 1981. Complements Moody (1.813).

1.813 **Moody**, T. W. (ed.), *Irish Historiography, 1936–70*, Dublin, 1971. A collection of bibliographical essays.

Italy

1.814 **Berengo**, M., 'Italian historical scholarship since the fascist era', *Daedalus*, C, 1971, 469–84.

1.815 **Jacobitti**, E. E., *Revolutionary Humanism and Historicism in Modern Italy*, 1981. Focuses particularly on Benedetto Croce.

Japan

1.816 **Brownlee**, J. S., *Political Thought in Japanese Historical Writing*, Waterloo, Ont., 1991.

1.817 **Maruyama**, M., *Studies in the Intellectual History of Tokugawa Japan*, Princeton, NJ, 1974.

1.818 **Mayo**, Marlene J., 'Some reflections on the new texts in Japanese history and the current state of American scholarship on Japan', *J. Asian Studs.*, XXXI, 1971, 157–66.

1.819 **Nakamura**, H., 'L'historie en Inde, en Chine et au Japon', *Diogène*, XLII, 1963, 48–63.

1.819a *Recent Trends in Japanese Historiography. Bibliographical Essays on Japan at the XIIIth International Congress of Historical Sciences in Moscow*, Tokyo, 1970.

1.820 **Wilson**, G. M., 'Time and history in Japan', *A.H.R.*, LXXXV, 1980, 557–71.

Jewish History

1.821 **Dawidowicz**, Lucy S., *What is the Use of Jewish History?*, New York, 1992.

1.822 **Meyer**, M. A., 'The emergence of modern Jewish historiography; motives and motifs', *Hist. and Theory*, XXVII, 1988, 160–75.

1.823 **Yerushalmi**, J. H., *Zakhor. Jewish History and Jewish Memory*, Seattle, WA, 1982.

Latin America

1.824 **Burns**, E. B., *Perspectives in Brazilian History*, New York, 1967. An invaluable collection of essays which includes chapters on 'Brazilian historiography in the nineteenth and twentieth centuries', 'Guide for the historiography of the Second Empire', 'Problems in Brazilian history and historiography', 'Periodization of Brazilian history' and 'Historical thought in twentieth-century Brazil'.

1.825 **Cline**, H. F., (ed.), *Latin American History. Essays on its Study and Teaching 1898–1965*, 2 vols, Austin, TX, 1967.

1.826 **Halperin**, D. T., 'The state of Latin American history', in C. Mitchell (ed.), *Changing Perspectives in Latin American Studies. Insights from Six Disciplines*, Stanford, CA, 1988, 13–62.

1.827 **Smith**, R. F., 'Twentieth-century Cuban historiography', *Hisp. Am. Hist.*, XLIV, 1964, 44–73.

The Middle East

1.828 **Chejne**, A. G., 'The use of history by modern Arab writers', *Middle East J.*, 1960, 382–96.

1.829 **Chesnaux**, J., 'For an Asian history of modern Asia', *Diogenes*, LI, 1966, 104–19.

1.830 **Farouk-Sluglett**, Marion and **Sluglett**, P., 'The historiography of modern Iraq', *A.H.R.*, XCVI, 1991, 1408–21.

1.831 **Hourani**, A., 'Islam and the philosophers of history', *Middle East Studs.*, III, 1967, 206–68.

1.832 **Lewis**, B. and **Holt**, R. (ed.), *Historians of the Middle East*, 1962. There are four general sections: Arabic, Persian and Turkish historiography to the twelfth century; European historical writing on the Near and Middle East from the Middle Ages to the present day; modern Middle Eastern historical writing: general themes.

1.833 **Owen**, R., 'Studying Islamic history', *J. Interdis. Hist.*, IV, 1973, 287–98.

1.834 **Peterson**, J. E., 'The Arabian peninsula in modern times; a historiographical survey', *A.H.R.*, XCVI, 1991, 1435–49.

1.835 **Rosenthal**, F., *A History of Muslim Historiography*, rev. ed., Leiden, 1968.

Scandinavia

1.836 **Aalto**, P., *Oriental Studies in Finland, 1828–1918*, Helsinki, 1971. Deals with the heritage of earlier centuries, with the nineteenth-century study of oriental literature, Old Testament philology, biblical archaeology, gypsy studies, social anthropology, and with the explorers. Bibliography, 159–63.

1.837 **Barton**, H. A., 'Historians of Scandinavia in the English-speaking world since 1945', *Scand. Studs.*, XL, 1968, 273–93.

1.838 **Smith**, L. F., *Modern Norwegian Historiography*, Oslo, 1962.

1.839 **Torsendahl**, R., 'Minimum demand and optimum norms in Swedish historical research, 1920–60; the Weibull school in Swedish historiography', *Scand. J. Hist.*, VI, 1981, 117–41.

South East Asia

1.840 **Harper**, T. N., 'Asian values and South East Asian histories', *Hist. J.*, XL, 1997, 507–18.

1.841 **Reid**, A. and **Marr**, D. (eds), *Perceptions of the Past in South East Asia*, Singapore, 1979.

Turkey

1.842 **Castellan**, G., 'Directions nouvelles de l'histoire des Balkans', *Rev. Hist.*, 236, 1966, 107–24.

1.843 **Guboglu**, M., 'L'historiographie ottomane des XVe–XVIIIe siècles; bref aperçu', *Rev. Etat Sud-est Europe*, III, 1965, 81–93.

1.844 **Kerim**, K., *Outline of Modern Turkish Historiography*, Istanbul, 1954.

1.845 **Mantran**, R., 'L'orientation des études historiques en Turquie', *Rev. Hist.*, 234, 1965, 311–22.

The Former USSR

1.846 **Allen**, R. V., 'Recent developments in the history of the Soviet Union and Eastern Europe', *Annals. Am. Acad. Pol. and Soc. Sci.*, 365, 1966, 147–60.

1.847 **Barber**, J., *Soviet Historians in Crisis, 1928–32*, 1981. Looks at the responses of Russian historians to the tense and confused environment which surrounded them and to Stalin's intervention in 1931.

1.848 **Baron**, S. H., 'The transition from feudalism to capitalism in Russia; a major Soviet historical controversy', *A.H.R.*, LXXVII, 1972, 715–29.

1.849 **Black**, C. E. (ed.), *Rewriting Russian History. Soviet Interpretations of Russia's Past*, 1956, 2nd ed. New York, 1962. A collection of essays divided into two sections on the evolution and application of theory. There are chapters on 'History and politics in the Soviet Union', 'The problem of periodization', 'The role of the individual in history', 'The formation of the great Russian state', 'Ivan the Terrible', 'Peter the Great', and on 'The campaign of 1812'.

1.850 **Bolkhovitinov**, N. N., 'The study of US history in the Soviet Union', *A.H.R.*, LXXIV, 1969, 1221–42.

1.851 **Davies**, R. W., *Soviet History in the Gorbachev Revolution*, Bloomington, IN, 1989.

1.852 **Enteen**, G. M., 'Marxists v. non-Marxists; Soviet historiography in the 1920s', *Slav. R.*, XXXV, 1976, 91–110.

1.853 **Gati**, C., 'History, social science and the study of Soviet foreign policy', *Slav. R.*, XXIX, 1970, 682–87.

1.854 **Heer**, Nancy W., *Politics and History in the Soviet Union*, Cambridge, MA, 1971. Discusses the historiography of the 1950s and 1960s under four heads: history as political sub-system, history as political record, history as the mirror of conscience, history as portent. Extensive bibliography.

1.855 **Kan**, A., 'Soviet historiography of the West under Stalin's pre-war dictatorship', *Storia de Storiog.*, XXI, 1992, 45–64.

1.856 **Keep**, J. (ed.), *Contemporary History in the Soviet Mirror*, 1964. A symposium of thirteen essays based on the proceedings of a conference. The topics covered include: 'Party histories from Lenin to Krushchev', 'Soviet historians and the Sino-Soviet alliance' and 'Soviet historians and American history'.

1.857 **Loone**, E., *Soviet Marxism and Analytical Philosophies of History*, 1992.

1.858 **Mendel**, A. P., 'Current Soviet theory of history; new trends or old?', *A.H.R.*, LXXII, 1966, 50–73.

1.859 **Pork**, A., 'Critical philosophy of history in Soviet thought', *Hist. and Theory*, XXVII, 1988, 135–45.

1.860 **Pundeff**, M. (ed.), *History in the USSR. Selected Readings*, San Francisco, 1967, Deals with the doctrines of Marx and Engels, Plekhanov and Lenin and with their application and development under Lenin, the first Interregnum (1924–27), under Stalin, the second Interregnum (1953–55) and under Krushchev (1955–64). Bibliography and suggestions for further reading, 298–309.

1.861 **Rogger**, H., 'Politics, ideology and history in the USSR; the search for coexistence', *Sov. Studs.*, XVI, 1965, 253–75.

1.862 **Shteppa**, K. F., *Russian Historians and the Soviet State*, 1962. Surveys the period from 1917 to the early 1950s.

1.863 **Thaden**, E. C., 'Encounters with Soviet historians', *Historian*, XX, 1957, 80–95.

The United States

1.864 **Auerbach**, J. S., 'New Deal, Old Deal or raw deal; some thoughts on New Left historiography', *J. Southern Hist.*, XXXV, 1969, 18–30.

1.865 **Ausubel**, H., *Historians and their Craft. A Study of the Presidential Addresses of the American Historical Association, 1884–1945*, New York, 1950. Discusses their changing views on the immediate utility of history, on history as literature, on historical facts, on the science and philosophy of history and on the role of individuals.

1.866 **Bailey**, T. A., 'The myth makers of American history', *J.A.H.*, LV, 1968, 5–21.

1.867 **Bass**, H. J. (ed.), *The State of American History*, Chicago, IL, 1970. Includes essays on agricultural history, urban history, psychohistory, quantitative history and on ethnic history.

1.868 **Bassett**, J. S., *The Middle Group of American Historians*, 1916, Freeport, NY, 1966. The chapters deal with the early progress of history in the United States, with Jared Sparks, George Bancroft, Prescott and Motley, Peter Force the compiler, and with historians' publishers.

1.869 **Beard**, C., 'Grounds for a reconsideration of historiography', *Theory and Practice in Historical Study. A Report on the Committee on Historiography*, New York, 1946.

1.870 **Benson**, L., *Toward the Scientific Study of History. Selected Essays*, Philadelphia, 1972. Chiefly concerned with the study of American political history.

1.871 **Binkley**, W. C., 'Two world wars and American historical scholarship', *Miss. Vall. H.R.* XXXIII, 1946, 3–26.

1.872 **Bogue**, A. G., 'United States; the "new" political history', *J. Contemp. Hist.*, III, 1968, 5–27.

1.873 **Breisach**, E. A., *American Progressive History. An Experiment in Modernization*, Chicago, IL, 1993. Covers the period 1890–1948 and provides extensive treatments of Turner, Beard and Becker. See also (1.893).

1.874 **Burton**, D. H. (ed.), *American History – British Historians*, Chicago, IL, 1978. There are two general essays on conceptions of American history.

1.875 **Cohen**, W. I., *The American Revisionists*, Chicago, IL, 1967.

1.876 **Commager**, H. S., *The Search for a Usable Past, and other Essays in Historiography*, New York, 1967. A mixture of general essays – such as the one which provides the title for the book – and case studies.

1.877 **Cunliffe**, M. and **Winks**, R. W. (eds), *Past Masters. Some Essays on American Historians*, New York, 1969. Includes essays on Adams, Beard, Miller and Boorstin.

1.878 **Curti**, M. (ed.), *American Scholarship in the Twentieth Century*, Cambridge, MA, 1953. Includes essays on history, philosophy and the social sciences.

1.879 —— 'The democratic theme in American historical literature', *Miss. Vall. H.R.*, XXXIX, 1952, 3–28.

1.880 **Donovan**, T. P., *Historical Thought in America. Postwar Patterns*, Norman, OK, 1973. Examines historians' responses to the changed conditions after 1945 and the expansion and redefinition of their subject. Extensive bibliography, 147–78.

1.881 **Eisenstadt**, A. S. (ed.), *The Craft of American History. Selected Essays*, 2 vols, New York, 1966. An invaluable collection arranged under seven heads: the nature and uses of history; objectivity and truth in history; history of American history; rewriting the American past; varieties of history; history and other disciplines; research and writing.

1.882 **Garraty**, J. A., *Interpreting American History. Conversations with Historians*, New York, 1970. An American equivalent of Cantor (9.25). Greene, Bailyn, Commager, Hofstadter and Billington are included.

1.883 **Gatell**, F. O. and **Weinstein**, A. (eds), *American Themes. Essays in Historiography*, New York, 1968. Arranged chronologically, these essays examine important debates in American history. J. R. Pole concludes by asking whether the American past is still usable, 450–66. Bibliography.

1.884 **Guggisberg**, H., 'The uses of the European past in American historiography', *J. Am. Hist.*, IV, 1970, 1–18.

1.885 **Hanke**, L., 'American historians and the world today; responsibilities and opportunities', *A.H.R.*, LXXX, 1975, 1–20.

1.886 **Higham**, J., 'American intellectual history; a critical appraisal', *Am. Q.*, XIII, 1961, 219–33.

1.887 —— 'Changing paradigms; the collapse of consensus history', *J.A.H.*, LXXVI, 1989, 460–6.

1.888 —— *History. The Development of Historical Studies in the United States*, 1968.

1.889 —— *The Reconstruction of American History*, 1962. Eleven essays which examine different facets of the changing face of American historiography. Useful guide to further reading.

1.890 —— 'The rise of American intellectural history', *A.H.R.*, LVI, 1951, 453–71.

1.891 —— 'The schism in American scholarship', *A.H.R.*, LXXII, 1966, 1–21.

1.892 —— *Writing American History. Essays on Modern Scholarship*, Bloomington, IN, 1970.

1.893 **Hofstadter**, R., *The Progressive Historians*, 1969. A well known study of Turner, Beard and Parrington, their context and their influence. See also (1.873).

1.894 **Hoggan**, D. L., *The Myth of the 'New History'. The Techniques and Tactics of the New Mythologists of American History*, Nutley, NJ, 1965. Deals with eight crises in American history and the changing theories and methods harnessed to deal with them. Bibliography, 237–44.

1.895 **Hollinger**, D. A., 'The problem of pragmatism in American history', *J.A.H.*, LXVII, 1980, 88–107.

1.896 **Holt**, W. S., *Historical Scholarship in the United States and other Essays*, Seattle, WA, 1967. Part One is specifically historiographical and includes essays on 'The idea of scientific history in America' and 'Historical scholarship in the twentieth century'.

1.897 **Hoover**, D. W., 'Some comments on recent US Historiography', *Am. Q.*, XVII, 1965, 299–318.

1.898 **Hosmer**, C. B., *Presence of the Past. A History of the Preservation Movement in the US before Williamsburg*, Charlottesville, VA, 1965.

1.899 —— *Preservation Comes of Age. From Williamsburg to the National Trust, 1926–49*, Charlottesville, VA, 1981.

1.900 **Jacobs**, W. R., *On Turner's Trail. 100 Years of Writing Western History*, Lawrence, KS, 1994.

1.901 **Jones**, H. G., *For History's Sake. The Preservation and Publication of North Carolina History, 1663–1903*, Chapel Hill, NC, 1966.

1.902 **Kammen**, M. (ed.), *The Past before Us. Contemporary Historical Writing in the United States*, Ithaca, NY, 1980. Looks at the current state of individual fields of history, at new and expanding areas (black history, for example) and at methodological changes.

1.903 —— *Selvages and Biases. The Fabric of History in American Culture*, Ithaca, NY, 1987.

1.904 **Kraditor**, Aileen S., 'American radical historians on their heritage', *P.P.*, 56, 1972, 136–53.

1.905 **Kramer**, L., **Reid**, D., and **Barney**, W. L., *Learning History in America. Schools, Cultures and Politics*, Minneapolis, MN, 1994.

1.906 **Kraus**, M., *The Writing of American History*, Norman, OK, 1953, 2nd ed., revised by D. D. Joyce, 1985. A survey of the writing of American history which extends from the Age of Discovery to the twentieth century. Francis Parkman and Henry Adams each receive a separate chapter.

1.907 **Kristol**, I., 'American historians and the democratic idea', *Am. Scholar*, XXXIX, 1970, 89–104.

1.908 **Kutler**, S. I. and **Katz**, S. N. (eds), *The Promise of American History*, Baltimore, MD, 1982.

1.909 **Lemisch**, J., *On Active Service in War and Peace. Politics and Ideology in the American Historical Profession*, Toronto, 1975.

1.910 **Loewenberg**, B. J., *American History in American Thought. Christopher Columbus to Henry Adams*, New York, 1972. A careful survey of the development of American historiography from its origins. There are separate chapters on the Revolution, nationalism, the Civil War. Individual historians such as Sparks, Bancroft, Hildreth, Burgess, Henry Baxter Adams and Henry Adams receive separate chapters. There is also a chapter on the impact of science and the science of history together with institutional studies of Johns Hopkins, Columbia and Harvard universities. Extensive bibliography, 659–96.

1.911 **Lowenheim**, F. L. (ed.), *The Historian and the Diplomat. The Role of History and Historians in American Foreign Policy*, New York, 1967. Concentrates chiefly on record keeping, on memory and on historical thought in the twentieth century.

1.912 **Mowry**, G. E., 'The uses of history by recent presidents', *J.A.H.*, 53, 1966, 5–18.

1.913 **Perkins**, D. and **Snell**, J. L., *The Education of Historians in the United States*, New York, 1962. Looks at the present position, problems and prospects of history in education in the United States.

1.914 **Pierre**, Bessie L., *Public Opinion and the Teaching of History in the United States*, New York, 1970.

1.915 **Rapson**, R. L. (ed.), *Major Interpretations of the American Past*, New York, 1971.

1.916 **Reinitz**, R., *Irony and Consciousness. American Historiography and Reinhold Niebuhr's Vision*, Lewisburg, PA, 1980.

1.917 **Robinson**, A. L., 'Beyond the realm of social consensus; new meanings of reconstruction in American history', *J.A.H.*, LXVIII, 1981, 276–97.

1.918 **Rundell**, W., *In Pursuit of American History. Research and Training in the United States*, Norman, OK, 1970.

1.919 **Russo**, D. J., *Clio Confused. Troubling Aspects of Historical Study from the Perspective of US History*, Westport, CT, 1995.

1.920 ——*Families and Communities. A New View of American History*, Nashville, TN, 1974.

1.921 **Sanders**, J. B., *Historical Interpretations and American Historianship*, Yellow Springs, OH, 1966. Includes chapters on history and its philosophic–scientific setting, historicism and relativism, historianship, citizenship and moral responsibility, the preparation and practice of the historian, and on the American character and American history.

1.922 **Shaffer**, A., 'John Day Burk's *History of Virginia* and the development of American national history', *Virginia Mag. Hist and Biog.*, LXXVII, 1969, 336–46.

1.923 **Shalhope**, R. E., 'Toward a Republican synthesis; the emergence of an understanding in American historiography', *Wm and Mary Q.*, XXIX, 1972, 49–80.

1.924 **Skotheim**, R. A., *American Intellectual Histories and Historians*, Princeton, NJ, 1966. Deals with early American chroniclers and historians from the seventeenth century to the nineteenth, with the progressive tradition (represented by Robinson, Beard, Becker, Parrington, Curti) and with its assailants (Morison, Miller *et al.*).

1.925 —— (ed.), *The Historian and the Climate of Opinion*, Reading, MA, 1969. An interesting collection on American historiography, though some of the essays – on the historian as moral critic and on the historian as participant – are of more general significance.

1.926 **Soltow**, J. H., 'Recent developments in United States history', *Annals Am. Acad. Pol. and Soc. Sci.*, 375, 1968, 176–95.

1.927 **Sternsher**, B., *Consensus, Conflict, and American Historians*, Bloomington, IN, 1975.

1.928 **Tejera**, V., *History as a Human Science. The Conception of History in some Classic American Philosophers*, Lanham, MD, 1984.

1.929 **Unger**, I., 'The New Left *v.* the New History', *A.H.R.*, LXXII, 1967, 1237–63.

1.930 **White**, M. W., *Pragmatism and the American Mind. Essays and Reviews in Philosophical and Intellectual History*, New York, 1973. Deals, *interalia*, with historicism, E. H. Carr and Richard Hofstadter.

1.931 **Wise**, G., *American Historical Explanations. A Strategy for Grounded Inquiry*, Homewood, IL, 1973. Deals with forms, ideas, reality, books, explanations, and offers strategies for grounded enquiry. There are case studies of Turner and the Progressives, Parrington, and the new consensus of Lewis, Miller and the counter-progressives.

1.932 **Wish**, H., *The American Historian. A Social and Intellectual History of Writings on the American Past*, New York, 1960. Surveys the development of American historiography from the seventeenth century to the present day, though it tends – anachronistically – to judge earlier historians by the standards of scientific history.

1.933 —— (ed.), *American Historians. A Selection*, New York, 1962. An anthology of lengthy extracts extending from William Bradford in the seventeenth century to Arthur M. Schlesinger Jr in the twentieth.

1.934 —— 'The American historian and the new conservatism', *S. Atlantic Q.*, LXV, 1966, 178–91.

1.935 —— 'The new formalism *v.* the progressive historians', *S. Atlantic Q.*, LXVII, 1968, 78–93.

1.936 **Woodward**, C. V., *American Attitudes toward History*, 1955.

1.937 **Young**, A. (ed.), *Beyond the American Revolution. Explorations in the History of American Radicalism*, DeKalb, IL, 1993.

2

ANCIENT
HISTORY

GENERAL

2.1 **Albrektson**, B., *History and the Gods. An Essay on the Idea of Historical Events as Divine Manifestations in the Ancient Near East and in Israel*, Lund, 1967.

2.2 **Burke**, P., 'A survey of the popularity of ancient historians, 1450–1700', *Hist. and Theory*, V, 1966, 135–52.

2.3 **Butterfield**, H., *The Origins of History*, 1981. Deals with the earliest stages in the development of historiography. Jews, Greeks and Chinese figure prominently, as does the establishment of a Christian historiography. Bibliography.

2.4 **Cameron**, A. (ed.), *History as Text. The Writing of Ancient History*, 1989.

2.5 **Clarke**, M. L., *Classical Education in Britain, 1500–1900*, 1959. Deals with the classical education provided in English grammar schools and universities. There are supplementary chapters on Scotland and on Trinity College, Dublin.

2.6 **Coleman**, Janet, *Ancient and Medieval Memories. Studies in the Reconstruction of the Past*, 1992.

2.7 **Dean-Boer**, W., 'Graeco-Roman historiography in its relation to biblical and modern thinking', *Hist. and Theory*, IX, 1968, 60–75.

2.8 **Dentan**, R. C. (ed.), *The Idea of History in the Ancient Near East*, New Haven, CT, 1966. Separate chapters deal with Egypt, Mesopotamia, Persia, Israel, the Hellenistic Orient, with Christianity and Islam.

2.9 **Dodds**, E. R., *The Ancient Concept of Progress, and other Essays on Greek Literature and Belief*, 1973. A collection of lectures. As well as the one which gives its title to the book, chapter 10 on 'supernormal phenomena in classical antiquity' may be noted.

2.10 **Edelstein**, L., *The Idea of Progress in Classical Antiquity*, Baltimore, MD, 1967. A portion of what was intended to be a larger work extending down to the sixth century A.D. The four chapters cover the development of the idea of progress down to 30 B.C. Bibliography, 181–98.

2.11 **Finley**, M. I., *The Use and Abuse of History*, 1975. Includes essays on 'Generalizations in ancient history', 'Archaeology and history' and 'Anthropology and the classics'.

2.12 ——*Ancient History. Evidence and Models*, 1985. Chapters on 'The ancient historian and his sources', on war and empire and on Max Weber and the Greek city state.

2.13 **Fornara**, C. W., *The Nature of History in Ancient Greece and Rome*, Berkeley, CA, 1983. Deals systematically with genres, aims and methods.

2.14 **Galasterer**, H., 'A man, a book, and a method: Sir Ronald Syme's *Roman Revolution* after fifty years', in K. Raaflaub and M. Toher (eds), *Between Republic and Empire. Interpretations of*

Augustus and his Principate, Berkeley, CA, 1990.

2.15 **Grant**, M., *The Ancient Historians*, 1970. Superior popularisation.

2.16 **Halpern**, B., *The First Historians. The Hebrew Bible and History*, San Francisco, CA 1988.

2.17 **Holborn**, H., 'History and the study of the classics', *J. Hist. Ideas*, XIV, 1953, 33–50.

2.18 **Jones**, T. B., *Paths to the Ancient Past. Applications of the Historical Method to Ancient History*, New York, 1967.

2.19 **Khalidi**, T., *Arabic Historical Thought in the Classical Period*, Cambridge, MA, 1994.

2.20 **Luce**, T. J. (ed.), *Ancient Writers. Greece and Rome*, 2 vols, New York, 1983. A useful reference work.

2.21 **McMullen**, D., *State and Scholars in T'ang China*, 1988.

2.22 **Mann**, W. R., 'The origins of the modern historiography of ancient philosophy', *Hist. and Theory*, XXXV, 1996, 165–95. See also (2.33).

2.23 **Markus**, R. A., *From Augustine to Gregory the Great. History and Christianity in late Antiquity*, 1983.

2.24 **Milburn**, R. L. P., *Early Christian Interpretations of History*, 1954. Includes chapters on the use of history in early apologetic, on Eusebius, on God's judgement in history, and on the treatment of history in early Christian art.

2.25 **Momigliano**, A., *Studies in Historiography*, 1966. Thirteen essays which include 'Gibbon's contribution to historical method', 'The place of Herodotus in the history of historiography' and 'Historicism in contemporary thought'.

2.26 —— 'The historians of the classical world and their audiences', *Am. Scholar*, XLVII, 1978, 193–204.

2.27 —— *The Classical Foundations of Modern Historiography*, 1990.

2.28 **Ogilvie**, R. M., *Latin and Greek. A History of the Influence of the Classics on English Life from 1600 to 1918*, 1964.

2.29 **Pathak**, V. S., *Ancient Historians and India*, Bombay, 1966.

2.30 **Press**, G. A., *The Development of the Idea of History in Antiquity*, Montreal, 1982. Looks at the supersession of Graeco-Roman ideas by Judaeo-Christian culture.

2.31 **Rabinowitz**, Nancy S. and **Kichlin**, Amy, *Feminist Theory and the Classics*, New York, 1993.

2.32 **Shotwell**, J. T., *An Introduction to the History of History*, New York, 1922. Devoted chiefly to ancient Jewish, Greek and Roman historiography and to the impact of Christianity.

2.33 **Twitchett**, D., *The Writing of Official History under the T'ang*, 1992.

2.34 **Usher**, S., *The Historians of Greece and Rome*, 1969. A well written introduction to Herodotus, Thucydides, Xenophon, Polybius, Sallust, Livy, Tacitus and others.

2.35 **Wilamowitz-Moellendorf**, U. von, *History of Classical Scholarship*, ed. H. Lloyd-Jones, 1982. A modern edition of a work first published in Germany in 1921. There is a substantial new introduction and annotations to the text.

2.36 **Woodman**, A. J., *Rhetoric in Classical Historiography*, 1988.

GREECE

2.37 **Adcock**, F. E., *Thucydides and his History*, 1963. A suggestive reconsideration of the *History* and its background. Purposes, ethics, politics, dialectic and narrative are examined.

2.38 **Anderson**, J. K., *Xenophon*, 1974.

2.39 **Austin**, N., *The Greek Historians. Herodotus, Thucydides, Polybius, Plutarch. Introduction and Selected Readings*, New York, 1969.

2.40 **Brown**, T., *The Greek Historians*, Lexington, MA, 1973.

2.41 **Bury**, J. B., *The Ancient Greek Historians*, 1909.

2.42 **Cochrane**, C. N., *Thucydides and the Science of History*, 1929.

2.43 **Cogan**, M., *The Human Thing. The Speeches and Principles of Thucydides' History* Chicago, IL, 1981.

2.44 **Dewald**, Caroline and **Marincola**, J. (eds), *Herodotus and the Invention of History*, Buffalo, NY, 1987.

2.45 **Dombrowski**, D. A., *Plato's Philosophy of History*, Washington, DC, 1981.

2.46 **Dover**, K. J., *Thucydides*, 1973.

2.47 —— 'Thucydides as "history" and as "literature" ', *Hist. and Theory*, XXII, 1983, 54–63.

2.48 **Drews**, R., *The Greek Accounts of Eastern History*, Cambridge, MA, 1973. Chapters on the archaic period, the earliest Greek accounts of Eastern history, Herodotus, and on Herodotus's successors. Bibliography, 211–14.

2.49 **Evans**, J. A. S., *Herodotus*, Boston, MA, 1983. A basic introduction.

2.50 —— *Herodotus, Explorer of the Past. Three Essays*, Princeton, NJ, 1991.

2.51 **Fehling**, D., *Herodotus and his 'Sources'. Citation, Invention and Narrative Art*, 1989.

2.52 **Finley**, J. W., *Thucydides*, Cambridge, MA, 1942.

2.53 —— *Three Essays on Thucydides*, Cambridge, MA, 1967.

2.54 **Finley**, M. I., *The Greek Historians*, 1959. Systematic, perceptive analysis.

2.55 **Gomme**, A. W., *The Greek Attitude to Poetry and History*, Berkeley, CA, 1954. Concentrates on Homer, Aristotle (in the *Poetics*), Herodotus, Aeschylus and Thucydides.

2.56 —— *A Historical Commentary on Thucydides*, 4 vols, 1945–70.

2.57 **Gould**, J., *Herodotus*, 1989.

2.58 **Grundy**, G. B., *Thucydides and the History of his Age*, 1911, 2nd ed., 2 vols, 1948. Detailed analysis of the composition of Thucydides' *History* against the background of the economic and military trends of the period.

2.59 **Hart**, J., *Herodotus and Greek History*, 1982. Deals straightforwardly with Herodotus's treatment of personalities, religion, war and politics.

2.60 **Hartog**, F., *The Mirror of Herodotus*, Berkeley, CA, 1988.

2.61 **Henry**, W. P., *Greek Historical Writing. A Historiographical Essays based on Xenophon's Hellenica*, Chicago, 1967.

2.62 **Hornblower**, S. (ed.), *Greek Historiography*, 1994.

2.63 —— *Thucydides*, 1987.

2.64 **Hunter**, Virginia, *Past and Process in Herodotus and Thucydides*, Princeton, NJ, 1982. Considers the dynamics of time and process in the light of problematics inspired by Braudel and Foucault.

2.65 **Hunter**, *Thucydides. The Artful Reporter*, Toronto, 1973.

2.66 **Immerwahr**, H. R., *Form and Thought in Herodotus*, Cleveland, OH, 1966. Has chapters on the subject matter of the *Histories*, on style and structure, Herodotus's dealings with both east and west, with the great battles of the Persian wars and with 'History and the order of nature'.

2.67 **Jenkyns**, R., *The Victorians and Ancient Greece*, 1980. A wide-ranging exploration of the many facets of the Hellenism favoured by the Victorians. See also Turner (2.85).

2.68 **Kateb**, G., 'Thucydides' *History*: a manual of statecraft', *Pol. Sci. Q.*, LXXIX, 1964, 481–503.

2.69 **Konstan**, D., 'Inventing ancient Greece', *Hist. and Theory*, XXXVI, 1997, 261–9.

2.70 **Kosso**, P., 'Historical evidence and epistemic justification: Thucydides as a case study', *Hist. and Theory*, XXXII, 1993, 1–13.

2.71 **Lang**, Mabel L., *Herodotean Narrative and Discourse*, Cambridge, MA, 1984.

2.72 **Lateiner**, D., *The Historical Method of Herodotus*, Toronto, 1989.

2.73 **Lewis**, D. M. (ed.), *The Greek Historians. Literature and History. Essays presented to A. E. Raubitschek*, Stanford, CA, 1986.

2.74 **Momigliano**, A., 'Greek historiography', *Hist. and Theory*, XVII, 1978, 1–28.

2.75 **Myres**, J. L., *Herodotus: the Father of History*, 1953.

2.76 **Page**, D. L., *History and the Homeric Iliad*, Berkeley, CA, 1959. Originally lectures. Supplements a close analysis of the *Iliad* with a detailed consideration of other available historical and archaeological evidence.

2.77 **Pearson**, L., *Early Ionian Historians*, 1939. Detailed, scholarly studies of Hecataeus of Miletus, Xanthus the Lydian, Charon of Lampsacus and Hellenicus of Lesbos.

2.78 **Pfeiffer**, R., *History of Classical Scholarship from the Beginnings to the End of the Hellenistic Age*, 1968. Though not chiefly concerned with historians as such this study does much to open up the intellectual ethos of the time.

2.79 **Powell**, J. E., *The History of Herodotus*, Amsterdam, 1967.

2.80 **Pritchett**, W. K., *The Liar School of Herodotus*, Amsterdam, 1993.

2.81 **Romilly**, J de, *Thucydides and Athenian Imperialism*, 1963.

2.82 **Shrimpton**, G., 'Time, memory and narrative in Thucydides', *Storia de Storiog.*, XXVIII, 1995, 47–54.

2.83 **Starr**, C. G., *The Awakening of the Greek Historical Spirit*, New York, 1968.

2.84 **Toynbee**, A. J. (ed.), *Greek Historical Thought*, 1950.

2.85 **Turner**, F. M., *The Greek Heritage in Victorian Britain*, New Haven, CT, 1981. A wide-ranging discussion of the appeal of Hellenism in the nineteenth century. Includes a discussion of Grote, Mitford, Arnold and Jowett. See also Jenkins (2.67).

2.86 **Verdin**, H., **Schepens**, G., and **de Keyser**, E., *Purposes of History. Studies in Greek Historiography from the Fourth to the Second Centuries BC*, Leuven, 1990.

2.87 **Walsh**, W. H., 'Plato and the philosophy of history; history and theory in the *Republic*', *Hist. and Theory*, II, 1962, 3–16.

2.88 **Waters**, K. H., 'The relationship of material and structure in the *History* of Herodotus', *Storia de Storiog.*, VII, 1985, 123–37.

2.89 **Westlake**, H. D., *Essays on the Greek Historians and Greek History*, 1969.
——*Individuals in Thucydides*, 1968.

2.90 **Wood**, Ellen, 'Marxism and ancient Greece', *Hist. Workshop J.*, XI, 1981, 3–23.

2.91 **Woodhead**, A. G., *Thucydides on the Nature of Power*, Cambridge, MA, 1970.

ROME

2.92 **Adcock**, F. E., *Caesar as Man of Letters*, 1956. Considers the form and purposes of Caesar's writing.

2.93 **Attridge**, H. W., *The Presentation of Biblical History in the 'Antiquates Judicae' of Flavius Josephus*, Missoula, MT, 1976.

2.94 **Baldwin**, B., *Suetonius*, Amsterdam, 1983.

2.95 **Barrow**, R. H., *Plutarch and his times*, 1967. Devotes most space to Plutarch as teacher and as commentator on the Roman empire.

2.96 **Bridenthal**, Renate, 'Was there a Roman Homer? Niebuhr's thesis and its critics', *Hist. and Theory*, XI, 1972, 193–213.

2.97 **Brown**, P., *Augustine of Hippo. A Biography*, 1967. See also Deane (2.103) and Figgis (2.113).

2.98 **Buchner**, K., *Cicero*, Heidelberg, 1964.

2.99 ——*Sallust*, Heidelberg, 1960.

2.100 **Cohen**, Shaye, *Josephus in Galilee and Rome. His Vita and Development as a Historian*, Leiden, 1979.

2.101 ——'History and historiography in the *Against Apion* of Josephus', *Hist. and Theory*, XXVII, 1988, 1–11.

2.102 **Crump**, G. A., *Ammianus Marcellinus as a Military Historian*, Wiesbaden, 1975.

2.103 **Deane**, H. A., *The Political and Social Ideas of St Augustine*, New York, 1963. See also Brown (2.97) and Figgis (2.113).

2.104 **Dorey**, T. A. (ed.), *Livy*, 1971.

2.105 ——(ed.), *Tacitus*, 1969.

2.106 ——(ed.), *Latin Historians*, 1966. Includes chapters on Polybius, Caesar, Livy and Bede.

2.107 **Dowling**, Linda, 'Roman decadence and Victorian historiography', *Vict. Studs.* XXVIII, 1985, 597–607.

2.108 **Dudley**, D. R., *The World of Tacitus*, 1968.

2.109 **Earl**, D. C., *The Political Thought of Sallust*, 1961. Examines Sallust's three major works in the light of his political and moral principles.

2.110 **Eckstein**, A. M., *Moral Vision in the Histories of Polybius*, Berkeley, CA, 1995.

2.111 **Erasmus**, H. J., *The Origins of Rome in Historiography from Petrarch to Perizonius*, Leiden, 1962.

2.112 **Feldman**, L. and G. H. (eds), *Josephus, Judaism and Christianity*, Detroit, MI, 1987

2.113 **Figgis**, J. N., *The Political Aspects of St Augustine's City of God*, 1921. See also Brown (2.97) and Deane (2.103).

2.114 **Grant**, R., *Eusebius as Church Historian*, 1980. A thematic treatment of the *Church History* considering its concern with apostolic succession, events, persons, heretics, the Jews, persecution and martyrdom, and the intervention and help of God.

2.115 **Hammond**, N. G. L., *Three Historians of Alexander the Great. The So-called Vulgate Authors, Diodorus, Justin and Curtius*, 1983. Detailed analysis of the texts.

2.116 **Laistner**, M. L. W., *The Greater Roman Historians*, 1947. Revaluations of Sallust, Livy, Tacitus and Ammianus Marcellinus.

2.117 **Luce**, T. J. and **Woodman**, A. J. (eds), *Tacitus and the Tacitean Tradition*, Princeton, NJ, 1993.

2.118 **Markus**, R. A., *Saeculum. History and Society in the Theology of St Augustine*, 1970. See also Brown (2.97), Deane (2.103) and Figgis (2.113).

2.119 **Miles**, G. B., *Livy. Reconstructing Early Rome*, Ithaca, NY, 1995.

2.120 **Plass**, P., *Wit and the Writing of History. The Rhetoric of Historiography in Imperial Rome*, Madison, WI, 1988.

2.121 **Rajak**, T., *Josephus. The Historian and his Society*, 1983. Considers Josephus's own circumstances, his educational, social and linguistic context and his treatment of revolt and civil war.

2.122 **Sacks**, K., *Polybius on the Writing of History*, Berkeley, CA, 1981.

2.123 **Saunders**, J. J., 'The debate on the fall of Rome', *Hist.*, XLVIII, 1963, 1–17.

2.124 **Stadter**, P. A., *Plutarch's Historical Methods. An Analysis of the Mulierum Virtues*, Cambridge, MA, 1965.

2.125 **Syme**, R., *Ammianus and the Historia Augusta*, 1968.

2.126 —— *Sallust*, Berkeley, CA, 1964.

2.127 —— *Tacitus*, 2 vols, 1985. The major work. Looks at the circumstances surrounding the composition of the *Histories* and the *Annals* and at their influence on author and readers.

2.128 **Thompson**, E. A., *The Historical Work of Ammianus Marcellinus*, 1947.

2.129 **Walbank**, F. W., *Polybius*, Berkeley, CA, 1972.

2.130 **Walker**, B., *The Annals of Tacitus*, 1952. Considers the ways in which Tacitus's approach to history was influenced by his republicanism, stoicism and training in rhetoric.

2.131 **Wallace-Hadrill**, A., *Suetonius. The Scholar and his Caesars*, 1983.

2.132 **Walsh**, P. G., *Livy. His Historical Aims and Methods*, 1961. Delivers the author from his tarnished reputation.

2.133 **Wiseman**, T. P., 'Practice and theory in Roman historiography', *Hist.*, LXVI, 1981, 375–93.

3

MEDIEVAL
HISTORY

GENERAL

3.1 **Brandt**, W. J., *The Shape of Medieval History. Studies in the Modes of Perception*, New Haven, CT, 1966. Concerned principally with English chroniclers of the twelfth to fourteenth centuries.

3.2 **Burrow**, J. W., *The Ages of Man. A Study in Medieval Writing and Thought*, 1986. Looks at the variety of medieval schematisations of the different stages of human life and history.

3.3 **Cantor**, N. F., 'Medieval historiography as modern political and social thought', *J. Contemp. Hist.*, III, 1968, 55–73.

3.4 ——*Inventing the Middle Ages. The Lives, Works and Ideas of the Great Medievalists of the Twentieth Century*, New York, 1991. Includes studies of Maitland, Kantorowicz, Bloch, Powicke, Haskins, Knowles, Southern, Huizinga, Postan and Eileen Power.

3.5 **Cate**, J. L. and **Anderson**, E. N. (eds), *Medieval and Historiographical Essays in Honour of J. W. Thompson*, 1938. Includes a study of twelfth-century interest in the antiquities of Rome. Bibliography of the writings of James Westfall Thompson, 493–9.

3.6 **Chandler**, Alice, *A Dream of Order. The Medieval Ideal in Nineteenth-Century English Literature*, 1971. Includes chapters on Scott, Cobbett, Carlyle, Disraeli, Ruskin and Morris. Bibliography, 249–64.

3.7 **Christianson**, G., 'G. G. Coulton; the medieval historian as controversialist', *Cath. H.R.*, LVII, 1971, 421–41.

3.8 **Dahmus**, J., *Seven Medieval Historians*, Chicago, IL, 1982. Extracts and commentary. Bede and Matthew Paris are among those included.

3.9 **Damico**, H. and **Zavadil**, J. B. (eds), *Medieval Scholarship. Biographical Studies on the Formation of a Discipline*. I, *History*, New York, 1995.

3.10 **Davis**, R. H. C. and **Wallace-Hadrill**, J. M. (ed.), *The Writing of History in the Middle Ages. Essays presented to R. W. Southern*, 1981. A substantial collection which includes chapters on Bede, on William of Malmesbury, on chivalry and history and on the town chronicles.

3.11 **Drew**, Katherine F. and **Lear**, F. S. (ed.), *Perspectives in Medieval History*, Chicago, IL, 1963. Includes 'The growth of a discipline: medieval studies in America' and 'Medieval foundations of modern history'.

3.12 **Fleischman**, S., 'On the representation of history and fiction in the Middle Ages', *Hist. and Theory*, XXII, 1983, 278–310.

3.13 **Funkenstein**, A., 'Periodization and self-understanding in the Middle Ages and early modern times', *Med. and Hum.*, n.s., V, 1974, 3–23.

3.14 **Galbraith**, V. H., *Historical Research in Medieval England*, 1951. Examines the relationship between peaks of monastic influence and historical writing.

3.15 **Gatrell**, P., 'Historians and peasants; studies of medieval English society in a Russian context', *P.P.*, 96, 1982, 22–50.

3.16 **Goldstein**, R. J., *The Matter of Scotland. Historical Narrative in Medieval Scotland*, Lincoln, NE, 1993.

3.17 **Gransden**, Antonia, *Legends, Traditions and History in Medieval England*, 1992. Collected essays. Includes 'Bede's reputation as a historian in medieval England', 'Prologues in the historiography of twelfth-century England', 'The chronicles of medieval England and Scotland' and 'Antiquarian studies in fifteenth-century England'.

3.18 **Knowles**, D., 'Some trends in scholarship, 1868–1968, in the field of medieval history', *T.R.H.S.*, 5th ser., XIX, 1969, 139–57.

3.19 **Linehan**, P. A., 'Making of the *Cambridge Medieval History*', *Speculum*, LVII, 1982, 463–94.

3.20 **Matthew**, D. J. A., 'Professor R. W. Southern and the study of medieval history' *Durham U.J.*, LXII, 1969–70, 160–71.

3.21 **Mommsen**, T. E., *Medieval and Renaissance Studies* ed. E. E. Rice, Ithaca, NY, 1959. Part Three is devoted to studies in early Christian historiography.

3.22 **Oakley**, F., 'Celestial hierarchies revisited: Walter Ullman's vision of medieval politics', *P.P.*, 60, 1973, 3–48.

3.23 **Poole**, R. L., *Chronicles and Annals*, 1926. A brief outline of their origin and growth.

3.24 ——*Studies in Chronology and History*, 1934. Includes a chapter on Bede's chronology.

3.25 **Power**, Eileen, 'On medieval history as a social study', *Economica*, n.s., I, 1934, 13–29.

3.26 **Smalley**, Beryl, *Historians in the Middle Ages*, 1974. An invaluable general survey which deals with the main influences on, and different categories of, historical writing in the Middle Ages.

3.27 ——*The Study of the Bible in the Middle Ages*, 1952.

3.28 **Spiegel**, Gabrielle M., 'Political writing in medieval historiography', *Hist. and Theory*, XIV, 1975, 314–25.

3.29 **Sterns**, I. (ed.), *The Greater Medieval Historians. A Reader*, Washington, DC, 1982. A generous selection.

3.30 ——*The Greater Medieval Historians. An Interpretation and a Bibliography*, Washington, DC, 1980. Useful, but catalogue-style historiography.

3.31 **Strayer**, J. R., *Medieval Statecraft and the Perspectives of History*, Princeton, NJ, 1971. Section VI contains four essays on the teaching of history.

3.32 **Ullmann**, W., *The Relevance of Medieval Ecclesiastical History*, 1966. Inaugural lecture.

PRE-CONQUEST ENGLAND

3.33 **Barker**, E. E., 'The Anglo-Saxon chronicle used by Aethelweard', *B.I.H.R.*, XI, 1967, 85–91.

3.34 **Beaven**, M. L. R., 'The beginning of the year in the Alfredian chronicle 806–77', *E.H.R.*, XXXIII, 1918, 328–42.

Bede

3.35 **Bately**, Janet, 'Bede and the *Anglo-Saxon Chronicle*' in Margot H. King and W. M. Stevens (eds), *Saints, Scholars and Heroes. Studies in Medieval Culture in Honour of Charles W. Jones*, Collegeville, MN, 1979, 233–54.

3.36 **Blair**, P. H., 'The historical writings of Bede', *La Storiografia Alto Medievale*, Spoleto, 1970, 196–221.

3.37 ——*The World of Bede*, 1970. The principal sections deal with the growth of Christianity and of monasticism, and with learning, teaching and writing. Bibliography, 310–28.

3.38 **Bonner**, G. (ed.), *Famulus Christi. Essays in Commemoration of the Thirteenth Centenary of the Birth of the Venerable Bede*, 1976. Twenty-two essays dealing with Bede's life, context and writing.

3.39 **Davidse**, J., 'The sense of history in the Venerable Bede', *Studi Medievali*, XXIII, 1982, 647–95.

3.40 **Higham**, N. J., *An English Empire. Bede and the Early Anglo-Saxon Kings*, 1995.

3.41 **Jones**, C. W., 'Bede as early medieval historian', *Med. and Hum.*, IV, 1946, 26–36.

3.42 **Kirby**, D. P., 'Bede's native sources for the *Historia Ecclesiastica*', *Bull. J. Ryl. Lib.*, XLVIII, 1966, 341–71.

3.43 **Markus**, R. A., *Bede and the Tradition of Ecclesiastical Biography*, Jarrow Lecture, 1975.

3.44 **Miller**, Molly, 'Bede's use of Gildas', *E.H.R.*, XG, 1975, 241–61.

3.45 **Rosenthal**, J. T., 'Bede's use of miracles in the *Ecclesiastical History*', *Traditio*, XXXI, 1975, 328–35.

3.46 —— 'Bede's *Ecclesiastical History* and the material conditions of Anglo-Saxon life', *J. Brit. Studs.*, XIX, 1979, 1–17.

3.47 **Stephens**, J. N., 'Bede's *Ecclesiastical History*', *Hist.*, LXII, 1977, 1–14. Argues that Bede's major work, its title notwithstanding, is principally a history of a nation.

3.48 **Thompson**, A. H. (ed.), *Bede. His Life, Times and Works*, 1935. A collection of essays to commemorate the twelfth centenary of Bede's death.

3.49 **Whitelock**, Dorothy, 'The Old English Bede', *Proc. Brit. Acad.*, XLVIII, 1962, 57–90. Considers the responsibility for the Anglo-Saxon translation of Bede's *History*.

3.50 **Wormald**, P., 'Bede, Beowulf and the conversion of the Anglo-Saxon aristocracy' in R. T. Farrell (ed.), *Bede and Anglo-Saxon England*, 1978, 32–90.

3.51 **Wynn**, J. B., 'The beginning of the year in Bede and the *Anglo-Saxon Chronicle*', *Medium Aevum*, XXI, 1956, 70–8.

3.52 **Binchy**, D. A., 'Patrick and his biographers; ancient and modern', *Studia Hibernica*, II, 1962, 7–173.

3.53 **Bolton**, W. F., *A History of Anglo-Latin Literature, 597–1066*, Princeton, NJ, 1967.

3.54 **Briggs**, A., *Saxons, Normans and Victorians*, 1966. Lecture.

3.55 **Brinkley**, R. F., *Arthurian Legend in the Seventeenth Century*, 1932.

3.56 **Brooke**, C. N. L., 'Geoffrey of Monmouth as a historian' in C. N. L. Brooke *et al.* (eds), *Church and Government in the Middle Ages*, 1976, 77–91. Concentrates on the author's literary significance.

3.57 —— 'Historical writing in England, 850–1150', *La Storiografia Alto Medievale*, Spoleto, 1970, 223–47.

3.58 **Conway Davies**, J., 'Giraldus Cambrensis, 1146–1946', *Arch. Cambrensis*, XCIX, 1947, 85–108, 256–80.

3.59 **Davies**, R. R., *Historical Perception. Celts and Saxons*, 1979. Inaugural lecture. Considers the treatment of this subject by three writers at widely separated moments in time.

3.60 **Davis**, R. H. C., 'Alfred the Great: propaganda and truth', *Hist.*, LVI, 1971, 173–77.

3.61 **Dickins**, B., *John Kemble and Old English Scholarship*, 1938. Lecture.

3.62 **Duckett**, Eleanor S., *Anglo-Saxon Saints and Scholars*, New York, 1947. Four biographical studies of Aldhelm of Malmesbury, Wilfred of York, Bede of Jarrow and Boniface of Devon. Bibliography.

3.63 **Dumville**, D. N., 'The Corpus Christi "Nennius"', *Bull. Bd. Celt. Studs.*, XXV, 1974, 369–80.

3.64 —— 'Nennius and the *Historia Brittonorum*', *Studia Celtica*, X–XI, 1975–6, 78–95.

3.65 —— 'Sub-Roman Britain: history and legend', *Hist.*, LXII, 1977, 973–92.

3.66 —— 'The historical value of the *Historia Brittonorum*', *Arthurian Lit.*, VI, 1986, 1–26.

3.67 **Fisher**, D. J. V., 'The early biographers of St Aethelwold', *E.H.R.*, LXVII, 1952, 381–91.

3.68 **Galbraith**, V. H., 'Research in action. Who wrote Asser's *Life of Alfred*?' in Galbraith (1.397), 88–128.

3.69 **Gransden**, Antonia, *Historical Writing in England, c. 550–c. 1307*, 1974. A weighty, 500 page study. The twenty-one chapters are sometimes devoted to individuals (Bede, William of Malmesbury, Matthew Paris), sometimes to genres (local history, sacred biography, chronicles), sometimes to particular centres (St Albans, Bury St Edmunds) or to particular eras (the Norman

Conquest, the reign of King John). Continued in (3.162).

3.70 **Hanning**, R. W., *The Vision of History in Early Britain. From Gildas to Geoffrey of Monmouth*, New York, 1966. Within the framework of an account of the formation of the early medieval historical imagination the author offers case studies of Gildas, Bede and Geoffrey of Monmouth.

3.71 **Harrison**, K., 'The beginning of the year in England, *c.* 500–900', *Anglo-Saxon England*, II, 1973, 51–70.

3.72 —— *The Framework of Anglo-Saxon History to A.D. 900*, 1976. Examines the systems of dating used in Anglo-Saxon England.

3.73 **Hodgkin**, R. H., 'The beginning of the year in the English Chronicle', *E.H.R.*, XXXIX, 1924, 497–510.

3.74 **Holdsworth**, C. and **Wiseman**, T. P. (eds), *The Inheritance of Historiography, 350–900*, 1986. Explores the extent to which early medieval historians were influenced by classical conventions. Includes chapters on Bede and Asser.

3.75 **Hughes**, Kathleen, *The Early Celtic Idea of History and the Modern Historian*, 1977. Inaugural lecture.

3.76 **Jones**, C. W., *Saints' Lives and Chronicles in Early England*, Ithaca, NY, 1947. Examines the chronicles, Bede's *Ecclesiastical History* and the development of historiography. There are translations of the lives of Gregory the Great and of St Guthlac.

3.77 **Jones**, T., 'The early evolution of the legend of Arthur', *Nottingham Med. Studs.*, VIII, 1964, 3–21.

3.78 **Keeler**, L., *Geoffrey of Monmouth and the Late Latin Chroniclers, 1300–1500*, Berkeley, CA, 1946. A discussion of the variety of uses – uncritical, selective, political, hostile – made of Geoffrey of Monmouth's work.

3.79 **Knowles**, D., *Saints and Scholars*, 1962. Twenty-five short biographies, including Giraldus Cambrensis and Matthew Paris.

3.80 **O'Sullivan**, T. D., *The Excidio of Gildas. Its Authenticity and Date*, Leiden, 1978.

3.81 **Rees**, J. F., 'Gerald of Wales' in Rees, *Studies in Welsh History. Collected Papers, Lectures and Reviews*, 1947.

3.82 **Rouse**, R. H. and **Goddu**, A. A., 'Gerald of Wales and the *Florilegum Anglicum*', *Speculum*, LII, 1977, 488–521.

3.83 **Sisam**, K., 'Anglo-Saxon royal genealogies', *Proc. Brit. Acad.*, XXXIX, 1953, 287–348.

3.84 **Stevens**, C. E., 'Gildas and the Civitates of Britain', *E.H.R.*, LII, 1937, 193–201.

3.85 —— 'Gildas sapiens', *E.H.R.*, LVI, 1941, 353–73.

3.86 **Tatlock**, J. S. P., *The Legendary History of Britain. Geoffrey of Monmouth's Historiae Regum Britanniae and its early Vernacular Versions*, Berkeley, CA, 1950.

3.87 **Thorogood**, A. J., 'The *Anglo-Saxon Chronicle* in the reign of Ecgbert', *E.H.R.*, XLVIII, 1933, 353–63.

3.88 **Vann**, R. T., 'The Free Anglo-Saxons: a historical myth', *J. Hist. Ideas*, XIX, 1958, 259–72.

3.89 **Wallace-Hadrill**, J. M., 'Gregory of Tours and Bede: their views on the personal qualities of kings', *Fruhmittelalterliche Studien*, II, 1968, 31–44.

3.90 **Whitelock**, Dorothy, *The Genuine Asser*, 1968.

3.91 **Williams**, E. A., 'A bibliography of Giraldus Cambrensis', *Nat. Lib. Wales J.*, XII, 1961, 97–140.

3.92 **Wright**, C. E., *The Cultivation of Saga in Anglo-Saxon England*, 1939. The body of the book consists of two long chapters relating to the early period and to the eleventh century. There are preparatory chapters on the historical and intellectual background.

POST-CONQUEST ENGLAND

3.93 **Appleby**, J. T., 'Richard of Devizes and the Annals of Winchester', *B.I.H.R.*, XXXVI, 1963, 70–5.

3.94 **Atiya**, A. S., *The Crusade. Historiography and Bibliography*, Bloomington. IN, 1962. An introduction to the patterns of crusade historiography precedes a sectionalised bibliography.

3.95 **Blacker**, Jean, *The Faces of Time. Portrayal of the Past in Old French and Latin Historical Narratives of the Anglo-Norman Regnum*, Austin, TX, 1994.

3.96 **Brooke**, C. N. L., *The Twelfth Century Renaissance*, 1969. A basic, well illustrated introduction to the various aspects of this period, including its historiography.

3.97 **Brown**, R. A., 'The Norman Conquest', *T.R.H.S.*, 5th ser., XVII, 1967, 109–30. Emphasises the 'anachronistic nationalism' often displayed in modern studies of the Conquest.

3.98 **Brown**, Shirley A., *The Bayeux Tapestry. History and Bibliography*, 1988.

3.99 **Brundage**, J. A., 'Recent crusade historiography: some observations and suggestions', *Cath. H.R.*, XLIX, 1964, 493–507.

3.100 **Carter**, J. M., *The Norman Conquest in English Historiography*, Manhattan, KS, 1980.

3.101 **Chibnall**, Marjorie, *The Debate on the Norman Conquest*, 1999. Surveys the historiography of the subject from the Bayeux Tapestry and the chronicles up to the present day.

3.102 —— *The World of Orderic Vitalis*, 1984.

3.103 **Clanchy**, M. T., 'Remembering the past and the good old law', *Hist.*, LV, 1970, 165–76.

3.104 —— *From Memory to Written Record: England, 1066–1307*, 1979.

3.105 **Darlington**, R. R., *Anglo-Norman Historians*, 1947. Inaugural lecture. William of Malmesbury is the chief centre of interest.

3.106 **Davis**, H. W. C., 'The chronicle of Battle Abbey', *E.H.R.*, XXIX, 1914, 426–34.

3.107 **Denholm-Young**, N., *History and Heraldry, 1254–1310*, 1965.

3.108 —— *Collected Papers. Cultural, Textual and Biographical Essays on Medieval Topics*, 1969. Includes chapters on the Winchester–Hyde chronicle, Thomas de Wykes and his chronicle, and on the authorship of the *Vita Edwardi Secondi*.

3.109 **Denton**, J. H., 'The crisis of 1297 from the Evesham Chronicle', *E.H.R.*, XCIII 1978, 560–79.

3.110 **Dickins**, B., 'A Yorkshire chronicler (William of Newburgh)', *Trans. Yorks. Dialect Soc.*, V, 1934, 15–26.

3.111 **Douglas**, D. C., *The Norman Conquest and British Historians*, 1946. Lecture.

3.112 **Edwards**, J. G., *Historians and the Medieval English Parliament*, 1960. Lecture.

3.113 **Flahiff**, G. B., 'Ralph Niger: an introduction to his life and works', *Med. Studs.*, II, 1940, 104–26.

3.114 **Galbraith**, V. H., *Roger Wendover and Matthew Paris*, 1944, Lecture.

3.115 —— 'The St Edmundsbury chronicle, 1296–1301', *E.H.R.*, LVIII, 1943, 51–78.

3.116 **Gransden**, Antonia, 'Propaganda in medieval historiography', *J. Med. Hist.*, I, 1975, 363–81.

3.117 **Hollister**, C. W., 'King John and the historians', *J. Brit. Studs.*, I, 1961, 1–19.

3.118 **Holt**, J. C., 'The St Albans chroniclers and Magna Carta', *T.R.H.S.*, 5th ser., XIV, 1964, 67–88.

3.119 **Jenkins**, C., *The Monastic Chronicler and the Early School of St Albans*, 1922.

3.120 **Ker**, N. R., *Medieval Libraries of Great Britain*, 1941, 2nd ed. 1964.

3.121 **Lewis**, Suzanne, *The Art of Matthew Paris in the Chronica Majora*, Berkeley, CA, 1987.

3.122 **Little**, A. G., 'Chronicles of the mendicant friars' in *Franciscan Papers, Lists and Documents*, 1943, 25–41.

3.123 **McKisack**, May, 'Edward III and the historians', *Hist. Today*, XLV, 1960, 1–15.

3.124 **Matthew**, D. J. A., 'The English cultivation of Norman history', in D. Bates and Anne Curry (eds), *England and Normandy in the Middle Ages* (1995), 1–18.

3.125 **Offler**, H. S., *Medieval Historians of Durham*, 1958.

3.126 **Pafford**, J. H. P., 'Robert of Gloucester's Chronicle' in J. Conway Davies (ed.), *Studies presented to Sir Hilary Jenkinson*, 1957, 304–19.

3.127 **Ray**, R. D., 'Orderic Vitalis and his readers', *Studia Monastica*, XIV, 1972, 17–33.

3.128 **Reader**, Rebecca, 'Matthew Paris and the Norman Conquest', in J. Blair and B. Golding, (eds), *The Cloister and the*

World. Essays in Medieval History in Honour of Barbara Harvey, 1996, 118–47.

3.129 **Smallwood**, T. M., 'The text of Langtoft's chronicle', *Med. Aevum*, XLVI, 1977, 219–30.

3.130 **Southern**, R. W., *St Anselm and his Biographer. A Study of Medieval Life and Thought, 1059–c. 1130*, 1963.

3.131 **Stenton**, Doris M., 'The Pipe Rolls and the historians, 1660–1883', *Camb. H.J.*, X, 1950–2, 271–92.

3.132 **Stenton**, F. M. (ed.), *The Bayeux Tapestry. A Comprehensive Survey*, 1957, 2nd ed. 1965.

3.133 **Taylor**, J., 'The development of the *Polychronicon* continuation', *E.H.R.*, LXXVI, 1961, 20–36.

3.134 —— 'The French "Brut" and the reign of Edward II', *E.H.R.*, LXXII, 1957, 423–37.

3.135 —— *The Kirkstall Abbey Chronicles*, 1952.

3.136 —— *Medieval Historical Writing in Yorkshire*, 1961.

3.137 —— *The Universal Chronicle of Ranulf Higden*, 1966.

3.138 —— *The Use of Medieval Chronicles*, 1965. Historical Ass. pamphlet. Brief discussion with bibliography and notes on standards of editing.

3.139 **Taylor**, J., *English Historical Literature in the Fourteenth Century*, 1987. Surveys the different kinds of presentations of history – chronicles, universal histories, chivalric writing, letters, and political poems and ballads. Bibliography, 325–39.

3.140 **Templeman**, G., 'Edward I and the historians', *Camb. H.J.*, X, 1950–52, 16–35.

3.141 **Tout**, T. F., 'The Westminster chronicle attributed to Robert of Reading', *E.H.R.*, XXXI, 1916, 450–64.

3.142 **Tyson**, M., 'The annals of Southwark and Merton', *Surrey Arch. Collns*, XXXVI, 1925, 24–57.

3.143 **van Houts**, E. M. C., 'The memory of 1066 in written and oral tradition', *Anglo-Norman Studies*, XIX, 167–79.

3.144 **Vaughan**, R., *Matthew Paris*, 1958. The major study of the writer's life as chronicler and hagiographer. Additionally there are chapters on the links with Roger of Wendover and on

the textual problems connected with his writings.

3.145 —— *The Chronicles of Matthew Paris. Monastic Life in the Thirteenth Century*, 1984.

3.146 **Werkmeister**, O. K., 'The political ideology of the Bayeux Tapestry', *Studi Medievali*, XVII, 1976, 535–95.

3.147 **Wolter**, H., *Ordericus Vitalis*, Wiesbaden, 1955.

3.148 **Zinn**, G. A. Jr, 'The influence of Hugh of St Victor's *Chronicon* on the *Abbreviatones Chronicorum* by Ralph of Diceto', *Speculum*, LII, 1977, 38–61.

William of Malmesbury

3.149 **Farmer**, H., 'William of Malmesbury's life and work', *J. Ecc. H.*, XIII, 1962, 39–54.

3.150 **Haahr**, J. G., 'The concept of kingship in William of Malmesbury's *Gesta Regum* and *Historia Novella*', *Med. Studs.*, XXXVIII, 1976, 351–71.

3.151 **Newell**, W. W., 'William of Malmesbury on the antiquity of Glastonbury', *Pub. Mod. Lang. Ass. America*, XVIII, 1903, 459–512.

3.152 **Schutt**, Marie, 'The literary form of William of Malmesbury's *Gesta Regum*', *E.H.R.*, XLVI, 1931, 255–60.

3.153 **Thomson**, R., *William of Malmesbury*, 1987. Looks at William's character and achievement and also at different aspects of his working practice.

THE LATER MIDDLE AGES

3.154 **Boardman**, S., 'Chronicle propaganda in late medieval Scotland. Robert the Steward, John of Fordun and the "Anonymous Chronicle" ', *Scot. H.R.*, LXXVI, 1997, 23–43.

3.155 **Britnell**, R. H. and **Pollard**, A. J., *The McFarlane Legacy. Studies in Late Medieval Politics and Society*, 1995. Includes an historiographical assessment of McFarlane's work.

3.156 **Cox**, D. C., 'The French Chronicle of London', *Medium Aevum*, XLV, 1976, 201–8.

3.157 **Dean**, R. J., 'Nicholas Trevet, historian', in J. J. G. Alexander and M. T. Gibson (eds), *Medieval Learning and Literature. Essays presented to R. W. Hunt*, 1976, 328–52.

3.158 **Duls**, Louisa D., *Richard II in the early Chronicles*, The Hague, 1975. The different traditions in chronicle presentation are examined through the treatment of six episodes.

3.159 **Dyer**, A., 'English town chronicles', *Loc. Historian*, XII, 1976–77, 285–92.

3.160 **Flenley**, R., *Six Town Chronicles of England*, 1911. The first two chapters place the writing of town chronicles in historiographical perspective.

3.161 **Gill**, P. E., 'Politics and propaganda in fifteenth-century England: the polemical writings of Sir John Fortescue', *Speculum*, XLVI, 1971, 333–47.

3.162 **Gransden**, Antonia, *Historical Writing in England*, II: *c. 1307 to the early Sixteenth Century*, 1982. A long and learned study which extends from the chroniclers of the reign of Edward II to humanist historians such as More and Polydore Vergil. Bibliography. Exceptionally full index.

3.163 **Hadwin**, J. F., 'The medieval lay subsidies and economic history', *Ec.H.R.*, 2nd ser., XXXVI, 1983, 200–17.

3.164 **Hallam**, H. E., 'The Postan thesis', *Hist. Studs.*, XV, 1971–73, 203–22. Criticises Postan's interpretation of demographic and economic history in the thirteenth and fourteenth centuries.

3.165 **Hanham**, Alison, *Richard III and his early Historians*, 1975. A case study in the development of an unsavoury reputation. Includes a discussion of the Crowland Chronicle, John Rous, Polydore Vergil and Sir Thomas More.

3.166 **Kingsford**, C. L., *English Historical Literature in the Fifteenth Century*, 1913. Broad-based discussion which takes account of Thomas Walsingham, the biographers of Henry V, the Brut and the chronicles.

3.167 **Lewis**, P. S., 'War, propaganda and historiography in fifteenth-century France and England', *T.R.H.S.*, 5th ser., XV, 1965, 1–21.

3.168 **McFarlane**, K. B., 'William Worcester: a preliminary survey', J. Conway Davies (ed.), *Studies presented to Sir Hilary Jenkinson*, 1957, 196–221.

3.169 **Mann**, J. G., 'Instances of antiquarian feeling in medieval and renaissance art', *Arch. J.*, LXXXIX, 1932, 254–74.

3.170 **Murph**, Roxane S., *Richard III. The Making of a Legend*, Metuchen, NJ, 1977.

3.171 **Myers**, A. R., 'Richard III and historical tradition', *Hist.*, LIII, 1968, 181–202.

3.172 **Palmer**, J. J. N., 'The authorship, date and historical value of the French chronicles on the Lancastrian revolution', *Bull. J. Ryl. Lib.*, LXI, 1978–79, 145–81, 398–421.

3.173 **Reid**, Rachel R., 'The date and authorship of Redmayne's *Life of Henry V*', *E.H.R.*, XXX, 1915, 74–8.

3.174 **Robinson**, J. A., 'An unrecognised Westminster chronicle, 1381–94', *Proc. Brit. Acad.*, III, 1907, 61–92.

3.175 **Roskell**, J. S. and **Taylor**, F., 'The authorship and purpose of the *Gesta Henrici Quinti*', 1–2, *Bull. J. Ryl. Lib.*, LIII, 1970–71, 428–64; LIV, 1971–72, 223–40.

3.176 **Rowe**, B. J. H., 'A contemporary account of the Hundred Years War, 1415–29', *E.H.R.*, XLI, 1926, 504–13.

3.177 **Stowe**, G. B., 'Thomas Walsingham, John Malvern and the *Vita Ricardi Secundi*, 1377–81: a reassessment', *Med. Studs.*, XXXIX, 1977, 490–7.

EUROPE

3.178 **Archambault**, P., *Seven French Chroniclers. Witness to History*, Syracuse, NY, 1974. Includes studies of Froissart, Joinville and Villehardouin.

3.179 **Brown**, Elizabeth A. R., 'The tyranny of a construct: feudalism and historians of medieval Europe', *A.H.R.*, LXXIX, 1974, 1063–88.

3.180 **Edbury**, P. W. and **Rowe**, J. G., *William of Tyre, Historian of the Latin East*, 1988.

3.181 **Gillingham**, J., 'Kingship, chivalry and love: political and cultural values in the earliest history written in French,

Geoffrey Gaimar's *Estoire des Engleis'*, in C. W. Hollister (ed.), *Anglo-Norman Political Culture in the Twelfth-Century Renaissance*, 1997, 33–58.

3.182 **Goffart**, W., *The Narrators of Barbarian History AD 550–800. Jordanes, Gregory of Tours, Bede, and Paul the Deacon*, Princeton, NJ, 1988.

3.183 **Kurbis**, Brygida, 'L'historiographie médiévale en Pologne', *Acta Poloniae Hist.*, VI, 1962, 7–34.

3.184 **Leclercq**, J., 'Monastic historiography from Leo IX to Callistus II', *Studia Monastica*, XII, 1970, 57–86.

3.185 **Linehan**, P., *History and the Historians of Medieval Spain*, 1993.

3.186 **McKitterick**, Rosamond, 'Constructing the past in the early Middle Ages: the case of the Royal Frankish Annals', *T.R.H.S.*, 6th ser., VII, 1997, 101–30.

3.187 **Mierow**, C. C., 'Otto of Freising: a medieval historian at work', *Philological Q.*, XIV, 1935, 344–62.

3.188 **Minnis**, A. J., *Medieval Theory of Authorship. Scholastic Literary Attitudes in the later Middle Ages*, 1984.

3.189 **Morgan**, D. O. (ed.), *Medieval Historical Writing in the Christian and Islamic Worlds*, 1982.

3.190 **Palmer**, J. J. (ed.), *Froissart. Historian*, 1981. A symposium dealing with various aspects of Froissart's work as a historian and the subject matter of his *History*.

3.191 **Petry**, R. C., 'Three medieval chroniclers: monastic historiography and biblical eschatology in Hugh of St Victor, Otto of Freising and Ordericus Vitalis', *Church Hist.*, XXXIV, 1965, 282–93.

3.192 **Reynolds**, B. R., 'Latin historiography: a survey, 1400–1600, *Studs. Renaiss.*, XI, 1955, 7–66.

3.193 **Southern**, R. W., 'Aspects of the European tradition of historical writing', 1, 'The classical tradition from Einhard to Geoffrey of Monmouth', *T.R.H.S.*, 5th ser., XX, 1970, 173–91; 2, 'Hugh of St Victor and the idea of historical development', *T.R.H.S.*, 5th ser. XXI, 1971, 159–79; 3, 'History as prophecy', *T.R.H.S.*, 5th ser., XXII, 1972, 159–80; 4, 'The sense of the past', *T.R.H.S.*, 5th ser., XXIII, 1973, 243–63.

3.194 **Spiegel**, Gabrielle, *Romancing the Past. The Rise of Vernacular Prose Historiography in Thirteenth-Century France*, Berkeley, CA, 1993.

3.195 **Tate**, R. B., 'Mythology in Spanish historiography of the Middle Ages and Renaissance', *Hispanic R.*, XXII, 1954, 1–18.

4

THE
RENAISSANCE

4.1 **Baker**, H., *The Race of Time. Three Lectures on Renaissance Historiography*, Toronto, 1967. Analyses the ways in which historians of this period understood their role and developed their methods.

4.2 **Baron**, H., *The Crisis of the Early Italian Renaissance*, rev. ed., Princeton, NJ, 1965. Sections on changes in politics and historical thought, promise and tradition in politico-historical literature about 1400, Leonardo Bruni's civic humanism, and on classicism and the Trecento tradition.

4.3 ——*Humanistic and Political Literature in Florence and Venice at the Beginning of the Quattrocento*, rev. ed., New York, 1968.

4.4 ——*From Petrarch to Leonardo Bruni. Studies in Humanistic and Political Literature*, Chicago, IL, 1968. A collection of related studies concerned with methodology, chronology and rhetoric.

4.5 ——'Machiavelli: the republican citizen', *E.H.R.*, LXXXVI, 1961, 217–53.

4.6 **Becker**, M., 'Individualism in the early Renaissance', *Studs. Renaiss.*, XIX, 1972, 273–97.

4.7 ——'Towards a Renaissance historiography in Florence' in A. Molho and J. A. Tedeschi (eds), *Renaissance Studies in Honor of Hans Baron*, DeKalb, IL, 1971, 141–71.

4.8 **Bietenholz**, P. G., *History and Biography in the Work of Erasmus of Rotterdam*, Geneva, 1966. Assesses Erasmus's place among the sixteenth-century interpreters of history and his criticisms of other historians of his age.

4.9 **Bolgar**, R. R. (ed.), *Classical Influences on European Culture, 500–1500*, 1971. Includes essays on 'Sallust in the Middle Ages' and 'Petrarch and the transmission of classical elements'.

4.10 **Bonfil**, R., 'How golden was the Age of the Renaissance in Jewish historiography?', *Hist. and Theory*, XXVII, 1988, 78–102.

4.11 **Borchardt**, F. L., *German Antiquity in Renaissance Myth*, Baltimore, MD, 1971. Considers the nature of the myths about the national past which were current in Renaissance Germany and the sources which fostered them.

4.12 **Burke**, P., *Culture and Society in Renaissance Italy*, 1972. Examines the context of Renaissance historiography.

4.13 ——*The Renaissance Sense of the Past*, 1969. A compact analysis of the new sense of the past which emerged in the Renaissance.

4.14 **Clough**, C. H. (ed.), *Cultural Aspects of the Italian Renaissance. Essays in Honour of Paul Oskar Kristeller*, 1976. Twenty-seven essays which include studies of the cult of antiquity and Renaissance libraries.

4.15 **Cochrane**, E., *Historians and Historiography in the Italian Renaissance*, Chicago, IL, 1981. A wide-ranging treatment of the development of humanist history between the fourteenth and sixteenth centuries. Unavoidably – since no fewer than 783 different writers are referred to – the survey is sometimes sketchy.

4.16 —— 'Profession of the historian in the Italian Renaissance', *J. Soc. Hist.*, XV, 1981, 51–72.

4.17 **Ferguson**, W. K., *The Renaissance in Historical Thought. Five Centuries of Interpretation*, Boston, MA, 1948. A major historiographical case study which takes account of the changing perspectives on the Renaissance associated with later humanism, the Reformation, rationalism, romanticism, and with Burckhardt and his successors. Bibliography.

4.18 **Franklin**, J. H., *Jean Bodin and the Sixteenth-Century Revolution in the Methodology of Law and History*, Columbia, NY, 1963. Examines the ways in which developments in the study of law led on to refinements in historical methodology.

4.19 **Fryde**, E. B., *Humanism and Renaissance Historiography*, 1983. Concentrates on the earlier Italian Renaissance.

4.20 **Geerken**, J. H., 'Pocock and Machiavelli: structuralist explanation in history', *J. Hist. Philos.*, XVII, 1979, 309–18.

4.21 **Gilbert**, F., 'Machiavelli's *Istorie Fiorentine*; an essay in interpretation' in M. P. Gilmore (ed.), *Studies on Machiavelli*, Florence, 1972, 73–99.

4.22 ——*Machiavelli and Guicciardini. Politics and History in Sixteenth-Century Florence*, Princeton, NJ, 1965. Locates Machiavelli chiefly within the framework of Florentine political institutions, issues and ideas of the late fifteenth century and connects Guicciardini with the Renaissance crisis in historiography. Bibliographical essays, 305–38.

4.23 **Gilmore**, M., 'Freedom and determination in Renaissance historians', *Studs. Renaiss.*, III, 1956, 49–60.

4.24 ——*Humanists and Jurists. Six Studies in the Renaissance*, Cambridge, MA, 1963. Includes chapters on Renaissance conceptions of the lessons of history, on individualism, on law and lawyers, and on Erasmus.

4.25 **Gombrich**, E. H., *Norm and Form*, 1966. Includes essays on Renaissance conceptions of artistic progress and its consequences; Renaissance and golden age; norm and form: the stylistic categories of art history and their origin in Renaissance ideals; and on mannerism: the historiographical background. Bibliographical note, 156.

4.26 **Green**, L. F., *Chronicle into History. An Essay on the Interpretation of History in Florentine Fourteenth-Century Chronicles*, 1972. Case studies of Giovanni and Matteo Villani, Goro Dati, and the Florentine chroniclers of the late fourteenth century.

4.27 **Hay**, D., 'Flavio Biondo and the Middle Ages', *Proc. Brit. Acad.*, XLV, 1959, 97–128.

4.28 **Huppert**, C., *The Idea of Perfect History. Historical Erudition and Historical Philosophy in Renaissance France*, Urbana, IL, 1970. Examines the work of Pasquier, Bodin and La Popelinière and their contribution to the development of the Renaissance sense of history in France.

4.29 —— 'The Renaissance background of historicism', *Hist. and Theory*, V, 1966, 48–60.

4.30 **Jackson**, G., 'The historical writing of Juan Vicens Vives', *A.H.R.*, LXXV, 1970, 808–15.

4.31 **Janik**, Linda G., 'Lorenzo Valla: the primacy of rhetoric and the demoralization of history', *Hist. and Theory*, XII, 1973, 389–404.

4.32 **Kelley**, D. R., *Foundations of Modern Historical Scholarship. Language, Law, and History in the French Renaissance*, New York, 1970. Considers the ways in which the search for a new design for history utilised the methods of the historical school of law.

4.33 —— 'Legal humanism and the sense of history', *Studs. Renaiss.*, XIII, 1966, 184–99.

4.34 —— 'The rise of legal history in the Renaissance', *Hist. and Theory*, IX, 1970, 174–94.

4.35 **Kennedy**, W. J., *Authorizing Petrarch*, Ithaca, NY, 1994.

4.36 **Mansfield**, B., *Phoenix of his Age. Interpretations of Erasmus, c. 1550–1750*, Toronto, 1979.

4.37 —— 'Erasmus, Luther, and the problem of Church history', *Aust. J. Pol. and Hist.*, VIII, 1962, 41–56. Looks at nineteenth and twentieth-century Roman Catholic views of Erasmus.

4.38 **Martines**, L., *The Social World of the Florentine Humanists*, Princeton, NJ, 1968.

4.39 **Mazzocco**, A., 'The antiquarianism of Francesco Petrarca', *J. Med. and Renaiss. Studs.*, VII, 1977, 203–24.

4.40 **Mommsen**, T. E., 'Petrarch's concept of the Dark Ages' in Mommsen, *Medieval and Renaissance Studies*, Ithaca, NY, 1959.

4.41 **Nugent**, Elizabeth M., *The Thought and Culture of the English Renaissance*, 1956. Sections on Tudor humanists, Tudor grammars, the political and social order, Tudor medicine, sermons and religious treatises, chronicles and histories, romances and tales.

4.42 **Oppel**, J. W., 'Peace and liberty in the Quattrocento', *J. Med. and Renaiss. Studs.*, IV, 1974, 221–65.

4.43 **Peddie**, R. A., *Printing at Brescia in the Fifteenth Century*, 1905.

4.44 **Pfeiffer**, R., *The History of Classical Scholarship from 1300 to 1850*, 1976.

4.45 **Phillips**, M., *Francesco Guicciardini. The Historian's Craft*, 1977. Pride of place is given to Guicciardini's *History of Italy* and its composition, but there is also some discussion of the *Ricordi* and other minor works.

4.46 —— 'Machiavelli, Guicciardini and the tradition of vernacular historiography in Florence', *A.H.R.*, LXXXIV, 1979, 86–105.

4.47 —— 'Representation and argument in Florentine historiography', *Storia de Storiog.*, X, 1986, 48–63.

4.48 **Quinones**, R. J., *The Renaissance Discovery of Time*, Cambridge, MA, 1972. Chiefly a literary study, with chapters on Dante, Petrarch, Rabelais, Montaigne, Spenser, Shakespeare and Milton.

4.49 **Ridolfi**, R., *The Life of Francesco Guicciardini*, 1967. The standard work.

4.50 **Ross**, B., 'Giovanni Colonna, historian at Avignon', *Speculum*, XLV, 1970, 533–63.

4.51 **Rowe**, J. G. and **Stockdale**, W. H. (eds), *Florilegium Historiae: Essays presented to Wallace K. Ferguson*, Toronto, 1971.

4.52 **Rummel**, Erika, *The Humanist–Scholatic Debate in the Renaissance and Reformation*, Cambridge, 1995.

4.53 **Schiffman**, Z. S., 'Renaissance historicism reconsidered', *Hist. and Theory*, XXIV, 1985, 170–82.

4.54 —— 'An anatomy of historical revolution in Renaissance France', *Renaissance Q.*, XLII, 1989, 507–33.

4.55 **Seigel**, J. E., *Rhetoric and Philosophy in Renaissance Humanism*, Princeton, NJ, 1968. Attempts to establish the intellectual and social setting of Renaissance humanism and to explore the adaptation of Ciceronian models by Petrarch, Bruni and Valla.

4.56 **Singleton**, C. S. (ed.). *Art, Science and History in the Renaissance*, Baltimore, MD, 1967. Part Three of the book is devoted to Renaissance historiography and includes essays by Felix Gilbert and J. H. Hexter.

4.57 **Strauss**, G., *Historian in an Age of Crisis. The Life and Work of Aventinus, 1477–1534*, Cambridge, MA, 1963. A biography of the humanist historian of Bavaria.

4.58 **Struever**, Nancy S., *The Language of History in the Renaissance*, Princeton, NJ, 1970. Using case studies of Bruni, Salvtati and Bracciolini, the author explores the connections between rhetoric, poetics, ethics and history.

4.59 **Sypher**, G. W., 'Similarities between the scientific and the historical revolutions at the end of the Renaissance', *J. Hist. Ideas*, XXVI, 1965, 353–68.

4.60 **Ullmann**, B. L., 'Leonardo Bruni and humanistic historiography', *Med. and Hum.*, IV, 1946, 45–61.

4.61 **Weinberg**, B., *A History of Literary Criticism in the Italian Renaissance*, Chicago, IL, 1961.

4.62 **Weisinger**, H., 'Ideas of history during the Renaissance', *J. Hist. Ideas*, VI, 1945, 415–35.

4.63 **Weiss**, R., *Humanism in England during the Fifteenth Century*, 1941, rev. ed. 1957. Deals with the origins of humanism in fifteenth-century England, with Humphrey of Gloucester and George Neville and their circles, with the English pupils of Guarino da Verona, and with humanism in Canterbury, Cambridge and Oxford.

4.64 —— *The Renaissance Discovery of Classical Antiquity*, 1960. Considers how and why the classical past was used by Renaissance scholars.

4.65 **Wilcox**, D. J., *The Development of Florentine Humanist Historiography in the Fifteenth Century*, Cambridge, MA, 1969. Studies of Bruni, Bracciolini and della Scala and their contribution to the development and the new style of historiography.

5

THE SIXTEENTH CENTURY

ENGLAND AND SCOTLAND

5.1 **Anderson**, Judith, *Biographical Truth. The Representation of Historical Persons in Tudor and Stuart Historical Writing*, New Haven, CT, 1984. Cavendish, More, Roper, Shakespeare, Bacon, Walton and others are carefully scrutinised.

5.2 **Anglo**, S., 'The "British History" in early Tudor propaganda', *Bull. J. Ryl. Lib.*, XLIV, 1961–2, 17–48. Considers the uses made of Geoffrey of Monmouth.

5.3 **Archer**, I., 'John Stow's *Survey of London*; the nostalgia of John Stow', in D. L. Smith *et al.* (eds), *The Theatrical City. Culture, Theatre and Politics in London, 1576–1649*, 1995, 17–34.

5.4 **Aston**, Margaret, 'English ruins and history; the Dissolution and the sense of the past', *J. Warburg and Courtauld Insts*, XXXVI, 1973, 231–55.

5.5 **Beer**, B. L., 'John Stow and the English Reformation, 1547–1559', *Sixteenth Century J.*, XVI, 1985, 257–71.

5.6 **Brooks**, C., **Kelley**, D., and **Sharpe**, K., 'Debate; history, English law and the Renaissance', *P. P.*, 72, 1976, 133–46. See Kelley (5.31).

5.7 **Brown**, D., 'The birth of Scottish history', *Scot. H.R.*, LXXVI, 1997, 4–22.

5.8 **Burke**, P., 'The politics of Reformation history; Burnet and Brandt' in A. C. Duke and C. A. Tamse (eds), *Clio's Mirror. Historiography in Britain and the Netherlands*, Zutphen, 1985, 73–86.

5.9 **Campbell**, Lily B., *Shakespeare's "Histories". Mirror of Elizabethan Policy*, San Marino, CA, 1947. Looks at the ways in which Shakespeare utilised historiography.

5.10 **Cantor**, N. F., 'The pursuit of the modern' in Cantor, *The English. A History of Politics and Society to 1760*, New York, 1969, 294–310. Considers changing perspectives on the Tudor period.

5.11 **Clegg**, Cyndia S., 'Which Holinshed? Holinshed's *Chronicles* at the Huntington Library', *Hunt. Lib. Q.*, LV, 1994, 559–77.

5.12 **Collinson**, P., 'Truth and legend; the veracity of John Foxe's *Book of Martyrs*' in Duke and Tames (5.8), 31–54.

5.13 —— 'Truth, lies and fiction in sixteenth-century Protestant historiography', in Kelley and Sacks (5.32), 37–68.

5.14 **Dean**, L., *Tudor Theories of Historical Writing*, Ann Arbor, MI, 1947. A concise account.

5.15 **Donno**, Elizabeth S., 'Some aspects of Shakespeare's Holinshed', *Hunt. Lib. Q.*, L, 1987, 229–48.

5.16 —— 'Thomas More and Richard III', *Renaissance Q.*, XXXV, 1982, 401–47.

5.17 **Edelen**, G., 'William Harrison, 1535–1593', *Studs. Renaiss.*, IX, 1962, 256–72.

5.18 **Fairfield**, L. P., *John Bale. Mythmaker for the English Reformation*, West Lafayette, IN, 1976.

5.19 **Ferguson**, A. B., *Clio Unbound. Perceptions of the Social and Cultural Past in Renaissance England*, Durham, NC, 1979. Concentrates on the ways in which historical consciousness was revealed in the uses of the past rather than in historical writing. The great religious and legal controversies of the age are examined from this perspective and in addition there are chapters on language, the concept of civilisation, and on the authority of the ancients.

5.20 **Firth**, Katherine R., *The Apocalyptic Tradition in Reformation Britain, 1530–1645*, 1979. Looks at the ways in which writers like Foxe, Bale, Knox and later Ralegh related modern history to biblical prophecy.

5.21 **Fox**, A., *Thomas More. History and Providence*, 1982. Places More's historical writing within the context of his whole *oeuvre* and his times.

5.22 **Fussner**, F. S., *Tudor History and the Historians*, New York, 1960. Examines the changing trends in twentieth-century historians' treatments of the Tudor period.

5.23 **Haigh**, C., 'The recent historiography of the English Reformation; review article', *Hist. J.*, XXV, 1982, 995–1007.

5.24 **Hale**, J. R., *England and the Italian Renaissance*, 1954, rev. ed. 1963. Looks at changes in the interpretation of the Italian Renaissance from the sixteenth century to the nineteenth.

5.25 **Haller**, W., *The Elect Nation. The Meaning and Relevance of Foxe's Book of Martyrs*, 1963. Considers the significance of Foxe's work as history and propaganda.

5.26 **Hanson**, D. W., *From Kingdom to Commonwealth. The Development of Civic Consciousness in English Political Thought*, Cambridge, MA, 1970.

5.27 **Hay**, D., 'The Historiographers Royal in England and Scotland', *Scot. H.R.*, XXX, 1951, 15–29.

5.28 ——*Polydore Vergil. Renaissance Historian and Man of Letters*, 1952. A biography of the writer and an evaluation of his work, especially the *Anglica Historia*.

5.29 **Helgerson**, R., 'Murder in Faversham; Holinshed's impertinent history', in Kelley and Sacks (5.32), 133–58.

5.30 **Hurstfield**, J., *The Historian as Moralist. Reflections on the Study of Tudor England*, 1974.

5.31 **Kelley**, D. R., 'History, English law and the Renaissance', *P.P.*, 65, 1974, 24–51. See Brooks *et al.* (5.6).

5.32 **Kelley**, D. R. and **Sacks**, D. H. (eds), *The Historical Imagination in Early Modern Britain. Historical Rhetoric and Fiction, 1500–1800*, 1997. Thirteen essays with an introduction ranging from More to Gibbon and addressing aspects of the overlap and interaction between history and fiction.

5.33 **Kelly**, H. A., *Divine Providence in the England of Shakespeare's Histories*, 1970. Includes a discussion of the views on causation entertained by Polydore Vergil, More, Holinshed and Shakespeare.

5.34 **Koebner**, R., '"The imperial crown of this realm"; Henry VIII, Constantine the Great and Polydore Vergil', *B.I.H.R.*, XXVI, 1953, 29–52.

5.35 **Lang**, A., 'Knox as historian', *Scot. H.R.*, II, 1905, 113–30.

5.36 **Lee**, M., 'John Knox and his history', *Scot. H.R.*, XLV, 1966, 79–88. Considers Knox's reasons for writing his work.

5.37 **Levine**, J. M., *Humanism and History. Origins of Modern English Historiography*, Ithaca, NY, 1987. Eight essays, wide-ranging in character, which extend from 'fact and fiction at the close of the Middle Ages' to 'eighteenth-century historicism and the first Gothic Revival'.

5.38 ——'Thomas More and the English Renaissance; history and fiction in Utopia', in Kelley and Sacks (5.32), 69–92.

5.39 **Levy**, F. J., *Tudor Historical Thought*, San Marino, CA, 1967. Assesses the impact of Italian humanism, the growing awareness of anachronism, the need for source criticism, and the stress on politics and political utility.

5.40 ——'The making of Camden's *Britannia*', *Bibliothèque d'Humanisme et Renaissance*, XXVI, 1964, 70–97.

5.41 **McKisack**, May, *Medieval History in the Tudor Age*, 1971. Considers Leland, Bale, Matthew Paris and his circle, patrons and collectors, archivists and record searchers, the Elizabethan Society of Antiquaries. There are separate chapters on general histories of Britain and on local historians and topographers.

5.42 **McNeill**, J. T., 'John Foxe; historiographer, disciplinarian, tolerationist', *Church Hist.*, XLIII, 1974, 216–29.

5.43 **Mason**, R. A., ' "Usable pasts"; history and identity in Reformation Scotland', *Scot. H.R.*, LXXVI, 1997, 54–68.

5.44 **O'Day**, Rosemary, *The Debate on the English Reformation*, 1986. A survey of changing trends in the historiography from the sixteenth century to the present day.

5.45 **Olsen**, V. N., *John Foxe and the Elizabethan Church*, Berkeley, CA, 1973.

5.46 **Parry**, G. J. R., 'William Harrison and Holinshed's *Chronicles*', *Hist. J.*, XXVII, 1984, 789–810.

5.47 **Patterson**, Annabel, 'Foul, his wife, the mayor and Foul's mare; the power of anecdote in Tudor historiography' in Kelley and Sacks (5.32), 159–78.

5.48 ——*Reading Holinshed's Chronicles*, Chicago, IL, 1994. An enterprising, lively, revisionist book which attempts a reappraisal of Holinshed's *Chronicles* and rescues their intentions and protocols. Part 2 establishes the ecclesiastical, religious and legal context. Part 3 deals with populism, women, censorship and readers.

5.49 **Pineas**, R., 'William Tyndale's influence on John Bale's polemical use of history', *Archiv für Reformationgeschichte*, LIII, 1962, 79–96.

5.50 ——'Robert Barnes's polemical use of history', *Bibliotheque d'Humanisme et Renaissance*, XXVI, 1964, 55–69.

5.51 **Pollard**, A. F., 'The making of Sir Thomas More's *Richard III*' in J. G. Edwards *et al.* (eds), *Historical Essays in Honour of James Tait*, 1933, 223–38.

5.52 **Power**, M. J., 'John Stow and his London', *J. Hist. Geog.*, XI, 1985, 1–20.

5.53 **Powicke**, F. M., 'William Camden', *Eng. Studs.*, n.s., I, 1948, 67–84.

5.54 **Ridley**, J., *John Knox*, 1968. A biography which gives due consideration to Knox's work as a historian.

5.55 **Rodgers**, C. P., 'Humanism, history and the common law', *J. Legal Hist.*, VI, 1985, 129–56. See also Kelley (4.32).

5.56 **Ross**, A., 'Some Scottish Catholic historians', *Innes R.*, I, 1950, 5–21. Considers the characteristics of a group of sixteenth to eighteenth-century historians.

5.57 **Saccio**, P., *Shakespeare's English Kings. History, Chronicle and Drama*, 1977.

5.58 **Salmon**, J. H. M., 'Precept, example, and truth; Degory Wheare and the *ars historica*' in Kelley and Sacks (5.32), 11–36.

5.59 **Slavin**, A. J., 'G. R. Elton; on *Reformation and Revolution*', *Hist. Teacher*, XXIII, 1990, 405–31.

5.60 **Strathmann**, E. A., *Sir Walter Ralegh. A Study in Elizabethan Skepticism*, New York, 1951. Includes a chapter on Ralegh as 'the judicious historian'.

5.61 **Terrill**, R. J., 'William Lambarde; Elizabethan humanist and legal historian', *J. Legal Hist.*, VI, 1985, 157–78.

5.62 **Trevor-Roper**, H. R., *Queen Elizabeth's First Historian. William Camden and the Beginnings of English Civil History*, 1971.

5.63 ——'George Buchanan and the ancient Scottish constitution', *E.H.R.* supplement 3, 1966, 1–53.

5.64 **Warnicke**, Retha M., *William Lambarde. Elizabethan Antiquary, 1536–1601*, 1973.

5.65 **Wooden**, W. W., *John Foxe*, Boston, MA, 1983.

5.66 **Wright**, C. E., 'The dispersal of the monastic libraries and the beginnings of Anglo-Saxon studies', *Trans Camb. Biblio. Soc.*, I, 1951, 208–37.

5.67 **Wright**, L. B., *Tudor and Stuart History. A Report of the Folger Library Conference on Needs and Opportunities*, Washington, DC, 1959. A collection of short reports and comments.

EUROPE

5.68 **Avis**, P., *The Foundations of Modern Historical Thought. From Machiavelli to Vico*, 1986. Discusses the philosophical contribution to the rise of historical consciousness.

5.69 **Bender**, H. S., 'The historiography of the Anabaptists', *Mennonite Q.R.*, XXXI, 1957, 88–104.

5.70 **Bouwsma**, W. J., 'Three types of historiography in post-Renaissance Italy', *Hist. and Theory*, IV, 1965, 303–14.

5.71 —— *Venice and the Defence of Republican Liberty. Renaissance Values in the Age of the Counter-Reformation*, Berkeley, CA, 1968. Contains a long chapter (556–623) on Renaissance liberty and the uses of the past. Bibliography, 629–56.

5.72 **Davis**, Natalie Zemon, 'Gender and genre; women as historical writers, 1400–1820', in Patricia Labalme (ed.), *Beyond their Sex. Learned Women of the European Past*, New York, 1980.

5.73 **Denzer**, H. (ed.), *Jean Bodin. Proceedings of the International Conference on Bodin in Munich*, Munich, 1973.

5.74 **Dickens**, A. G., *Contemporary Historians of the German Reformation*, 1979. Lecture.

5.75 —— 'Johannes Sleiden and Reformation history' in R. Knox (ed.), *Reformation Conformity and Dissent. Essays in Honour of Geoffrey Nuttall*, 1977, 17–43.

5.76 —— and **Tonkin**, J. M., *The Reformation in Historical Thought*, 1986. A major work which traces changing tendencies in writing about the European and English Reformations from the sixteenth century to the present day. There is no bibliography, unfortunately, but the footnotes are a mine of information.

5.77 **Fenlon**, D., '*Encore une question*; Lucien Febvre, the Reformation and the school of *Annales*', *Hist. Studs.*, XI, 1974, 65–81.

5.78 **Friesen**, A., 'The Marxist interpretation of the Reformation', *Archiv für Reformationgesichte*, LXIV, 1973, 34–54.

5.79 —— 'Philipp Melanchthon, Wilhelm Zimmermann and the dilemma of Muntzer historiography', *Church Hist.*, XLIII, 1974, 164–82.

5.80 —— 'Thomas Muntzer in Marxist thought', *Church Hist.*, XXXIV, 1965, 306–27.

5.81 **Headley**, J., *Luther's View of Church History*, New Haven, CT, 1963. Has chapters on the defining of Church history, the problem of tradition, the problem of periodisation, the early church, the appearance of Antichrist, and on the Antichrist and the last times. Bibliography, 272–84.

5.82 **Ianziti**, G., *Humanistic Historiography under the Sforzas. Politics and Propaganda in Fifteenth-Century Milan*, 1988.

5.83 **Kelley**, D. R., 'Johann Sleiden and the origins of history as a profession', *J.M.H.*, LII, 1980, 573–98.

5.84 **Logan**, O., *Culture and Society in Venice, 1470–1790*, 1972. Emphasises the central position of attitudes to the past.

5.85 **Maskell**, D., *The Historical Epic in France, 1500–1700*, 1973.

5.86 **Mousnier**, R. and **Pillorget**, R., 'Contemporary history and historians of the sixteenth and seventeenth centuries', *J. Contemp. Hist.*, III, 1968, 93–109.

5.87 **O'Malley**, J., 'Historical thought and the Reformation crisis of the early sixteenth century', *Theol. Studs.*, XXVIII, 1967, 531–48.

5.88 **Pauck**, W., 'The historiography of the German Reformation during the past twenty years', *Church Hist.*, IX, 1940, 305–40.

5.89 —— *The Heritage of the Reformation*, Boston, MA, 1950, 2nd ed. Glencoe, IL, 1961.

5.90 **Pullapilly**, C. K., *Caesar Baronius, Counter-Reformation Historian*, 1975.

5.91 **Regosin**, R., 'D'Aubigné's *Les Tragiques*; a Protestant apocalypse', *Pub. Mod. Lang. Ass. America*, LXXXI, 1966, 363–8.

5.92 **Ryan**, E., *The Historical Scholarship of Robert Bellarmine*, Louvain, 1936.

5.93 **Scott**, T., 'The Peasants' War; a historiographical review', *Hist. J.*, XXII, 1979, 693–720, 953–74.

5.94 **Scribner**, R. W., 'Is there a social

history of the Reformation?', *Soc. Hist.*, IV, 1977, 483–503.

5.95 —— 'Communalism; universal category or ideological construct? A debate in the historiography of early modern Germany and Switzerland', *Hist. J.*, XXXVII, 1994, 199–208.

5.96 **Simpler**, S. H., *Roland H. Bainton. An Examination of his Reformation Historiography*, Lewiston, NY, 1985.

5.97 **Strauss**, G., *Sixteenth-Century Germany. Its Topography and Topographers*, Madison, WI, 1959.

5.98 **Tilmans**, Karin, *Historiography and Humanism in Holland in the Age of Erasmus*, Nieuwkoop, 1992.

5.99 **Williams**, G., *Reformation Views on Church History*, 1970. The central chapters deal with Tyndale, Bale and Foxe. Bibliography, 75–7.

5.100 **Witschi-Bernz**, Astrid, 'Main trends in historical method literature; sixteenth to eighteenth centuries', *Hist. and Theory*, supplement, 12, 1972, 50–90.

5.101 **Wootton**, D., 'Lucien Febvre and the problem of unbelief in the early modern period', *J.M.H.*, LX, 1988, 695–730.

5.102 —— *Paolo Sarpi. Between Renaissance and Enlightenment*, 1983. The most substantial study of the Italian political and ecclesiastical historian.

5.103 **Yates**, Frances A., 'Paolo Sarpi's *History of the Council of Trent*', *J. Warburg and Coutauld Insts*, VII, 1944, 123–43.

6

THE SEVENTEENTH CENTURY

ENGLAND

6.1 **Abbott**, W. C., 'The historic Cromwell' in Abbott, *Adventures in Reputation*, Cambridge, MA, 1935, 94–117.

6.2 **Ashley**, M., 'King James II and the revolution of 1688; some reflections on the historiography' in H. E. Bell and R. L. Ollard (eds), *Historical Essays, 1600–1750, presented to David Ogg*, 1963, 185–202.

6.3 **Ashton**, R., 'Cavaliers and capitalists; reflections on current controversies on the role of material factors in the genesis of the English civil war', *Renaiss. and Mod. Studs.*, V, 1961, 149–75.

Francis Bacon

6.4 **Clark**, D. S. T., 'Bacon's Henry VII; a case study in the science of man', *Hist. and Theory*, XIII, 1974, 97–118.

6.5 **Guibbory**, A., 'Francis Bacon's view of history; the cycles of error and the progress of truth', *J. Eng. and Germanic Philology*, LXXIV, 1975, 336–50.

6.6 **Nadel**, G. H., 'History as psychology in Francis Bacon's theory of history', *Hist. and Theory*, V, 1966, 275–87.

6.7 **White**, H. B., 'The English Solomon; Francis Bacon on Henry VII', *Soc. Research*, XXIV, 1957, 457–81.

6.8 **Beer**, Anna R., *Sir Walter Ralegh and his Readers in the Seventeenth Century*, 1997.

Includes a full discussion of Ralegh's *History of the World* and charts the phases of its author's reputation. Bibliography. See also May (6.61).

6.9 **Bowle**, J., *Hobbes and his Critics*, 1951. Clarendon was a prominent figure in this group. See also Goldsmith (6.36) and MacGillivray (6.57).

6.10 **Breward**, I., 'The abolition of Puritanism', *J. Relig. Hist.*, VII, 1974. See also George (6.35).

6.11 **Burgess**, G., 'On revisionism; an analysis of early Stuart historiography in the 1970s and 1980s', *Hist. J.*, XXXIII, 1990, 609–28.

6.12 —— 'Revisionism, politics and political ideas in early Stuart England', *Hist. J.*, XXXIV, 1991, 465–78.

6.13 **Butterfield**, H., *Magna Carta in the Historiography of the Sixteenth and Seventeenth Centuries*, 1969. See also Thompson (6.80).

6.14 **Callincos**, A., 'Bourgeois revolutions and historical materialism', *Internat. Socialism*, XLIII, 1989, 113–71.

Clarendon

6.15 **Brownley**, M. W., *Clarendon and the Rhetoric of Historical Form*, Philadelphia, PA, 1985. Essentially a literary approach, concentrating on Clarendon's style and on his identification of moral and political lessons.

6.16 **Finlayson**, M., 'Clarendon, Providence and the historical revolution', *Albion*, XXII, 1990, 607–32.

6.17 **Firth**, C. H., 'Clarendon's *History of the Rebellion*', *E.H.R.*, XIX, 1904, 26–54; *E.H.R.*, XX, 1905, 246–62; *E.H.R.*, XX, 1905, 464–83. Examines the way in which Clarendon's *History* came to be written and assembled.

6.18 **Harris**, R. W., *Clarendon and the English Revolution*, 1983. A biography, but one that pays due attention to Clarendon's work as a historian.

6.19 **Hill**, C., 'Lord Clarendon and the Puritan Revolution' in Hill, *Puritanism and Revolution*, 1958, 199–214. Examines Clarendon's diagnosis of the social causes of the mid-seventeenth-century upheavals.

6.20 **Hutton**, R., 'Clarendon's *History of the Rebellion*', *E.H.R.*, XCVII, 1982.

6.21 **Roebuck**, G., *Clarendon and Cultural Continuity. A Bibliographical Study*, New York, 1981. After a brief introduction the author provides a bibliography of Clarendon's own writings and of his subsequent reassessment.

6.22 **Trevor-Roper**, H. R., 'Clarendon and the practice of history' in F. R. Foyle and H. R. Trevor-Roper, *Milton and Clarendon*, Los Angeles, CA, 1965, 21–50.

6.23 **Wormald**, B. H. G., *Clarendon. Politics, History and Religion, 1640–60*, 1951. A well known study which places Clarendon firmly in his seventeenth-century context.

6.24 **Zagorin**, P., 'Clarendon and Hobbes', *J.M.H.*, LVII, 1985, 593–616. See also Bowle (6.9), Goldsmith (6.36) and MacGillivray (6.57).

6.25 **Davis**, J. C., *Fear, Myth and History. The Ranters and the Historians*, 1986. Argues that the Ranters were the mythical construct of their seventeenth-century adversaries and of modern left-wing historians whose concept of 'revolt within the revolution' depends on their existence. There is a substantial appendix of seventeenth-century tracts.

6.26 ——'Puritanism and revolution; themes, categories, methods, and conclusions', *Hist. J.*, XXXIV, 1991, 479–90.

6.27 **Douglas**, D. C., *English Scholars, 1660–1730*, 1939, 2nd ed. 1951. Considers the work of Brady, Wharton, Hearne, Rymer and others and the relations between late seventeenth-century antiquarianism and politics.

6.28 **Dray**, W. H., 'J. H. Hexter, neo-Whiggism and early Stuart historiography', *Hist. and Theory*, XXVI, 1987, 133–49.

6.29 **Finlayson**, M. G., *Historians, Puritanism and the English Revolution. The Religious Factor in English Politics before and after the Interregnum*, 1983. Looks at the ways in which historical interpretations of this period – mistakenly, in the author's view – have centred on Puritanism. See also Breward (6.10) and George (6.35).

6.30 **Firth**, C. H., 'The development of the study of seventeenth-century history', *T.R.H.S.*, 3rd ser., VII, 1913, 25–48.

6.31 ——'Sir Walter Ralegh's *History of the World*', *Proc. Brit. Acad.*, VIII, 1917–18. Reprinted in Firth, *Essays Historical and Literary*, 1938, 34–60.

6.32 **Fox**, L. (ed.), *English Historical Scholarship in the Sixteenth and Seventeenth Centuries*, 1956. The proceedings of the Dugdale tercentenary conference. Included are chapters on 'The public records in the sixteenth and seventeenth centuries', 'Politics and historical research in the early seventeenth century' and 'Antiquarian thought in the sixteenth and seventeenth centuries'.

6.33 **Fulbrook**, Mary, 'The English Revolution and the revisionist revolt', *Soc. Hist.*, VII, 1982, 249–64. Complements Richardson's survey (6.73).

6.34 **Fussner**, F. S., *The Historical Revolution. English Historical Writing and Thought, 1580–1640*, 1962. Looks at the ways in which changes in the intellectual, social and political context produced new kinds and new understandings of history.

6.35 **George**, C. H., 'Puritanism as history and historiography', *P.P.*, 41, 1968, 77–104. See also Breward (6.10).

6.36 **Goldsmith**, M. M., *Hobbes's Science of Politics*, New York, 1966. Analyses the ideas that informed Hobbes's approach to philosophy, human nature and history.

6.37 **Gough**, J. W., 'James Tyrrell, Whig historian and friend of John Locke', *Hist. J.*, XIX, 1976, 581–610.

6.38 **Greaves**, R. L., 'The Puritan/Nonconformist tradition, 1560–1700; historiographical reflections', *Albion*, XVII, 1985, 449–86.

6.39 **Greenleaf**, W. H., 'Filmer's patriarchal history', *Hist. J.*, IX, 1966, 157–71.

6.40 **Herrup**, Cynthia, 'The counties and the country; some thoughts on seventeenth-century historiography', *Soc. Hist.*, VIII, 1983, 169–81.

6.41 **Hexter**, J. H., 'The early Stuart Parliament; old hat and the *nouvelle vague*', *Parl. Hist.*, I, 1982, 181–215.

6.42 **Hicks**, P., *Neoclassical History and English Culture. From Clarendon to Hume*, 1996. Places Clarendon, Brady, Burnet, Bolingbroke, Rapin, Hume and others within the context of neoclassicism. Bibliography.

6.43 **Hill**, C., 'The English Civil War interpreted by Marx and Engels', *Sci. and Soc.*, XII, 1948, 130–56.

6.44 —— *England's Turning Point. Essays on Seventeenth-Century English History*, 1998. Mainly a collection of short occasional pieces and reviews, the earliest of them going back to 1938. H. A. L. Fisher, Lawrence Stone, R. H. Tawney, G. M. Trevelyan are among the historians who come under discussion.

6.45 —— *Intellectual Origins of the English Revolution*, 1965, 2nd ed. 1997. Includes a chapter on 'Ralegh; science, history and politics', 131–224.

6.46 —— 'The Norman yoke' in Hill, *Puritanism and Revolution*, 1958, 50–122. A classic study of the political uses of history.

6.47 **Hunter**, M., *John Aubrey and the Realm of Learning*, 1975.

6.48 **Jessup**, F. W., *Sir Roger Twysden, 1597–1672*, 1965. A study of one of the leading mid-seventeenth-century antiquarians.

6.49 **Johnson**, L. M., *Thucydides, Hobbes, and the Interpretation of Realism*, DeKalb, IL, 1993.

6.50 **Johnston**, D., *The Rhetoric of Leviathan. Thomas Hobbes and the Rhetoric of Cultural Transformation*, Princeton, NJ, 1987.

6.51 **Josten**, C. H., *Elias Ashmole, 1617–92*, I, 1966. A biography and evaluation of the major seventeenth-century antiquary.

6.52 **Kliger**, S. T., *The Goths in England. A Study in Seventeenth and Eighteenth Century Thought*, Cambridge, MA, 1952. Examines the political uses made of 'Gothic' history to serve the purposes of the present. There are chapters on 'Gothic parliaments' and on the Levellers.

6.53 **Kraynack**, R. P., *History and Modernity in the Thought of Thomas Hobbes*, Ithaca, NY, 1990.

6.54 **Levine**, J. M., 'Ancients, moderns and history; the continuity of English historical writing in the later seventeenth century' in P. J. Korshin (ed.), *Studies in Change and Revolution. Aspects of English Intellectual History, 1640–1800*, 1972, 43–75.

6.55 **Levy**, F. J., 'The background of Hobbes's *Behemoth*' in Kelley and Sacks (5.32), 243–66.

6.56 **McDougall**, D. J., 'Oliver Cromwell and his biographers', *Hist. Bull.*, XXXIII, 1954–5, 131–48. See also Abbott (6.1).

6.57 **MacGillivray**, R., *Restoration Historians and the English Civil War*, The Hague, 1974. Critically examines the Royalist and Parliamentarian perspectives. Excellent bibliography.

6.58 **MacLachlan**, A. *The Rise of Revolutionary England. An Essay on the Fabrication of Seventeenth-Century History*, 1996. A hard-hitting study of the celebration of the English Revolution by Marxist and other radical historians and of the revisionist challenge.

6.59 **Manley**, L., *Convention, 1500–1700*, Cambridge, MA, 1980. Considers – *inter alia* – the literary conventions expressed in the development of English Renaissance historiography.

6.60 **Manuel**, F. E., *Isaac Newton, Historian*, Cambridge, MA, 1963. Examines Newton's interest in the history of science, the Church and the classical world.

6.61 **May**, S. W., *Sir Walter Ralegh*, Boston, MA, 1989. A short guide to the different facets of Ralegh's career and to his historical and other writings.

Bibliography, 154–60. See also Beer (6.8).

6.62 **Mendyk**, S. A. E., *'Speculum Britanniae'. Regional Study, Antiquarianism and Science in Britain to 1700*, 1989. Camden, Dugdale, Lambarde, Norden and Plot rub shoulders here with Bacon and the Royal Society. Extensive bibliography, 331–45.

6.63 **Merchant**, W. M., 'Lord Herbert of Cherbury and seventeenth-century historical writing', *Trans. Hon. Soc. Cymmrodorion*, 1956, 47–63.

6.64 **Morrill**, J., 'Textalising and contextualising Cromwell', *Hist. J.*, XXXIII, 1990, 629–40.

6.65 **Parry**, G., *The Trophies of Time. English Antiquarianism of the Seventeenth Century*, 1999. A substantial study of the place of Camden, Cotton, Selden, Ussher, Spelman, Somner, Dugdale, Fuller, Aubrey and others within the seventeenth-century antiquarian tradition.

6.66 **Piggott**, S., *Ruins in a Landscape. Essays in Antiquarianism*, 1976. Includes studies of sixteenth and seventeenth-century antiquarian thought, William Camden, of Celts, Saxons and the early antiquaries, and the origins of the English county archaeological societies.

6.67 **Pocock**, J. G. A., *The Ancient Constitution and the Feudal Law. A Study of English Historical Thought in the Seventeenth Century*, 1957. A classic study of seventeenth-century scholarship and uses of the past. Spelman, Harrington and Brady are among those included.

6.68 —— 'Time, history and eschatology in the thought of Thomas Hobbes' in Pocock, *Politics, Language and Time. Essays on Political Thought and History*, 1972, 148–201.

6.69 —— 'Robert Brady, 1627–1700; a Cambridge historian of the Restoration', *Camb. Hist. J.*, X, 1950–52, 186–204.

6.70 **Preston**, J. H., 'English ecclesiastical historians and the problem of bias, 1559–1742', *J. Hist. Ideas*, XXXII, 1971, 203–20.

6.71 **Raab**, F., *The English Face of Machiavelli*, 1964. Explores the reception of Machiavelli's ideas in England.

6.72 **Richardson**, R. C. (ed.), *The English Civil Wars. Local Aspects*, 1997. The editor's introduction surveys the historiography.

6.73 —— *The Debate on the English Revolution*, 1977, 3rd ed., 1998. Examines changing perceptions of the mid-seventeenth-century upheavals, arguably the most controversial period in the whole of English history, from the initial responses of contemporaries up to the very different collisions of interpretation which abound today.

6.74 —— and **Ridden**, G. M. (ed.), *Freedom and the English Revolution*, 1986. The introduction is to a large extent historiographical. Bibliography.

6.75 —— (ed.), *Images of Oliver Cromwell. Essays for and by Roger Howell*, 1993. A collection of essays which survey the changing historical reputation of Cromwell in England, Ireland and America.

6.76 **Sanderson**, J., 'Reflections upon Marxist historiography; the case of the English Civil War' in B. Chapman and A. Potter (eds), *W.J.M.M. Political Questions*, 1975, 226–51.

6.77 **Sharpe**, K., *Sir Robert Cotton, 1586–1631. History and Politics in Early Modern England*, 1979. Relates Cotton's antiquarianism to the political world of his day.

6.78 **Springborg**, Patricia, *'Leviathan, mythic history and national historiography'* in Kelley and Sacks (5.32), 267–97.

6.79 **Tawney**, R. H., 'Harrington's interpretation of his age', *Proc. Brit. Acad.*, XXVII, 1941, 199–223. A major landmark in the twentieth-century rediscovery of Harrington and his integration into modern studies of the Civil War period.

6.80 **Thompson**, Faith, *Magna Carta. Its Role in the Making of the English Constitution, 1300–1629*, Minneapolis, MN, 1948. See also Butterfield (6.13).

6.81 **Tomlinson**, H., 'The causes of war; a historiographical survey' in Tomlinson (ed.), *Before the English Civil War*, 1983, 7–26. Complements Richardson's survey (6.73).

6.82 **von Maltzahn**, N., *Milton's History of Britain. Republican Historiography in the English Revolution*, 1991. Looks at the background to the composition of Milton's *History* and at his accounts of the ancient Britons, the early Church and the Saxons. Milton's use of Gildas is assessed, as are his contributions to the discussion of the ancient constitution and feudalism. Bibliography.

6.83 **Walcott**, R., 'The idea of party in the writing of later Stuart history', *J. Brit. Studs.*, I, 1962, 54–61.

6.84 **Wilson**, R. B., 'The evolution of local history writing in Warwickshire', *Birm. Arch. Soc. Trans. and Proc.*, LXXI, 1953, 63–75. Looks at Dugdale and his successors.

6.85 **Woolf**, D. R., 'A feminine past? Gender, genre, and historical knowledge in England, 1500–1800', *A.H.R.*, CII, 1997, 645–79.

6.86 ——*The Idea of History in Early Stuart England. Erudition, Ideology and the 'Light of Truth' from the Accession of Charles I to the Civil War*, Toronto and Buffalo, NY, 1990. Connects the historical writing of this period with its political and intellectual context and explores the breakdown in consensus among historians. History's changing relations with poetry, antiquarianism, chorography and legal studies are carefully examined in the discussion of unfamiliar as well as celebrated writers.

6.87 **Wright**, C. J. (ed.), *Sir Robert Cotton as Collector. Essays on an Early Stuart Courtier and his Legacy*, 1997. A motley collection of essays on this leading early seventeenth-century antiquarian. The most weighty contributions are those by Kevin Sharpe ('Rewriting Sir Robert Cotton') and by David Howarth (Sir Robert Cotton and the Commonwealth of Famous Men').

EUROPE

6.88 **Aston**, T. and **Philpin**, C. H. E. (eds), *The Brenner Debate. Agrarian Class Structure and Economic Development in Preindustrial Europe*, 1985. Collects together the different contributions to a famous controversy which originally raged in the journal *Past and Present*.

6.89 **Barrett-Kreigel**, B., *Jean Mabillon*, Paris, 1988.

6.90 **Burke**, P., 'Structural history in the sixteenth and seventeenth centuries', *Storia de Storiog.*, X, 1986, 71–6.

6.91 **Cochrane**, E., 'The transition from Renaissance to Baroque; the case of historiography', *Hist. and Theory*, XIX, 1980, 21–38.

6.92 **Kelley**, D. R., 'History as a calling; the case of La Popelinière' in A. Molho and J. A. Tedeschi (eds), *Renaissance Studies in Honour of Hans Baron*, DeKalb, IL, 1971, 771–89.

6.93 **Kinser**, S., *The Works of Jacques Auguste de Thou*, The Hague, 1996. A bibliographical study of this neglected historian. There are chapters on the various editions, reprints and translations of his writings.

6.94 **Pocock**, J. G. A., *The Machiavellian Moment. Florentine Political Thought and the Atlantic Republican Tradition*, Princeton, NJ, 1975. Discusses the development of the historical outlook from the Renaissance.

6.95 **Ranum**, O., *Artisans of Glory. Writers and Historical Thought in Seventeenth-Century France*, Chapel Hill, NC, 1980. Looks at the rhetorical and ideological ramifications of historiography and the contribution of the royal historians to the *gloire* of the monarchy and nobility.

6.96 ——(ed.), *National Consciousness, History and Political Culture in Early Modern Europe*, Baltimore, MD, 1975. Has chapters on Italy, France, Germany, Russia, Spain and England.

6.97 **Sypher**, G. W., 'La Popelinière's *Histoire de France;* a case of historical objectivity and religious censorship', *J. Hist. Ideas*, XXIV, 1963, 41–54.

6.98 **Whelan**, Ruth, *The Anatomy of Superstition. A Study of the Historical Theory and Practice of Pierre Bayle*, 1989.

COLONIAL HISTORY

6.99 **Billington**, R. A. (ed.), *The Reinterpretation of Early American History. Essays in Honour of John Edwin Pomfret*, San Marino, CA, 1966. A *festschrift* which includes essays on the historians of early New England, the middle and southern colonies, and the American Revolution.

6.100 **Gay**, P., *A Loss of Mastery. Puritan Historians in Colonial America*, Berkeley, CA, 1966. Memorable partly for the collision between the author's scepticism and the piety of the colonial historians.

6.101 **Howard**, A. B., 'Art and history in Bradford's *Of Plymouth Plantation*', *Wm and Mary Q.*, XXVIII, 1971, 239–66.

6.102 **van Tassel**, D. D., *Recording America's Past. An Interpretation of the Development of Historical Studies in America, 1607–84*, Chicago, IL, 1960.

6.103 **Wilgus**, A. C., *The Historiography of Latin America. A Guide to Historical Writing, 1500–1800*, Metuchen, NJ, 1975.

7

THE EIGHTEENTH CENTURY

BRITAIN

7.1 **Allan**, D., ' "This inquisitive age"; past and present in the Scottish Enlightenment', *Scot. H.R.*, LXXVI, 1997, 69–85.

7.2 **Baxter**, S., 'John Strype, biographer of the Church of England' in J. D. Browning (ed.), *Biography in the Eighteenth Century*, New York, 1980, 69–84.

7.3 **Bennett**, G. V., *White Kennett, 1660–1728, Bishop of Peterborough. A Study in the Political and Ecclesiastical History of the Early Eighteenth Century*, 1957. Though chiefly a study in churchmanship the book includes an assessment of Kennett's work as a historian.

7.4 **Black**, J. B., *The Art of History. A Study of Four Great Historians of the Eighteenth Century*, 1926. Voltaire, Hume, Robertson and Gibbon are the historians included.

7.5 **Bowles**, P., 'The origin of property and the development of Scottish historical science', *J. Hist. Ideas*, XLVI, 1985, 197–209.

7.6 **Boyle**, J., *In Quest of Hasted*, 1984. A short study of the eighteenth-century antiquarian and his surviving manuscripts.

7.7 **Braudy**, L., *Narrative Form in History and Fiction. Hume, Fielding and Gibbon*, Princeton, NJ, 1970. Provides some account of Clarendon and Bolingbroke as well as those writers referred to in the title. Bibliography, 293–308.

7.8 **Butterfield**, H., *George III and the Historians*, 1957. A well known historiographical case study. Walpole, Croker, Erskine May, Lecky and G. O. Trevelyan are dealt with, but the longest section is that devoted to 'George III and the Namier school'.

7.9 **Camil**, C., *Experience and Enlightenment. Socialisation for Cultural Change in Eighteenth-Century Scotland*, 1983.

7.10 **Chitnis**, A., *The Scottish Enlightenment. A Social History*, 1977. See also Rendall (7.34).

7.11 **Christie**, I. R., '*George III and the Historians* thirty years on', *Hist.*, LXXI, 1986, 205–21.

7.12 **Colley**, Linda, 'The politics of eighteenth-century British historiography', *J. Brit. Studs.*, XXV, 1986, 359–79.

7.13 **Davis**, H., 'The Augustan conception of history' in J. A. Mazzeo (ed.), *Reason and Imagination. Studies in the History of Ideas, 1600–1800*, New York, 1962.

7.14 **Earl**, D. W. L., 'Procrustean feudalism; an interpretative dilemma in English historical narrative, 1700–25', *Hist. J.*, XIX, 1976, 33–51.

7.15 **Edgar**, I. I., 'Historiography and the great English triumvirate of the eighteenth century' in Edgar, *Essays in English Literature and History*, New York, 1972, 89–128.

7.15a **Fearney-Sander**, Mary, 'Philosophical history and the Scottish Reformation; William Robertson and the Knoxian tradition', *Hist. J.*, XXXIII, 1990, 323–38.

7.16 **Firth**, C. H., 'Modern history at Oxford, 1724–1841', *E.H.R.*, XXXII, 1917, 1–21.

Edward Gibbon

7.17 **Carnochan**, W. B., *Gibbon's Solitude. The Inward World of the Historian*, Stanford, CA, 1987.

7.18 **Craddock**, Patricia B., *Edward Gibbon. Luminous Historian, 1772–94*, Baltimore, MD, 1989. The major modern biography of the author of the *Decline and Fall* which systematically explores his place in the eighteenth-century European Enlightenment.

7.19 **de Beer**, G., *Gibbon and his World*, 1968. Informative and generously illustrated.

7.20 **Bond**, H. L., *The Literary Art of Edward Gibbon*, 1960. Analyses Gibbon's epic.

7.21 **Bowersock**, G. W., **Clive**, J., and **Graubard**, S. R. (eds), *Edward Gibbon and the Fall of the Roman Empire*, Cambridge, MA, 1977. Collects the papers given at a symposium.

7.22 **Burrow**, J. W., *Gibbon*, 1978. Focuses chiefly on *The Decline and Fall* and its genesis rather than on the biography of the historian.

7.23 **Dickinson**, H. T., 'The politics of Edward Gibbon', *Lit. and Hist.*, VIII, 1978, 175–96. Examines the ways in which the eighteenth-century constitution conditioned Gibbon's view of the past.

7.24 **Fuglum**, P., *Edward Gibbon. His View of Life and Conception of History*, Oslo, 1953. Has chapters on Gibbon the man, the philosopher and the historian, with discussions of the politics, social problems, economics and religion of the period. Bibliography, 163–5.

7.25 **Gossmann**, L., *The Empire Unpossess'd. An Essay on Gibbon's Decline and Fall*, 1981. Analyses the rhetoric, thematic structure and autobiographical undertones of Gibbon's *History*.

7.26 **Jordan**, D. P., 'Gibbon's Age of Constantine and the fall of Rome',

Hist. and Theory, VIII, 1969, 71–96.

7.27 —— *Gibbon and his Roman Empire*, Urbana, IL, 1971. Explores the subjectivity of Gibbon's account of the Roman empire.

7.28 **Low**, D. M., *Edward Gibbon, 1737–94*, 1937. Still the standard biography.

7.29 **McKitterick**, Rosamond (ed.), *Edward Gibbon and Empire*, 1996.

7.30 **Parkinson**, R. N., *Edward Gibbon*, New York, 1973. Concentrates chiefly on literary aspects.

7.31 **Plumb**, J. H., 'Gibbon and history', *Hist. Today*, XIX, 1969, 737–43.

7.32 **Pocock**, J. G. A., 'Gibbon's *Decline and Fall* and the world view of the late Enlightenment', *Eighteenth Century Studs.*, X, 1976–77, 287–303.

7.33 **Porter**, R., *Gibbon. Making History*, 1988. A compact study which places Gibbon and his *Decline and Fall* within the context of eighteenth-century historiography, politics and religion.

7.34 **Rendall**, Jane, *The Origins of the Scottish Enlightenment, 1707–76*. 1978. See also Chitnis (7.10).

7.35 **Swain**, J. W., *Gibbon the Historian*, 1966. An introductory study.

7.36 **Thompson**, M. A., *Gibbon*, 1946. Historical Ass. pamphlet.

7.37 **Trevor-Roper**, H. R., 'The idea of the *Decline and Fall of the Roman Empire*' in W. H. Barber *et al.* (eds), *The Age of the Enlightenment*, 1967, 413–30.

7.38 **Wedgwood**, C. V., *Edward Gibbon*, 1955. Pamphlet.

7.39 **Womersley**, D., *The Transformation of the Decline and Fall of the Roman Empire*, 1988.

7.40 —— (ed.), *Edward Gibbon. Bicentenary Essays*, 1997. Sixteen essays grouped into three categories, 'Gibbon and Europe'; 'The *Decline and Fall*; milieu, substance and reception'; 'After the *Decline and Fall*'.

7.41 **Wootton**, D., 'Narrative, irony and faith in Gibbon's *Decline and Fall*', *Hist. and Theory*, XXXIII, 1994, 77–105.

7.42 **Young**, G. M., *Gibbon*, 1932, new ed. 1948. A brief, ebullient biography.

7.43 **Gibbs**, G. C., 'The contribution of Abel Boyer to contemporary history in England in the early eighteenth century' in Duke and Tamse (5.8), 87–108.

7.44 **Girard D'Albissin**, Nelly, *Un Précurseur de Montesquieu. Rapin Thoyras, premier historien français des institutions anglaises*, Paris, 1969.

7.45 **Haywood**, I., 'The making of history: historiography and literary forgery in the eighteenth century', *Lit. and Hist.*, IX, 1983, 139–51.

7.46 **Hill**, Bridget, *The Republican Virago. The Life and Times of Catharine Macaulay, Historian*, 1992. A thorough study of the first major woman historian in England and of her place in the radical politics of the late eighteenth century.

7.47 ——and C., 'Catharine Macaulay's *History* and her catalogue of tracts', *Seventeenth Century*, VIII, 1993, 269–85.

7.48 **Hopel**, H. M., 'From savage to Scotsman: conjectural history in the Scottish Enlightenment', *J. Brit. Studs.*, XVII, 1977, 19–40.

7.49 **Hoppit**, J., 'Counting the industrial revolution', *Ec.H.R.*, XLIII, 1990, 173–93.

7.50 **Horn**, D. B., 'Some Scottish writers of history in the eighteenth century', *Scot. H.R.*, XL, 1961, 1–18.

7.51 **Hudson**, Pat, *The Industrial Revolution*, 1992. A survey of the writing and rewriting of the various histories of the industrial revolution. Particular debates and controversies are explored. Demography, capital formation, economic growth, consumption, class and gender all receive attention.

David Hume

7.52 **Abbott**, W. C., 'David Hume: philosopher-historian' in Abbott, *Adventures in Reputation*, Cambridge, MA., 1935, 118–48.

7.53 **Berry**, C. J., 'Hume on rationality in history and social life', *Hist. and Theory*, XXI, 1982, 234–47.

7.54 **Bongie**, L. L., *David Hume. Prophet of the Counter-revolution*, 1965. Discusses the uses made of Hume's writings by the late eighteenth-century French conservatives.

7.55 **Burke**, J. J., 'Hume's *History of England*; waking the English from a dogmatic slumber', *Studs. Eighteenth Century Culture*, VII, 1978, 235–50. Looks at the scepticism employed by Hume to combat the Whig interpretation of history.

7.56 **Davies**, G., 'Hume's history of the reign of James I' in H. Davis and Helen Gardner (eds), *Elizabethan and Jacobean Studies*, 1959, 231–49.

7.57 **Forbes**, D., *Hume's Philosophical Politics*, 1975. Carefully relates Hume's *History* to the Whig/Tory divisions of the eighteenth century.

7.58 **Mossner**, E. C., *The Life of David Hume*, 2nd ed., 1980. The standard work.

7.59 ——'Was Hume a Tory historian?', *J. Hist. Ideas*, II, 1941, 225–36.

7.60 **Norton**, D. F. and **Popkin**, R. H., *David Hume. Philosopher-Historian*, New York, 1965.

7.61 **Popkin**, R. H., 'Hume; philsophical *v.* prophetic historian' in K. R. Merrill and R. W. Shahan (eds), *David Hume. Many-sided Genius*, Norman, OK, 1976, 83–95.

7.62 **Price**, J. V., 'Hume's concept of liberty and the *History of England*', *Studs. Romanticism*, V, 1965–6, 139–57.

7.63 **Stevenson**, D. R., 'David Hume, historicist', *Historian*, LII, 1990, 209–18.

7.64 **Stockton**, C. N., 'Hume: historian of the English court', *Eighteenth-Century Studs.*, IV, 1970–71, 277–93.

7.65 **Trevor-Roper**, H. R., 'Hume as a historian' in D. F. Pears (ed.), *David Hume. A Symposium*, 1963, 89–100.

7.66 **Wexler**, E. E. G., *David Hume and the History of England*, Philadelphia, PA, 1979. Traces the development of Hume's career and the impact of his *History* on British historiography.

7.67 **Jackman**, S. W., *Man of Mercury. An Appreciation of the Mind of Henry St John Viscount Bolingbroke*, 1965. Includes a chapter on his historical writings.

7.68 **Jenkins**, H. and **Carodog-Jones**, D., 'The social class of Cambridge university *alumni* of the eighteenth and nineteenth centuries', *Brit. J. Sociol.*, I, 1950, 93–116.

7.69 **Johnson**, J. W., *The Formation of English Neoclassical Thought*, Princeton, NJ,

1967. Has a chapter on the role of historiography.

7.70 —— 'Swift's historical outlook', *J. Brit. Studs.*, IV, 1965, 52–77. See also Moore (7.75).

7.71 **Kidd**, C., *Subverting Scotland's Past. Scottish Whig Historians and the Creation of an Anglo-British Identity, 1689–c. 1830*, 1993.

7.72 **Klein**, L. E., 'Gender and the public/private distinction in the eighteenth century; some questions about evidence and analytic procedure', *Eighteenth Century Studs.*, XXIX, 1995, 97–109.

7.73 **Kramnick**, I., 'Augustan politics and English historiography: the debate on the English past, 1730–35', *Hist. and Theory*, VI, 1967, 33–56. Illustrates the expedient confusion of Whig and Tory principles at this time.

7.74 **Marshall**, P. J. and **Williams**, G., *The Great Map of Mankind. British Perceptions of the World in the Age of the Enlightenment*, 1982. Hume and Robertson are among those whose views are considered.

7.75 **Moore**, J. R., 'Swift as historian', *Studs. Philology*, XLIX, 1952, 583–604. See also Johnson (7.70).

7.76 **Okie**, L., *Augustan Historical Writing. Histories in the English Enlightenment*, Lanham, MD, 1991. Considers history's place and functions in the eighteenth-century political arena, the innovations of historians and the circumstances of publication.

7.77 **Phillips**, M. S., 'Reconsiderations on history and antiquarianism; Arnoldo Momigliano and the historiography of eighteenth-century Britain', *J. Hist. Ideas*, LVII, 1996, 296–316.

7.78 **Piggott**, S., *William Stukeley. An Eighteenth-Century Antiquarian*, 1950.

7.79 **Rae**, T. I., 'Historical scepticism in Scotland before David Hume', *Studs. Eighteenth Century*, II, 1973, 205–21. Focuses on MacKenzie and Innes.

7.80 **Reedy**, C., 'Rymer and history', *Clio*, VII, 1978, 409–22.

7.81 **Reill**, P. H., 'Narrative and structure in late eighteenth-century historical thought', *Hist. and Theory*, XXV, 1986, 286–98.

7.82 —— 'Narration and structure in late eighteenth-century historical thought', *Storia de Storiog.*, X, 1986, 77–90.

7.83 **Stephen**, Deborah, 'Lawrence Echard, Whig historian', *Hist. J.*, XXXII, 1989, 843–66. Contentious reassessment.

7.84 **Sutherland**, Lucy S., *The University of Oxford in the Eighteenth Century. A Reconsideration*, 1973. Lecture.

7.85 **Thompson**, M. A., *Some Developments in English Historiography during the Eighteenth Century*, 1956. Inaugural lecture.

7.86 **Trevor-Roper**, H. R., 'The Scottish Enlightenment', *Studs. Voltaire and the Eighteenth Century*, LVIII, 1967, 1635–58.

7.87 **Vance**, J. A., *Samuel Johnson and the Sense of History*, Athens, GA, 1984.

7.88 **Weisinger**, H., 'The Middle Ages and the late eighteenth-century historians', *Philological Q.*, XXVII, 1948, 63–79.

7.89 **Withey**, Lynne E., 'Catherine Macaulay and the uses of history; ancient rights, perfectionism and propaganda', *J. Brit. Studs.*, XVI, 1976, 59–83. See also Hill (7.46).

7.90 **Youngson**, A. J., *The Prince and the Pretender. A Study in the Writing of History*, 1985. Examines the uncertain dividing line between historical reporting and propaganda.

EUROPE

7.91 **Alagoa**, E. J., 'The encounter between African and Western historiography before 1800', *Storia de Storiog.*, XIX, 1991, 73–86.

7.92 **Alonso**, F. W. and **Andreotti**, G. C., 'On ancient history and the Enlightenment; two Spanish histories of the eighteenth century', *Storia de Storiog.*, XXIII, 1993, 75–94.

7.93 **Amariglio**, J. and **Norton**, B., 'Marxist historians and the question of class in the French Revolution', *Hist. and Theory*, XXX, 1991, 37–55.

7.94 **Barnes**, S. B., *Historiography under the Impact of Rationalism and*

Revolution, Kent, OH, 1952. A brief survey.

7.95 **Ben Israel**, Hedva, *English Historians on the French Revolution*, 1968. Concentrates particularly on Smyth, Carlyle, Croker and Acton.

7.96 **Berlin**, I., *Vico and Herder. Two Studies in the History of Ideas*, 1976. Places Vico's theory of knowledge within his intellectual system and looks at Herder's relationship to the Enlightenment.

7.97 **Berry**, T. M., *The Historical Theory of Giambattista Vico*, Washington, DC, 1949.

7.98 **Besterman**, T., *Voltaire*, 1969, 3rd ed. 1976. A full-scale biography which includes a discussion of Voltaire's historical writings.

7.99 **Brumfitt**, J. H., 'History and propaganda in Voltaire', *Studs. Voltaire and the Eighteenth Century*, XXIV, 1963, 271–87.

7.100 —— *Voltaire. Historian*, 1958. Chapters on Voltaire's major works, his philosophy and methodology.

7.101 **Burke**, P., *Vico*, 1985. Concerned primarily to locate Vico within his own age and to assess his contemporary and later influence.

7.102 **Cavanaugh**, G. C., 'The present state of French Revolutionary historiography; Alfred Cobban and beyond', *French. Hist. Studs.*, VII, 1972, 587–606.

7.103 **Cobban**, A., *Aspects of the French Revolution*, 1968. Includes essays on 'The state of Revolutionary historiography', 'Historians and the causes of the French Revolution', 'Carlyle's *French Revolution*', 'Historians of the French Revolution'.

7.104 **Cochrane**, E., 'Muratori; the vocation of a historian', *Cath. Hist. R.*, LI, 1965, 153–72.

7.105 **Comninel**, G. C., *Rethinking the French Revolution. Marxism and the Revisionist Challenge*, 1987. A lively defence of historical materialism though not of simplistic versions of the French 'bourgeois revolution'.

7.106 **Crocker**, L. G., 'Recent interpretations of the French Enlightenment', *J. World Hist.*, VIII, 1964, 426–56.

7.107 **Darnton**, R., 'In search of the Enlightenment; recent attempts to create a social history of ideas', *J.M.H.*, XLIII, 1971, 113–32.

7.108 **Davillé**, L., *Leibniz. Historien*, Paris, 1909.

7.109 **Duchet**, Michèle, *Anthropologie et histoire au siècle des lumières. Buffon, Voltaire, Rousseau, Helvetius, Diderot*, Paris, 1971.

7.110 **Epp**, A. R., 'Voltaire's view of the Anabaptists', *Mennonite Q.R.*, XLV, 1971, 145–51.

7.111 **Friedman**, B. R., *Fabricating History. English Writers on the French Revolution*, Princeton, NJ, 1988. An interdisciplinary cultural approach which takes in the different responses of Blake, Scott, Hazlitt, Carlyle, Dickens and Hardy to the revolutionary upheavals in France.

7.112 **Fryer**, W. R., *The Character of the French Revolution, or, Historians at Loggerheads*, 1969. Inaugural lecture.

7.113 **Furet**, F., *Interpreting the French Revolution*, 1981. Examines conceptualisations of the French Revolution. The views of de Tocqueville and Cochin on its tragic relevance receive particular attention.

7.114 **Gay**, P., *Voltaire's Politics*, 2nd ed., New Haven, CT, 1988.

7.115 **Gentile**, G., 'Eighteenth-century historical methodology; De Soria's *Institutiones*', *Hist. and Theory*, IV, 1965, 315–27.

7.116 **Hampson**, N., *The Enlightenment*, 1968. Wide-ranging discussion of the ethos of the Enlightenment.

7.117 **Hazard**, P., *European Thought in the Eighteenth Century*, 1954. Examines some of the targets of Enlightenment scepticism and the stress on reason and nature.

7.118 **Hefferman**, J. A. W. (ed.), *Representing the French Revolution. Literature, Historiography and Art*, Hanover, NH, 1992. A valuable interdisciplinary collection which examines images of the Revolution in France, England, Germany and elsewhere. The histories of Michelet and Carlyle come under review, as do Burke, Blake and Wordsworth. Discourse studies are well represented.

Iconography, caricature and theatricality also receive attention.

7.119 **Hobsbawm**, E. J., *Echoes of the Marseillaise. Two Centuries look back on the French Revolution*, 1990. A bicentenary retrospective on changing views and fashions in the historiography of the French Revolution.

7.120 **Hook**, S., 'The Enlightenment and Marxism', *J. Hist. Ideas*, XXIX, 1968, 93–108.

7.121 **Hutton**, P. H., 'The role of memory in the historiography of the French Revolution', *Hist. and Theory*, XXX, 1991, 56–69.

7.122 **Iggers**, G. G., 'The idea of progress; a critical reassessment', *A.H.R.*, LXXI, 1965, 1–17.

7.123 ——'The University of Göttingen, 1760–1800, and the transformation of historical scholarship', *Storia de Storiog.*, XII, 1982, 11–37.

7.124 **Jacques**, T. G., 'From savages and barbarians to primitives; Africa, social typologies and history in eighteenth-century French philosophy', *Hist. and Theory*, XXXIV, 1997, 190–215.

7.125 **Kelley**, D. R., *Historians and the Law in post-Revolution France*, Princeton, NJ, 1984.

7.126 **Kelly**, G. A., 'Rousseau, Kant and history', *J. Hist. Ideas*, XXIX, 1968, 347–64.

7.127 **Kley**, E. J. van, 'Europe's "discovery" of China and the writing of world history', *A.H.R.*, LXXVI, 1971, 358–85.

7.128 **Langlois**, C., **Bien**, D. D. *et al.* (eds), 'François Furet's interpretation of the French Revolution', *French Hist. Studs.*, XVI, 1990, 766–80.

7.129 **Leffler**, P. K., 'The "histoire raisonné", 1660–1720; a pre-Enlightenment genre', *J. Hist. Ideas*, XXXVII, 1976, 219–40.

7.130 **Liebel**, Helen P., 'The Enlightenment and the rise of historicism in German thought', *Eighteenth-Century Studs.*, IV, 1970, 359–85.

7.131 **Lilla**, M., *G. B. Vico. The Making of an Anti-modern*, Cambridge, MA, 1993.

7.132 **Mali**, J., *The Rehabilitation of Myth. Vico's New Science*, New York, 1992.

7.133 **Manuel**, F. E., *The Eighteenth Century Confronts the Gods*, 1959. Discusses the eighteenth-century mind and sensibility and its religious and anthropological interests.

7.134 **Meinecke**, F., *Historism. The Rise of a New Historical Outlook*, 1972. An exploration of English Enlightenment historiography, of the English pre-Romantics and of the German movement centred on Herder and Goethe.

7.135 **Nadel**, G. H., 'Philosophy of history before historicism', *Hist. and Theory*, III, 1964, 291–315.

7.136 **Orr**, Linda, *Headless History. Nineteenth-Century French Historiography of the Revolution*, Ithaca, NY, 1990.

7.137 **Parker**, N., *Portrayals of Revolution. Images, Debates and Patterns of Thought in the French Revolution*, 1990. Looks both at contemporary representations of the French Revolution and at later refashioning at the hands of liberals, romantics, socialists, Marxists and conservatives.

7.138 **Pompa**, L., 'Vico's science', *Hist. and Theory*, X, 1969, 49–83.

7.139 ——*Human Nature and Historical Knowledge. Hume. Hegel and Vico*, New York, 1990.

7.140 **Popkin**, J., 'The concept of public opinion in the historiography of the French Revolution; a critique', *Storia de Storiog.*, XX, 1991, 77–92.

7.141 **Reill**, P. H., *The German Enlightenment and the Rise of Historicism*, Berkeley, CA, 1975. Examines the eighteenth-century background which impinged on Ranke.

7.142 **Renaldo**, J., 'Antecedants of Vico; the Jesuit historians', *Archivum Historicum Societatis Jesu*, XXXIX, 1970, 349–55.

7.143 **Ricuperati**, G., 'A long journey. Italian historiography on the Enlightenment and its political significance, 1980–90', *Storia de Storiog.*, XX, 1991, 77–92.

7.144 **Rigney**, Ann, *The Rhetoric of Historical Representation. Three Narrative Histories of the French Revolution*, 1990. An assessment of the work of Lamartine, Michelet and Blanc.

7.145 **Robertson**, J., 'Franco Venturi's Enlightenment', *P.P.*, CXXVII, 1992, 183–206.

7.146 **Rosenthal**, J., 'Voltaire's philosophy of history', *J. Hist. Ideas*, XVI, 1955, 151–78.

7.147 **Sakmann**, P., 'The problems of historical method and the philosophy of history in Voltaire', *Hist. and Theory*, X, 1971, supplement 11, 24–59.

7.148 **Salvatorelli**, L., 'L'historiographie italienne au XVIIIe siècle', *Cahiers Hist. Mond.*, VII, 1963, 321–40.

7.149 **Schargo**, N. N., *History in the Encyclopédie*, 1947. Stresses the important contribution made by the *Encyclopédie* to the development of historical studies.

7.150 **Spitz**, L. W., 'The significance of Leibniz for historiography', *J. Hist. Ideas*, XIII, 1952, 333–48.

7.151 **Stromberg**, R. N., 'History in the eighteenth century', *J. Hist. Ideas*, XII, 1951, 295–304.

7.152 **Tagliacozzo**, G. and **White**, H. V. (eds), *Giambattista Vico. An International Symposium*, Baltimore, MD, 1969. A wide-ranging discussion of Vico's influence. Includes a chapter on 'the supposed influence of Vico on England and Scotland in the eighteenth century'.

7.153 **Trevor-Roper**, H. R., 'The historical philosophy of the Enlightenment', *Studs. Voltaire and the Eighteenth Century*, XXVII, 1963, 1667–87.

7.154 **Venturi**, F., 'History and reform in the middle of the eighteenth century' in J. H. Elliott and H. G. Koenigsberger (eds), *The Diversity of History*, 1970, 223–44.

7.155 **Vyerberg**, H., *Historical Pessimism in the French Enlightenment*, Cambridge, MA, 1958.

7.156 **Yovel**, Y., *Kant and the Philosophy of History*, Princeton, NJ, 1980. Examines Kant's concept of rational history as the central and supreme feature of his work.

7.157 **Zbinden**, J., 'Heterogeneity, irony, ambivalence. The idea of progress in the universal histories and histories of mankind in the German Enlightenment', *Storia de Storiog.*, XXIX, 1996, 21–46.

COLONIAL HISTORY

7.158 **Colbourn**, H. T., *The Lamp of Experience. Whig History and the Intellectual Origins of the American Revolution*, Chapel Hill, NC, 1965.

7.159 **Fisher**, S. G., 'The legendary and myth-making process in histories of the American Revolution', *Proc. Am. Phil. Soc.*, LI, 1912, 53–75.

7.160 **Greene**, J. P., *Interpreting Early America. Historiographical Essays*, Charlottesville, VA, 1996. Twenty-three essays originally published between 1962 and 1995 dealing with the colonial and Revolutionary periods and addressing the changing impulses, strategies and methodologies involved in the refashioning of the past.

7.161 **Marling**, Karal Ann, *George Washington Slept Here. Colonial Revivals and American Culture, 1876–1986*, Cambridge, MA, 1988. Explores Washington's talismanic significance in American culture and iconography. Centennial and bicentennial celebrations are examined, as are the efforts by later American politicians to enlist Washington's incorruptible image to serve their purposes. Profusely illustrated. See also Schwarz (7.166).

7.162 **Mason**, B., 'The heritage of Carl Becker; the historiography of the American Revolution', *New York Hist. Soc. Q.*, LIII, 1969, 127–47.

7.163 **Merrell**, J. H., 'Some thoughts on colonial historians and American Indians', *Wm and Mary Q.*, XLVI, 1989, 94–119.

7.164 **Middleton**, R., 'British historians and the American Revolution', *J. Am. Studs.*, V, 1971, 43–58.

7.165 **Pole**, J. R., 'Historians and the problem of early American democracy', *A.H.R.*, LXVII, 1962, 626–46.

7.166 **Schwarz**, B., *George Washington. The Making of an American Symbol*, New York, 1987. Explores the ubiquitous commemoration and idealisation of Washington in the United States. Marling (7.161).

7.167 **Sellers**, C. G., 'Andrew Jackson v. the

historians', *Miss. Vall. H.R.*, XLIV, 1958, 615–34.

7.168 **Shaffer**, A. H., *The Politics of History. Writing the History of the American Revolution, 1783–1815*, Chicago, IL, 1975. Analyses the contemporary attempts made to justify the revolution and develop ideas of national identity.

7.169 **Shalhope**, R. E., 'Republican and early American historiography' *Wm and Mary Q.*, XXXIX, 1982, 334–56.

7.170 —— 'Toward a republican synthesis; the emergence of an understanding of republicanism in American historiography', *Wm and Mary Q.*, XXIX, 1972, 49–80.

7.171 **Smith**, W. R., *History as Argument. Three Patriot Historians of the American Revolution*, The Hague, 1966.

7.172 **Starr**, R., 'Historians and the origins of British North American slavery', *Historian*, XXXVI, 1975, 1–19.

8

THE NINETEENTH CENTURY

BRITAIN

Trends and Tendencies

8.1 **Aarsleff**, H., *The Study of Language in England, 1780–1860*, Princeton, NJ, 1967.

8.2 **Alaya**, Flavia M., 'Arnold and Renan on the popular uses of history', *J. Hist. Ideas*, XXVIII, 1967, 551–74.

8.3 **Annan**, N. G., 'The intellectual aristocracy' in J. H. Plumb (ed.), *Studies in Social History presented to G. M. Trevelyan*, 1955, 243–86.

8.4 **Anderson**, Olive, 'The political uses of history in mid-nineteenth-century England', *P.P.*, 36, 1967, 87–105.

8.5 **Arx**, J. P. von, *Progress and Pessimism. Religion, Politics and History in late Nineteenth Century Britain*, Cambridge, MA, 1985. A consideration of four writers – Leslie Stephen, Lecky, Morley and Froude – within the context of the Victorian crisis of faith.

8.6 **Ash**, M., *The Strange Death of Scottish History*, 1980. Explores the declining interest in Scottish history after Scott.

8.7 **Ausubel**, H. J., **Brebner**, J. B., and **Hunt**, E. M. (eds), *Some Modern Historians of Britain*, New York, 1951. A *festschrift* which includes studies of Hallam, Gardiner, Firth, Tawney and Namier.

8.8 **Bann**, S., *The Clothing of Clio. A Study of the Representation of History in Nineteenth-Century Britain and France*, 1984. Embraces art and literature as well as historiography.

8.9 ——*Romanticism and the Rise of History*, New York, 1995. A succinct study dealing with the context of romanticism's historical-mindedness and its impact on the representation of the past and the subject's discourse.

8.10 **Bentley**, E. L., *A Century of Hero Worship*, Philadelphia, PA, 1944. Considers Carlyle and others. See also Lehman (8.130).

8.11 **Berdahl**, R. O., *British Universities and the State*, 1959.

8.12 **Bill**, E. G. W., *University Reform in Nineteenth-Century Oxford. A Study of H. H. Vaughan, 1811–85*, 1973. Vaughan was Regius Professor of Modern History and a radical reformer.

8.13 **Blaas**, P. B. M., *Continuity and Anachronism. Parliamentary and Constitutional Development in Whig Historiography and in the anti-Whig Reaction between 1890 and 1930*, The Hague, 1978. A critique of nineteenth-century Whig historiography which sees Maitland, Pollard and Tout together as constituting the major turning point.

8.14 **Blum**, Antoinette, 'The uses of literature in nineteenth and twentieth-century British historiography', *Lit. and Hist.*, 11:2, 1985, 176–202.

8.15 **Brooks**, R. A. E., 'The development of the historical mind' in J. E. Baker (ed.), *The Reinterpretation of Victorian Literature*, Princeton, NJ, 1950, 130–53.

8.16 **Buckley**, J. H., *The Triumph of Time. A Study of the Victorian Concepts of Time, History, Progress and Decadence*, Cambridge, MA, 1967. Predominantly a literary study, though historians such as Macaulay are discussed.

8.17 **Burrow**, J. W., *Evolution and Society. A Study in Victorian Social Theory*, 1966. Considers the Victorian preoccupation with evolutionary social theory. Henry Maine, Herbert Spencer and Edward Tylor each receive a separate chapter. Bibliography, 278–88.

8.18 ——*A Liberal Descent. Victorian Historians and the English Past*, 1981. A perceptive study of Victorian uses of the past and the complexity of the Whig tradition. Macaulay, Froude, Freeman and Stubbs are thoughtfully reassessed.

8.19 ——'The uses of philology in Victorian England' in R. Robson (ed.), *Ideas and Institutions in Victorian Britain*, 1967, 180–204. Examines the ways in which in England – as in Ranke's Germany – philology contributed to scientific history.

8.20 ——'"The village community" and the uses of history in late nineteenth-century England' in N. McKendrick (ed.), *Historical Perspectives. Studies in English Thought and Society in Honour of J. H. Plumb*, 1974, 255–84.

8.21 ——'Victorian historians and the Royal Historical Society', *T.R.H.S.*, 5th ser., XXXIX, 1989, 125–40.

8.22 **Butterfield**, H., 'History as a branch of literature' in Butterfield, *History and Human Relations*, 1951, 225–54. Focuses on Macaulay, Carlyle and Froude.

8.23 **Cannadine**, D., 'The past and the present in the English industrial revolution, 1880–1980', *P.P.*, 103, 1984, 131–72.

8.24 **Carrard**, P., 'Disciplining Clio; the rhetoric of positivism', *Clio*, XIV, 1995, 189–204.

8.25 **Chancellor**, Valerie E., *History for their Masters. Opinion in the English History Textbook, 1800–1914*, 1970.

8.26 **Clive**, J., 'English cliographers; a preliminary inquiry' in D. Aron (ed.), *Studies in Biography*, Cambridge, MA, 1978, 27–39. Considers the reasons why Macaulay, Acton, Green and Carlyle wrote history.

8.27 ——'Why read the great nineteenth-century historians?', *American Scholar*, XLVIII, 1978, 37–48.

8.28 **Collini**, S., **Winch**, D., and **Burrow**, J. W., *That Noble Science of Politics. A Study in Nineteenth-Century Intellectual History*, 1983.

8.29 **Culler**, A. D., *The Victorian Mirror of History*, New Haven, CT, 1986. A wide-ranging discussion of the historical dimension present in the philosophical, scientific, religious and artistic writing of the nineteenth century.

8.30 **Curtis**, L. P., *Anglo-Saxons and Celts. A Study of anti-Irish Prejudice in Victorian England*, Bridgeport, NY, 1968. Examines one of the consequences of the cult of Anglo-Saxonism.

8.31 **Dale**, P. A., *The Victorian Critic and the Idea of History*, Cambridge, MA, 1977.

8.32 **Dellheim**, C., *The Face of the Past. The Preservation of the Medieval Inheritance in Victorian England*, 1982. Deals with aspects of the vision of history that formed part of the paradoxes of progress and provincial liberalism in the Victorian period. Well illustrated. Bibliographical essay, 201–6.

8.33 **Ellis**, R. H., 'The building of the Public Record Office' in A. E. J. Hollaender (ed.), *Essays in Memory of Sir Hilary Jenkinson*, 1962, 9–30.

8.34 ——'The History Manuscripts Commission', *J. Soc. Archivists*, XI, 1962, 233–42. See also Roberts (8.87).

8.35 **Engel**, A. J., *From Clergyman to Don. The Rise of the Academic Profession in Nineteenth-Century Oxford*, 1983. See also Rothblatt (8.88).

8.36 **Firth**, C. H., *Modern History in Oxford, 1841–1918*, 1920.

8.37 **Forbes**, D., '"Historismus" in England', *Camb. H.J.*, IV, 1950–51, 387–400. Argues that the German influence was not strong in nineteenth-century England.

8.38 ——*The Liberal Anglican Idea of History*, 1952. Examines the shift away from rationalism displayed in the works of Arnold, Thirlwall, Milman, Stanley and others.

8.39 **Francis**, M., 'Who still has "sweetness and light" in studies of Victorian culture and politics?', *Hist. J.*, XXXIX, 1996, 1079–96.

8.40 **Fredericq**, P., *The Study of History in England and Scotland*, Johns Hopkins University Studies in History and Political Science, 5th ser., X, 1887.

8.41 **Garland**, M. M., *Cambridge before Darwin. The Ideal of a Liberal Education 1800–60*, 1980.

8.42 **Gilbert**, E. L., 'Rescuing reality; Carlyle, Froude and biographical truth-telling', *Vict. Studs.*, XXXIV, 1991, 295–314.

8.43 **Goldstein**, Doris S., 'The origins and early years of the *English Historical Review*', *E.H.R.*, CI, 1986, 20–41.

8.44 ——'The professionalisation of history in Britain in the late nineteenth and early twentieth centuries', *Storia de Storiog.*, III, 1983, 3–27.

8.45 **Gooch**, G. P., *History and Historians in the Nineteenth Century*, 1913, 2nd ed. 1952. One of the major works on the development of historiography in this period. Densely detailed.

8.46 ——*Maria Theresa and other Studies*, 1951. Reprints some items from (8.47) and adds other studies of 'modern historiography', 'Lord Acton; apostle of liberty' and 'Harold Temperley'.

8.47 ——*Studies in Modern History*, 1931. Has a pronounced historiographical dimension with essays on 'The study of Bismarck', 'German historical studies since the war' and 'The Cambridge Chair of modern history'.

8.48 **Greenlee**, J. G., '"A succession of Seeleys"; the "old school" re-examined', *J. Imp. and Comm. Hist.*, IV, 1976, 266–82.

8.49 **Gruner**, R., 'Historism; its rise and decline', *Clio*, VIII, 1978, 25–39.

8.50 **Haines**, D., 'Scientific history as a teaching method; the formative years', *J.A.H.*, LXIII, 1977, 893–912.

8.51 **Harte**, N. B., *One Hundred and Fifty Years of History Teaching at University College London*, 1982.

8.52 **Harvie**, C., *The Lights of Liberalism. University Liberals and the Challenge of Democracy, 1860–86*, 1976. The historians discussed include G. O. Trevelyan, Bryce, Freeman and Morley.

8.53 **Hayek**, F. A. (ed.), *Capitalism and the Historians*, 1954. A historiographical case study of the industrial revolution.

8.54 **Heyck**, T. W., *The Transformation of Intellectual Life in Victorian England*, 1982.

8.55 **Himmelfarb**, Gertrude, *Victorian Minds*, 1968. Includes chapters on J. S. Mill, Acton, Leslie Stephen, Bagehot and Froude. There are also chapters on the Victorian *Angst* and on 'Varieties of Social Darwinism'.

8.56 **Humphreys**, R. A., *The Royal Historical Society, 1868–1968*, 1969. A centenary memoir of the organisation whose growth reflects the development of professionalism among British historians.

8.57 **Jann**, Rosemary, *The Art and Science of Victorian History*, Columbus, OH, 1985. A reconsideration of Arnold, Carlyle, Macaulay, Froude, Green and Freeman.

8.58 ——'From amateur to professional; the case of the Oxbridge historians', *J. Brit. Studs.*, XXII, 1983, 122–47.

8.59 **Kelley**, D., 'Robert Flint, historian of ideas', *Storia de Storiog.*, XXVII, 1995, 39–62. A study of the now largely forgotten Victorian author of the *History of the Philosophy of History* (1874).

8.60 **Kidd**, C., '*The Strange Death of Scottish History* revisited; constructions of the past in Scotland, *c*. 1790–1914', *Scot. H. R.*, LXXVI, 1997, 86–102.

8.61 **Knowles**, D., *Great Historical Enterprises. Problems in Monastic History*, 1963. The historical enterprises discussed include the *Monumenta Germaniae Historica* and the Rolls series.

8.62 **Lang**, T., *The Victorians and the Stuart Heritage. Interpretations of a Discordant Past*, 1995. A new stocktaking of the huge Victorian outpouring on seventeenth-century history. The Victorians' own religious preoccupations are underlined as their bridge to the Puritans. Hallam, Macaulay and Gardiner are given separate chapters.

8.63 **Laqueur**, W. and **Mosse**, G. L., *Historians in Politics*, 1974. Includes an important essay on Bryce, 113–28.

8.64 **Lawson**, F. H., *The Oxford Law School, 1850–1965*, 1968. Since until the late nineteenth century the study of law and history were closely linked, there is much here on Victorian historiography.

8.65 **Levine**, G., *The Boundaries of Fiction. Carlyle, Macaulay and Newman*, Princeton, NJ, 1968.

8.66 **Levine**, Phillipa J. A., *The Amateur and the Professional. Historians, Antiquarians and Archaeologists in Nineteenth Century England, 1838–86*, 1986. Considers the various ways in which the new professionals consolidated their position and distinguished themselves from the amateurs. Bibliography, 186–200.

8.67 **McLachlan**, Jean O., 'The origin and early development of the Cambridge historical tripos', *Camb. Hist. J.*, 1947–9, 78–105.

8.68 **McClelland**, C. E., *The German Historians and England. A Study of Nineteenth-Century Views*, 1971. Looks at the changing relationship between the two countries and the ways in which it was expressed historiographically.

8.69 **MacDougall**, H. A., *Racial Myth in English History. Trojans, Teutons and Anglo-Saxons*, Montreal, 1982. Looks at the contributions made to the development of Anglo-Saxonism by Turner, Kemble, Buckle, Stubbs and others.

8.70 **Maitzen**, R., '"This Feminine Preserve"; historical biographies by Victorian women', *Vict. Studs.*, XXXVIII, 1995, 371–93.

8.71 **Mandler**, P., '"In the Olden Time"; romantic history and English national identity, 1820–50' in L. Brockliss and D. Eastwood (eds), *A Union of Multiple Identities*, 1997, 78–92.

8.72 **Miller**, E. F. *et al.*, 'Positivism, historicism and political inquiry', *Am. Pol. Sci. R.*, LXVI, 1972, 796–873.

8.73 **Morgan**, P., 'George Harris of Rugby and the prehistory of the Historical Manuscripts Commission', *Trans. Birm. Arch. Soc.*, LXXXII, 1967, 28–37. See also Ellis (8.34) and Roberts (8.87).

8.74 **Myres**, J. L., *Learned Societies*, 1922. Pamphlet.

8.75 **Neff**, E., *The Poetry of History. The Contribution of Literature and Literary Scholarship to the Writing of History since Voltaire*, New York, 1947. The central core of the book is an exploration of Romantic historiography.

8.76 **Owen**, Dorothy M., 'The Chichele professorship of modern history, 1862', *B.I.H.R.*, XXXIV, 1961, 217–20.

8.77 **Parker**, C. J. W., 'Academic history; paradigms and dialectic', *Lit. and Hist.*, 5:2, 1979, 165–82.

8.78 —— 'English historians and the opposition to positivism', *Hist. and Theory*, XXIII, 1983, 120–45.

8.79 —— *History as Present Politics*, 1980. Brief discussion of the political concerns of historians since the nineteenth century.

8.80 **Peardon**, T. P., *The Transition in English Historical Writing, 1760–1830*, New York, 1933. Considers the ways in which early nineteenth-century historians such as Hallam and Lingard departed from the characteristics of historiography established in the Age of the Enlightenment.

8.81 **Penny**, A. D., 'John Foxe's Victorian reception', *Hist. J.*, XL, 1997, 111–42.

8.82 **Prothero**, G. W., 'Historical science in Great Britain', *Am. Hist. Ass. Rep.*, 1909, 231–42.

8.83 **Ramsay**, G. D., 'Victorian historiography and the guilds of London; the report of the Royal Commission on the livery companies of London, 1884', *London J.*, X, 1984, 155–66.

8.84 **Reader**, W. J., *Professional Men. The Rise of the Professional Classes in Nineteenth Century England*, 1966. Deals with the wider social process of which the professionalisation of history was part.

8.85 **Roach**, J. P. C., 'Liberalism and the Victorian intelligentsia', *Camb. Hist. J.*, XIII, 1957, 58–81.

8.86 —— 'Victorian universities and the national intelligentsia', *Vict. Studs.*, III, 1959–60, 131–50.

8.87 **Roberts**, R. A., 'The Historical Manuscripts Commission', *T.R.H.S.*, 3rd ser., IV, 1910, 63–81. See also Ellis (8.34).

8.88 **Rothblatt**, S., *The Revolution of the Dons. Cambridge and Society in Victorian England*, 1968. Examines the ways in which the University of Cambridge accommodated itself to the changing world of the nineteenth century. See also Engel (8.35).

8.89 —— *Tradition and Change in English Liberal Education. An Essay in History and Culture*, 1976.

8.90 **Sheey**, Jeanne, *The Rediscovery of Ireland's Past. The Celtic Revival, 1830–1930*, 1980. A well rounded study which takes in painting, sculpture and architecture as well as the writers. Bibliography.

8.91 **Soffer**, Reba, 'Nation, duty, character and confidence; history at Oxford, 1850–1914', *Hist. J.*, XXX, 1987, 77–104.

8.92 **Sparrow**, J., *Mark Pattison and the Idea of a University*, 1967.

8.93 **Steeves**, H. R., *Learned Societies and English Literary Scholarship in Britain and America*, New York, 1913. See also Brown (9.21), Hay (9.49) and Stieg (8.94).

8.94 **Stieg**, Margaret F., 'The emergence of the *English Historical Review*', *Lib. Q.*, XLVI, 1976, 119–36.

8.95 **Strong**, R., *And when did you last See your Father? The Victorian Painter and British History*, 1978.

8.96 —— *Recreating the Past. British History and the Victorian Painter*, 1978. Written by the then Director of the Victoria and Albert Museum. Looks at the contribution of painters to Victorian depictions of history. Divided into three parts' – 'The century of history', 'Recreators and recreations' and 'Themes and obsessions' – the book is profusely illustrated.

8.97 **Taylor**, M., 'Rethinking the Chartist; searching for synthesis in the historiography of Chartism', *Hist. J.*, XXXIX, 1996, 479–96.

8.98 **Tosh**, J., 'What should historians do with masculinity? Reflections on nineteenth-century Britain', *Hist. Workshop J.*, XXXVIII, 1994, 179–202.

8.99 **Trevor-Roper**, H. R., *The Romantic Movement and the Study of History*, 1969. Lecture. Considers – *inter alia* – Scott's influence on Macaulay.

8.100 **Voget**, F. W., 'Progress; science, history and evolution in eighteenth and nineteenth-century anthropology', *J. Hist. Behavioral Sciences*, III, 1967, 132–55.

8.101 **Ward**, W. R., *Victorian Oxford*, 1965. See also Winstanley (8.106–7).

8.102 **Welch**, E., *The Peripatetic University. Cambridge Local Lectures, 1873–1973*, 1973.

8.103 **Wells**, G. A., 'The critics of Buckle', *P.P.*, 9, 1956, 65–89.

8.104 **Wernham**, R. B., 'The Public Record Office', *Hist.*, n.s., XXIII, 1968, 222–35.

8.105 **Wiener**, M. J., 'The changing image of William Cobbett', *J. Brit. Studs.*, XIII, 1974, 135–54.

8.106 **Winstanley**, D. A., *Early Victorian Cambridge*, 1940.

8.107 —— *Later Victorian Cambridge*, 1947. See also Ward (8.101). Chapters 5–8 deal with the reform of the university and with the place of historical studies in that process.

8.108 **Wood**, C. T., 'Beginnings of historical fiction', *Historian*, LIV, 1992, 305–14.

8.109 **Wood**, L. S., *Selected Epigraphs. The Inaugural Lectures of the Regius Professors of Modern History at Oxford and Cambridge since 1841*, 1930.

8.110 **Woodward**, E. L., 'The rise of the professional historian in England' in K. Bourne and D. C. Watt (eds), *Studies in International History*, 1967, 16–34.

8.111 **Wortham**, H. E., *Victorian Eton and Cambridge, being the Life and Times of Oscar Browning*, 1956.

Individual Historians

Lord Acton

8.112 **Butterfield**, H., 'Acton; his training, methods and intellectual system' in A. O. Sarkissian (ed.), *Studies in Diplomatic History and Historiography in Honour of G. P. Gooch*, 1961, 169–98.

8.113 **Chadwick**, O., *Acton and Gladstone*, 1976. Lecture.

8.114 —— *Acton and History*, 1998. A study of aspects of Acton's career and work as a historian. The final chapter is devoted to the famous library.

8.115 **Fasnacht**, G. E., *Acton's Political Philosophy. An Analysis*, 1952. Demonstrates that the concept of freedom was the dominant motif.

8.116 **Finer**, H., 'Acton as historian and political scientist', *J. Pol.*, X, 1948, 603–35.

8.117 **Himmelfarb**, Gertrude, *Lord Acton. A Study in Conscience and Politics*, Chicago, IL, 1952. Devotes chapters to Acton's projected history of liberty, to his liberal politics and to his regius professorship. Bibliography, 242–52.

8.118 **Kochan**, L., *Acton on History*, 1954. Exposes some of the contradictions (not necessarily irreconcilable) in Acton's position.

8.119 **Kohn**, H., 'Lord Acton and human liberty' in Kohn, *Reflections*, 1963, 60–70.

8.120 **Matthew**, D., *Acton. The Formative Years*, 1946. Vol. I of a biography continued in (8.121).

8.121 ——*Lord Acton and his Times*, 1968. A full discussion of Acton as liberal and historian.

8.122 **Schuettinger**, R. L., *Lord Acton. Historian of Liberty*, 1978.

8.123 **Tulloch**, H., *Acton*, 1988. A brief study of the liberal Catholic historian and his reputation.

8.124 **Watson**, G., *Lord Acton's History of Liberty. A Study of his Library, with an edited Text of his History of Liberty Notes*, 1994.

Thomas Arnold

8.125 **Williamson**, E. L., *The Liberalism of Thomas Arnold. A Study of his Religious and Political Writings*, Alabama, 1964. See also Forbes (8.38).

William Ashley

8.126 **Semmel**, B., 'Sir William Ashley as "socialist of the chair"', *Economica*, n.s., XXIV, 1957, 343–53.

H. T. Buckle

8.127 **St Aubyn**, G., *A Victorian Eminence. The Life and Works of H. T. Buckle*, 1958. Rescues Buckle from his 'undeserved obscurity'.

8.128 **Semmel**, B., 'H. T. Buckle; the liberal faith and the science of history', *Brit. J. Sociol.*, XXVII, 1976, 370–86.

Thomas Carlyle

8.129 **Childers**, J. W., 'Carlyle's *Past and Present*', *Clio*, XIII, 1984, 247–58.

8.130 **Lehman**, B. H., *Carlyle's Theory of the Hero. Its Sources, Development, History and Influence on Carlyle's Work*, Durham, NC, 1928. See also Bentley (8.10).

8.131 **Neff**, E., *Carlyle*, 1932. An enthusiastic portrait of the great Romantic.

8.132 **Rigney**, Anne, 'The untenanted places of the past; Thomas Carlyle and the varieties of historical ignorance', *Hist. and Theory*, XXXIV, 1996, 338–57.

8.133 **Rosenberg**, J. D., *Carlyle and the Burden of History*, 1985. A literary evocation of Carlyle's historical writing.

8.134 **Sharrock**, R., 'Carlyle and the sense of history', *Essays and Studies*, n.s., XIX, 1966, 74–91.

8.135 **Young**, Louise M., *Thomas Carlyle and the Art of History*, Philadelphia, PA, 1939. Has chapters on the rationalist and Romantic backgrounds, on Carlyle's philosophy of history, on the art of history in theory and practice and on Carlyle's position as a historian. Bibliography, 209–16.

William Cunningham

8.136 **Cunningham**, Audrey, *William Cunningham. Teacher and Priest*, 1950. A biography by his daughter of a distinguished pioneer of economic history.

R. W. Dixon

8.137 **Rupp**, E. G., 'The Victorian churchman as historian; a reconsideration of R. W. Dixon's *History of the Church of England*' in G. V. Bennett and J. D. Walsh (eds), *Essays in Modern English Church History in Memory of Norman Sykes*, 1966, 206–16.

J. N. Figgis

8.138 **Tucker**, M. G., *John Neville Figgis. A Study*, 1950. An appreciation of the underrated author of *The Divine Right of Kings*, 1896.

E. A. Freeman

8.139 **Bratchel**, M. E., *Edward Augustus Freeman and the Victorian Interpretation of the Norman Conquest*, 1969. Pamphlet.

8.140 **Cronne**, H. A., 'Edward Augustus Freeman, 1823–92', *Hist.*, XXVIII, 1943, 78–92.

8.141 **Parker**, C. J. W., 'The failure of liberal racialism; the racial ideas of E. A. Freeman', *Hist. J.*, XXIV, 1981, 825–46.

J. A. Froude

8.142 **Dunn**, W. H., *James Anthony Froude. A Biography*, 2 vols, 1961–63.

8.143 **Elton**, G. R., 'J. A. Froude and his *History of England*' in Elton, *Studies in Tudor and Stuart Politics and Government*, III: *Papers and Reviews, 1973–81*, 1983, 391–412.

S. R. Gardiner

8.144 **Adamson**, J. S. A., 'Eminent Victorians; S. R. Gardiner and the liberal as hero', *Hist. J.*, XXXIII, 1990, 641–58.

8.145 **Fahey**, D. M., 'Gardiner and Usher in perspective', *J. Hist. Studs.*, I, 1967–68, 137–50.

8.146 **Firth**, C. H., 'Samuel Rawson Gardiner', *Quarterly R.*, 195, 1902, 547–66. An admiring estimate penned by a disciple.

8.147 **Usher**, R. G., *A Critical Study of the Historical Method of S. R. Gardiner*, Washington University Studies, III, Part 2:1, 1915. A deflationary treatment.

Cardinal Gasquet

8.148 **Knowles**, M. D. *Cardinal Gasquet as a Historian*, 1957. Lecture.

William Godwin

8.149 **Morrow**, J., 'Republicanism and public virtue; William Godwin's *History of the Commonwealth of England*', *Hist. J.*, XXXIV, 1991, 645–64.

J. R. Green

8.150 **Brundage**, A., *The People's Historian. John Richard Green and the Writing of History in Victorian England*, Westport, CT, 1994. Chiefly a biography of this Victorian misfit and his people-centred *History*.

8.151 **Schuyler**, R. L., 'J. R. Green and his *Short History*', *Pol. Sci. Q.*, LXIV, 1949, 321–54.

George Grote

8.152 **Clarke**, M. L., *George Grote. A Biography*, 1962. A full-scale study of the leisured scholar who wrote the *History of Greece*.

Henry Hallam

8.153 **Clark**, P., *Henry Hallam*, Boston, MA, 1983. A compact study of Hallam's life, major works and place in English historiography. Bibliography.

Charles Kingsley

8.154 **Chadwick**, O., 'Charles Kingsley at Cambridge', *Hist. J.*, XVIII, 1975, 303–25.

William Lecky

8.155 **Auchmuty**, J. J., *Lecky. A Biographical and Critical Study*, 1945.

8.156 **McCartney**, D., *W. E. H. Lecky. Historian and Politician, 1838–1903*, Dublin, 1994.

John Lingard

8.157 **Jones**, E., 'John Lingard and the Simancas archives', *Hist. J.*, X, 1967, 57–76.

8.158 **Shea**, D. F., *The English Ranke. John Lingard*, New York, 1969. The claims made here for Lingard rest chiefly on his critical attitude to sources.

T. B. Macaulay

8.159 **Abbott**, W. C., 'Thomas Babington Macaulay, historian' in Abbott,

Adventures in Reputation, Cambridge, MA, 1935, 3–27.

8.160 **Clive**, J., *Thomas Babington Macaulay. The Shaping of the Historian*, 1973. The major work on the young Macaulay. There are chapters on his Cambridge background, his Whiggism, his work for the *Edinburgh Review* and on his period as a civil servant in India.

8.161 **Cruikshank**, Margaret, *Thomas Babington Macaulay*, Boston, MA, 1978. Devotes considerable space to the essays and speeches.

8.162 **Firth**, C. H., *A Commentary on Macaulay's History of England*, 1938. Originally a course of lectures which cover, *inter alia*, Macaulay's conception of history, his methodology, his errors, his treatment of individuals and his handling of social, naval and military history.

8.163 **Griffin**, J. R., *The Intellectual Milieu of Lord Macaulay*, Ottawa, 1965.

8.164 **Hamburger**, J., *Macaulay and the Whig Tradition*, Chicago, IL, 1977. A revisionist – at times overstated – view which presents Macaulay as an agile trimmer rather than a complacent Whig.

8.165 **Millgate**, Jane, *Macaulay*, 1973. Concentrates chiefly on Macaulay's literary achievement.

8.166 **Potter**, G. P., *Macaulay*, 1959. Pamphlet.

8.167 **Schuyler**, R. L., 'Macaulay and his *History*; 100 years after', *Pol. Sci. Q.*, LXIII, 1948, 161–93.

Sir Henry Maine

8.168 **Feaver**, G., *From Status to Contract. A Biography of Sir Henry Maine*, 1969. A thorough study of this important nineteenth-century specialist in legal and comparative history.

8.169 **Kuper**, A., 'Ancestors; Henry Maine and the constitution of primitive society', *Hist. and Anthropology*, I, 1985, 265–86.

F. W. Maitland

8.170 **Cameron**, J. R., *F. W. Maitland and the History of English Law*, Norman, OK, 1961.

8.171 **Bell**, H. E., *Maitland. A Critical Examination and Reassessment*, 1965.

8.172 **Elton**, G. R., *F. W. Maitland*, 1985. An admiring biography. Four case studies explore Maitland's historical method in more detail.

8.173 **Fifoot**, C. H. S., *F. W. Maitland. A Life*, 1971.

8.174 **Montpensier**, R. S. de, 'Maitland and the interpretation of history', *Am. J. Legal Hist.*, X, 1966, 259–81.

John Morley

8.175 **Alexander**, E., *John Morley*, New York, 1972.

8.176 **Hamer**, D. A., *John Morley. Liberal Intellectual in Politics*, 1968. A useful study of Gladstone's biographer.

Cardinal Newman

8.177 **Altholz**, J. L., 'Newman and history', *Vict. Studs.*, VII, 1964, 285–94.

Sir Walter Scott

8.178 **Anderson**, J., *Sir Walter Scott and History, with other Papers*, 1981. A systematic exploration of Scott's historical erudition.

8.179 **Brown**, D., *Walter Scott and the Historical Imagination*, 1979. As well as chapters on individual novels the book includes more general essays on historical authenticity in the Waverly novels and on Scott's outlook on history.

8.180 **Garside**, P. D., 'Scott and the philosophical historians', *J. Hist. Ideas*, XXX, 1975, 497–512.

8.181 **Robertson**, Fiona, *Legitimate Histories. Scott, Gothic and the Authorities of Fiction*, 1994.

8.182 **Vakil**, C., 'Sir Walter Scott and the historicism of Scottish Enlightenment philosophical history' in J. H. Alexander and D. Hewitt (eds), *Scott in Carnival*, 1993, 404–18.

Sir John Seeley

8.183 **Burroughs**, P., 'Sir John Seeley and British imperial history', *J. Imp. and Comm. Hist.*, I, 1973, 191–211.

8.184 **Herkless**, J. L., 'Seeley and Ranke', *Historian*, XLIII, 1980, 1–22.

8.185 **Peardon**, T. P., 'Sir John Seeley; pragmatic historian in a nationalistic age' in E. M. Earle (ed.), *Nationalism and Internationalism*, New York, 1950, 285–302.

8.186 **Wormell**, Deborah, *Sir John Seeley and the Uses of History*, 1980. A penetrating study of the nineteenth-century regius professor who established the study of history as a school of statesmanship at Cambridge. Bibliography, 211–24.

Goldwin Smith

8.187 **Wallace**, Elizabeth, *Goldwin Smith. Victorian Liberal*, Toronto, 1957.

William Smyth

8.189 **Butler**, K. T. B., 'A "petty" professor of modern history; William Smyth', *Camb. Hist. J.*, IX, 1948, 217–38.

Robert Southey

8.188 **Eastwood**, D., 'Robert Southey and the intellectual origins of Romantic Conservatism', *E.H.R.*, CIV, 1989, 308–31.

William Stubbs

8.190 **Brentano**, R., 'The sound of Stubbs', *J. Brit. Studs.*, VI, 1967, 1–14. Deals with Stubbs's style.

8.191 **Cam**, Helen M., 'Stubbs seventy years after', *Camb. Hist. J.*, IX, 1947–49, 129–47.

8.192 **Edwards**, J. G., *William Stubbs*, 1952. Pamphlet.

8.193 **Williams**, N. J., 'Stubbs's appointment as regius professor, 1866', *B.I.H.R.* XXXIII, 1960, 121–5.

J. A. Symonds

8.194 **Dale**, P. A., 'Beyond humanism; J. A. Symonds and the replotting of the Renaissance', *Clio*, XVII, 1988, 109–37.

EUROPE

General

8.195 **Ankersmit**, F. R., 'Historicism; an attempt at synthesis', *Hist. and Theory*, XXXIV, 1995, 143–61.

8.196 **Bann**, S., *The Inventions of History*, 1990. Reprinted essays dealing with the multiplicity of historians' vantage points and the complexities of historical discourse. Victor Hugo, Goya and Jean Renoir are among those creative contributors to the depiction of history drawn into the discussion.

8.197 **Butterfield**, H., *Man on his Past*, 1955. Originally delivered as lectures. Chapters on the history of historiography, on the rise of the German historical school, Lord Acton and the nineteenth-century historical movement, Ranke and the conception of general history, and two case studies dealing with the origins of the Seven Years War and the Massacre of St Bartholomew's Day.

8.198 **Chadwick**, O., *Catholicism and History. The Opening of the Vatican Archives*, 1978. Acton figures prominently in this account of relations between the Roman Catholic Church and historians.

8.199 —— *The Secularization of the European Mind in the Nineteenth Century*, 1975. A general exploration of a major intellectual and cultural phenomenon; the place of historical studies in this process is properly recognised.

8.200 **De Vries**, P., 'The writing and study of history in the nineteenth century', *Acta Hist. Neerlandica*, III, 1968, 247–65.

8.201 **Grafton**, A., 'The footnote from de Thou to Ranke', *Hist. and Theory*, XXXIII, 1994, 53–76.

8.202 **Iggers**, G. G., 'Historicism; the history and meaning of the term', *J. Hist. Ideas*, LVI, 1995, 129–52.

8.203 —— 'The *Methodenstreit* in international perspective; the reorientation of historical studies at the turn from the nineteenth to the twentieth century', *Storia de Storiog.*, VI, 1984, 21–32.

8.204 **Mandelbaum**, M., *History, Man and Reason. A Study in Nineteenth-Century Thought*, Baltimore, MD, 1971. Deals –

inter alia – with historicism and its philosophical background and with idealism, positivism and the rebellion against reason. Bibliography, 521–34.

8.205 **Peckham**, M., 'The function of history in nineteenth-century culture', *Survey*, XVII, 1971, 31–6.

8.206 **Pomata**, G., 'Versions of narrative; overt and covert narrators in nineteenth-century historiography', *Hist. Workshop J.*, XXVII, 1989, 1–17.

8.207 **Rudé**, G., *Debate on Europe, 1815–50*, New York, 1972. Surveys the recent historiography.

8.208 **Rüsen**, J., 'Jacob Burckhardt; political standpoint and historical insight on the border of postmodernism', *Hist. and Theory*, XXIV, 1985, 235–46.

8.209 **Varonyi**, Agnes R., 'The impact of scientific thinking on Hungarian historiography about the middle of the nineteenth century', *Acta Hist. Acad. Sci. Hungaricae*, XIV, 1968, 1–20.

8.210 ——'Buckle and Hungarian bourgeois historiography', *Acta Hist. Acad. Sci. Hungaricae*, X, 1963, 49–87.

8.211 **West**, P., 'Jacob Burckhardt and the "ideal past"', *S. Atlantic Q.*, LXII, 1963, 335–46.

8.212 **White**, A. D. (ed.), *European Schools of History and Politics*, Baltimore, MD, 1887.

8.213 **White**, H. V., *Metahistory. The Historical Imagination in Nineteenth-Century Europe*, Baltimore, MD, 1973. A demanding analysis of nineteenth-century realism in historical writing, its relation to the Enlightenment and its repudiation by Marx, Nietzsche, Croce and others. Bibliography. See (1.301).

France

8.214 **Arcangeli**, Bianca, 'The historical treatises and the image of history in France between the nineteenth and twentieth centuries', *Storia de Storiog.*, XXII, 1992, 57–78.

8.215 **Atherton**, J., 'Michelet; three conceptions of historical becoming', *Studs. Romanticism*, IV, 1965, 220–39.

8.216 **Barzun**, J., 'Romantic historiography as a political force in France', *J. Hist. Ideas*, II, 1941, 318–29.

8.217 **Bergin**, M. J., *Tocqueville as Historian. An Examination of the Influences on his Thought and on his Approach to History*, Ann Arbor, MI, 1986.

8.218 **Biddiss**, M. D., 'Prophecy and pragmatism; Gobineau's confrontation with Tocqueville', *Hist. J.*, XIII, 1970, 611–33.

8.219 **Burton**, J. K., *Napoleon and Clio. Historical Writing, Teaching and Thinking during the First Empire*, Durham, NC, 1979.

8.220 **Campbell**, S. L., *The Second Empire Revisited. A Study in French Historiography*, New Brunswick, NJ, 1978. Relates successive depictions of the Second Empire to the changing regimes, circumstances and political climates in which they were produced. Excellent bibliography, 201–24.

8.221 **Carbonell**, C. O., *Histoire et historiens. Une mutation idéologique des historiens français, 1865–85*, Toulouse, 1976. Examines the context out of which the *Revue Historique* emerged.

8.222 **Clark**, T. N., *Prophets and Patrons. The French University and the Emergence of the Social Sciences*, Cambridge, MA, 1973. The three major sections deal with organisation and innovation in the French system of higher education, with the institutionalisation of the social sciences, and with continuities and discontinuities since 1914.

8.223 **Cobban**, A., *France since the Revolution*, 1970. Includes a section – largely drawn from his editorial work for the journal *History* – of historiographical notes.

8.224 ——'Hippolyte Taine, historian of the French Revolution', *Hist.*, LIII, 1968, 331–41.

8.225 **Cormier**, Anne D., *Augustin Thierry. L'histoire autrement*, Paris, 1996.

8.226 **Cox**, M. R., 'Tocqueville's bourgeois revolution', *Hist. Reflections*, XIX, 1993, 279–307.

8.227 **Crossley**, Ceri, *French Historians and Romanticism. Thierry, Guizot, the Saint Simonians, Quinet, Michelet*, 1993. Compares and contrasts these major figures in early nineteenth-century

French historiography. Bibliography, 270–80.

8.228 **Engel Janosi**, F., *Four Studies in French Romantic Historical Writing*, Baltimore, MD, 1955. Contains studies of Chateaubriand, Prosper de Baronte, Thierry and de Tocqueville.

8.229 **Geyl**, P., *Napoleon. For and Against*, 1949. A classic historiographical case study which looks at the creation of the Napoleonic legend and its later vicissitudes in the hands of admirers and critics. Thiers, Taine, Sorel and Lefebvre figure prominently.

8.230 **Gooch**, G. P., *French Profiles. Prophets and Pioneers*, 1961. Includes essays on Voltaire, Michelet and Taine.

8.231 **Green**, F. C., A *Comparative View of French and British Civilisation, 1850–70*, 1965.

8.232 **Herrick**, Jane, *The Historical Thought of Fustel de Coulanges*, Washington, DC, 1954. A doctoral dissertation. The main chapters are on the nature, method and practice of history. There is a list of the publications of Fustel de Coulanges, 123–29, and a bibliography of secondary sources, 130–7.

8.233 **Johnson**, D., *Guizot. Aspects of French History, 1787–1874*, 1963. Has a chapter on Guizot as a historian which deals, *inter alia*, with his work on the English Revolution. See also O'Connor (8.241).

8.234 **Keylor**, W. R., *Academy and Community. The Foundation of the French Historical Profession*, Cambridge, MA, 1975. Places the professionalism of history within its social context.

8.235 **Kippur**, S. A., *Jules Michelet. A Study of Mind and Sensibility*, Albany, NY, 1981.

8.236 **Lombardo**, Patrizia, 'Hyppolyte Taine; between art and science', *Yale French Studs.*, LXXVII, 1990, 117–33.

8.237 **Mellon**, S., *The Political Uses of History. A Study of the Historians of the French Restoration*, Stanford, CA, 1958. Examines the interconnection of history and politics under the restored monarchy, looking particularly at Guizot, Thierry, Daunou, Barante and Montgaillard. Bibliography, 214–22.

8.238 **Michell**, A., 'German history in France after 1870', *J. Contemp. Hist.*, II, 1967, 81–100.

8.239 **Mitchell**, H., *Individual Choice and the Structures of History. Alexis de Tocqueville as Historian Reappraised*, 1996.

8.240 **Mitzman**, A., *Michelet, Historian. Rebirth and Romanticism in Nineteenth-Century France*, New Haven, CT, 1990.

8.241 **O'Connor**, M. C., *The Historical Thought of François Guizot*, Washington, DC, 1955. See also Johnson (8.233).

8.242 **Orr**, Linda, *Jules Michelet. Nature, History and Language*, 1976. A study of the ways in which Michelet's interests in history and natural history interacted.

8.243 **Pickering**, Mary, *Auguste Comte. An Intellectual Biography*, 1993.

8.244 **Roney**, J. B., *The Inside of History. Jean Henri Merle d'Aubigné and Romantic Historiography*, Westport, CT, 1996.

8.245 **Scharff**, R. C., *Comte after Postivism*, 1995.

8.246 **Schulkind**, E., 'Imagination and revolution; guidelines for a historiography of the literature of the Paris Commune of 1871', *Internat. R. Soc. Hist.*, XVII, 1972, 539–51.

8.247 **Siedentop**, L., *Tocqueville*, New York, 1994.

8.248 **Siegel**, M., 'Gabriel Monod and the ideological foundations of the *Revue Historique*', *Studia Metodol.*, IX, 1972, 3–15.

8.249 —— 'Clio at the Ecole Normale Supérieure; historical studies at an elite institution in France, 1870–1904', *Storia de Storiog.*, VIII, 1985, 37–46.

8.250 **Smithson**, R. N., *Augustin Thierry. Social and Political Consciousness in the Evolution of a Historical Method*, Geneva, 1972. A full study dealing with Thierry as journalist and as the author of the *History of the Norman Conquest of England*. Other chapters deal with Thierry's lesser works. Bibliography, 307–16.

8.251 **Waeber**, P., *Sismondi. Une biographie*, Geneva, 1991. A study of the French historian and economist (1773–1842).

Germany

8.252 **Anderson**, J., 'German romanticism as an ideology of cultural crisis', *J. Hist. Ideas*, II, 1941, 301–17.

8.253 **Andrews**, H. D., 'Bismarck's foreign policy and German historiography', *J.M.H.*, XXXVII, 1965, 345–56.

8.254 **Beller**, S., 'Modern owls fly by night; recent literature on *fin de siècle* Vienna', *Hist. J.*, XXXI, 1988, 665–84.

8.255 **Berthold-Bond**, D., 'Hegel's eschatological vision; does history have a future?', *Hist. and Theory*, XXVII, 1988, 14–29.

8.256 **Diehl**, C., *Americans and German Scholarship, 1770–1870*, 1978. Considers the influence of the German universities on the scholarly methods and ideals of American academics in the late eighteenth and nineteenth centuries.

8.257 **Echevarria**, A. J., 'Heroic history and vicarious war; nineteenth-century German military history writing', *Historian*, LIX, 1997, 573–90.

8.258 **Engel Janosi**, F., *The Growth of German Historicism*, Baltimore, MA, 1944. An overview containing short studies of Herder, Niebuhr, Ranke, Marx and Burckhardt.

8.259 **Ermath**, M., *William Dilthey. The Critique of Historical Reason*, Chicago, IL, 1978. A perceptive intellectual biography which explores Dilthey's goals, his debates with his critics and his place in German scholarship.

8.260 **Gerhard**, D., 'Otto Hintze; his work and significance in historiography', *Cen. European Hist.*, III, 1970, 17–48.

8.261 **Gilbert**, F. (ed.), *The Historical Essays of Otto Hintze*, 1975. The third section of the book – devoted to history and theory – includes 'The individualist and collective approach to history' and 'Troeltsch and the problems of historicism'.

8.262 **Hinde**, J. R., 'Jacob Burckhardt; the art of his *History*', *Storia de Storiog.*, XXX, 1996, 107–24.

8.263 **Iggers**, G. G., *The German Conception of History*, Middletown, CT, 1968. Deals with the origins, theoretical foundations, high point, crisis and decline of German historicism. There are separate chapters on von Humboldt, Ranke and the Prussian school. Bibliography, 349–56.

8.264 **Labuda**, G., 'The Slavs in nineteenth-century German historiography', *Polish W. Affairs*, X, 1969, 177–234.

8.265 **Lee**, D. E. and **Beck**, R. N., 'The meaning of historicism', *A.H.R.*, LIX, 1954, 568–77.

8.266 **McClelland**, C. E., 'Berlin historians and German politics', *J. Contemp. Hist.*, VIII, 1973, 3–34.

8.267 —— 'History in the service of politics; a reassessment of G. G. Gervinus', *Cen. European Hist.*, IV, 1971, 371–88.

8.268 —— *State, Society and University in Germany, 1700–1914*, 1980. Explores the circumstances which produced the distinctive university system in Germany.

Karl Marx

8.269 **Adamson**, W. L., 'Marx's four histories; an approach to his intellectual development', *Hist. and Theory*, XX, 1981, 379–402.

8.270 **Axelos**, K., *Alienation, Praxis, and Techne in the Thought of Karl Marx*, Austin, TX, 1976.

8.271 **Bendix**, R. and **Lipset**, S. M., 'Karl Marx's theory of social class' in R. Bendix and S. M. Lipset (eds), *Class, Status and Power*, Glencoe, IL, 1953, 26–35.

8.272 **Bober**, M. M., *Karl Marx's Interpretation of History*, New York, 1927, 2nd ed. 1948. A clear exposition and evaluation of the ideas of both Marx and Engels. Bibliography.

8.273 **Cohen**, G. A., *Karl Marx's Theory of History. A Defence*, 1978. A favourable account of historical materialism. Chapters on 'Images of history in Hegel and Marx', 'The economic structure', 'The primacy of the productive forces' and 'Base and superstructure'.

8.274 **Domarchi**, J., *Marx et l'histoire*, Paris, 1972.

8.275 **Enfield**, R., 'Marx and historical laws', *Hist. and Theory*, XV, 1976, 267–77.

8.276 **Gandy**, D. R., *Marx and History. From Primitive Society to the Communist Future*, Austin, TX, 1979. A lucid account of Marx's ideas on capitalism, class and revolution. Bibliography.

8.277 **Hobsbawm**, E. J. (ed.), *The History of Marxism*, I: *Marxism in Marx's Day*,

1982. Includes essays on 'The materialist concept of history', 'Marx and the concept of history', 'Engels and the history of Marxism', and on 'The fortunes of Marx's and Engels's writings'.

8.278 —— 'Karl Marx's contribution to historiography' in R. Blackburn (ed.), *Ideology in Social Science*, 1972, 265–83.

8.279 **Kain**, P. J., 'Marx's dialectic method', *Hist. and Theory*, XIX, 1980, 294–312.

8.280 —— 'Marx's theory of ideas', *Hist. and Theory*, XX, 1981, 357–78.

8.281 **King**, J. E., 'Marx as a historian of economic thought', *Hist. Pol. Econ.*, XI, 1979, 382–94.

8.282 **Krieger**, L., 'The uses of Marx for history', *Pol. Sci. Q.*, LXXV, 1960, 255–78.

8.283 **Lekas**, P., *Marx on Classical Antiquity. Problems of Historical Methodology*, 1988.

8.284 **Loewenstein**, J. I., *Marx against Marxism*, 1980. Deals with the formative influences on Marx's ideas, his own concepts and their effects on others. Bibliography.

8.285 **McGovern**, A. F., 'Young Marx on the role of ideas in history', *Philos. Today*, XV, 1971, 204–16.

8.286 **McLellan**, D., *Marx*, 1975. A brief introduction to the man and his ideas.

8.287 **Nicolaievesky**, B. and **Maenchen-Helfen**, O., *Karl Marx. Man and Fighter*, 1936, 2nd ed. 1973. A biographical rather than an intellectual study.

8.288 **Rader**, M., *Marx's Interpretation of History*, New York, 1979. Identifies three models in Marx's schema – dialectical development, organic totality and base/superstructure – and attempts to reconcile them.

8.289 **Shaw**, W. H., *Marx's Theory of History*, 1978. A useful, lucid survey of Marx's views on the anatomy of production, technological determinism, capitalism and socialism, Bibliography, 191–8.

8.290 **Simon**, L. H., 'Vico and Marx; perspectives on historical development', *J. Hist. Ideas*, XLII, 1981, 317–34.

8.291 **Wolf**, R. P., *Understanding Marx. A Reconstruction and Critique of Marx*, 1985.

See also the section on twentieth-century Marxist interpretations of history (pp. 101–3).

8.292 **Mommsen**, W. J., 'Jacob Burckhardt; defender of culture, prophet of doom', *Government and Opposition*, XVIII, 1983, 458–75.

8.293 **O'Brien**, G. D., 'Does Hegel have a philosophy of history?', *Hist. and Theory* X, 1971, 295–317.

Leopold von Ranke

8.294 **Dickens**, A. G., *Ranke as Reformation Historian*, 1980. Lecture.

8.295 **Gilbert**, F., *History. Politics or Culture? Reflections on Ranke and Burckhardt*, Princeton, NJ, 1990. Shows the common bonds as well as the contrasts between these two great nineteenth-century historians.

8.296 **Iggers**, G. G., 'The image of Ranke in American and German historical thought', *Hist. and Theory*, II, 1962, 17–40.

8.297 —— and **Powell**, J. M., *Leopold von Ranke and the Shaping of the Historical Discipline*, New York, 1990.

8.298 **Krieger**, L., *Ranke. The Meaning of History*, 1977. A sophisticated and systematic account of the justaposition of differences and opposites in Ranke's philosophy and methodology of history.

8.299 **Laue**, T. H. von, *Leopold Ranke. The Formative Years*, Princeton, NJ, 1950. Looks at the ways in which Ranke's religion and his training in philology contributed to his distinctive historical outlook.

8.300 **Southard**, R., *Droysen and the Prussian School of History*, Lexington, KY, 1995.

8.301 **Taylor**, C., *Hegel*, 1975. Combines history of ideas with intellectual biography and offers copious accounts of the main writings.

8.302 **Thiele**, L. P., 'Heidegger, history and hermeneutics', *J.M.H.*, LXIX, 1997, 534–56.

8.303 **Tuttle**, H. N., *Wilhelm Dilthey's Philosophy of Historical understanding. A Critical Analysis*, Leiden, 1969.

8.304 —— *The Dawn of Historical Reason. The Historiography of Human Experience in* the Thought of Dilthey, Heidegger, and Ortega y Gasset, New York, 1994.

8.305 **Wilkins**, B. T., *Hegel's Philosophy of History*, Ithaca, NY, 1974.

UNITED STATES

8.306 **Adas**, M., *'High' Imperialism and the 'New' History*, Washington, DC, 1994.

8.307 **Appleby**, Joyce, *Liberalism and Republicanism in the Historical Imagination*, Cambridge, MA, 1992.

8.308 **Baym**, Nina, *American Women Writers and the Work of History, 1790–1860*, New Brunswick, NJ, 1995.

8.309 **Becker**, C. L., *Everyman his own Historian. Essays on History and Politics*, Chicago, IL, 1935. Has essays on Marxist history, Bryce, Henry Adams and Turner.

8.310 **Beckmann**, A. C., 'Hidden themes in the frontier thesis; an application of psychoanalysis to historiography', *Comp. Studs. Soc. and Hist.*, VIII, 1966, 361–82.

8.311 **Bellot**, H. H., *American History and American Historians*, Norman, OK, 1952.

8.312 **Billington**, R. A., *Frederick Jackson Turner. Historian, Scholar, Teacher*, New York, 1973.

8.313 ——— *The Frontier Thesis. Valid Interpretation of American History?*, Chicago, IL, 1966.

8.314 **Blumenthal**, H., 'George Bancroft in Berlin, 1867–74', *New England Q.*, XXXVII, 1964, 224–41.

8.315 **Bonner**, T. N., 'Civil War historians and the "needless war"', *J. Hist. Ideas*, XVII, 1956, 193–216.

8.316 **Burich**, K. R., ' "Our power is always running ahead of our mind"; Henry Adams's phases of history', *New England Q.*, LXII, 1989, 163–86.

8.317 **Calcott**, G. H., *History in the United States, 1800–1860. Its Practice and Purpose*, Baltimore, MD, 1970.

8.318 **Cline**, H. F., **Gardiner**, C. H., and **Gibson**, C. (ed.), *William Hickling Prescott. A Memorial*, Durham, NC, 1959. Chapters on Prescott's research, style and interpretation; reprints

contemporary reviews of his chief works.

8.319 **Cooke**, J. E., *George Bancroft, Historian*, Norman, OK, 1957.

8.320 **Cronin**, W., 'Revisiting the vanishing frontier; the legacy of Frederick Jackson Turner', *Western Hist. Q.*, XVIII, 1987, 157–76.

8.321 **Cunningham**, R. J., 'The German historical world of Herbert Baxter Adams, 1874–76', *J.A.H.*, LXVIII, 1981, 261–75.

8.322 ——— 'Is history past politics? Herbert Baxter Adams as precursor of the "new" history', *Hist. Teacher*, IX, 1976, 244–57.

8.323 **Curti**, M., *The Growth of American Thought*, 1943, 3rd ed. New York, 1964. Though not specifically historiographical, ideas about history – firmly connected with their social context and social uses – figure in this general, seven-part survey. Extensive bibliography, 795–900.

8.324 **Dawes**, N. H. and **Nichols**, F. T., 'Revaluing Bancroft', *New England Q.*, VI, 1933, 278–93.

8.325 **Doughty**, H., *Francis Parkman*, Cambridge, MA, 1983. Chiefly a study of Parkman's histories.

8.326 **Faragher**, J. M., *Re-reading Frederick Jackson Turner. The Significance of the Frontier in American History, and other Essays*, New York, 1994.

8.327 **Fleming**, R., 'Picturesque history and the medieval in nineteenth-century America', *A.H.R.*, C, 1995, 1061–94.

8.328 **Gale**, R. L., *Francis Parkman*, New York, 1973.

8.329 **Hays**, S. P., 'The social analysis of American political history, 1880–1920', *Pol. Sci. Q.*, LXXX, 1965, 373–94.

8.330 **Hendricks**, L. V., *James Harvey Robinson. Teacher of History*, New York, 1946.

8.331 **Herbst**, J., *The German Historical School in American Scholarship. A Study in the Transfer of Culture*, Ithaca, NY, 1965. Considers the rise and decline of the influence of the German historical school of social science in the United States between 1876 (the founding of Johns Hopkins University) and the outbreak of the First World War.

8.332 **Higby**, C. P., *John Lothrop Motley*, New York, 1939.

8.333 **Hook**, A., 'Macaulay and America', *J. Am. Studs.*, IX, 1975, 335–46. Considers the historian's popularity on the other side of the Atlantic.

8.334 **Ions**, E., *James Bryce and American Democracy, 1870–1922*, 1968. A biography of the historian/diplomat author of *The American Commonwealth*. See also Robbins (8.349).

8.335 **Jacobs**, W. R., *The Historical World of Frederick Jackson Turner, with Selections from his Correspondence*, New Haven, CT, 1968. Deals with Turner as both historian and educationalist. Bibliography.

8.336 ——*Francis Parkman. Historian as Hero*, Austin, TX, 1991. A painstaking biography of the American romantic historian.

8.337 **Levin**, D., *History as Romantic Art*, New York, 1967. Deals with the romantic attitudes, conventional characters, and artistic achievements displayed in Bancroft, Prescott, Motley and Parkman.

8.338 **Levenson**, J. C., *The Mind and Art of Henry Adams*, Boston, MA, 1957.

8.339 **Maddox**, R. F., 'Wider frontiers; questions of war and conflict in American history. The strange solution of F. J. Turner', *Cal. Hist. Soc. Q.*, XXXVII, 1968, 291–336.

8.340 **Marshall**, L. L. and **Drescher**, S., 'American historians and Tocqueville's *Democracy*', *J.A.H.*, LV, 1968, 512–32.

8.341 **Nevins**, A., *James Truslow Adams. Historian of the American Dream*, Urbana, IL, 1968.

8.342 **Noble**, D., *Historians against History. The Frontier Thesis and the National Covenant in American Historical Writing since 1830*, Minneapolis, MN, 1965. American historiography from Bancroft to Boorstin.

8.343 **Novick**, P., *The Noble Dream. The 'Objectivity Question' and the American Historical Profession*, 1988. Surveys the development of professionalised history in the United States from the 1880s to the Cold War.

8.344 **Nye**, R. B., *George Bancroft. Brahmin Rebel*, New York, 1945.

8.345 **Parish**, P. J., *Slavery. History and Historians*, New York, 1989.

8.346 **Pease**, O. A., *Parkman's History. The Historian as Literary Artist*, New Haven, CT, 1953.

8.347 **Peterson**, M. D., *Lincoln in American Memory*, New York, 1994. A systematic examination of Lincoln's place in American thought and imagination and of the ways in which archetypes of Lincoln were variously used to further later political agendas.

8.348 **Ridge**, M. (ed.), *Frederick Jackson Turner. Wisconsin's Historian of the Frontier*, Madison, WI, 1986.

8.349 **Robbins**, K., 'Historians in politics; James Bryce', *J. Contemp. Hist.*, VII, 1972, 37–52. See also Ions (8.334).

8.350 **Rosenberg**, J. S., 'Toward a new Civil War revisionism', *Am. Scholar*, XXXVIII, 1969, 250–72.

8.351 **Russo**, D. J., *Keepers of our Past. Local Historical Writing in the United States, 1820s–1930s*, Westport, CT, 1988.

8.352 **Salamone**, A. W., 'The nineteenth-century discovery of Italy; an essay in American cultural history. Prolegomena to a historiographical problem', *A.H.R.*, LXXIII, 1968, 1359–91.

8.353 **Shaw**, P., 'Blood is thicker than irony; Henry Adams' *History*', *New England Q.*, XL, 1967, 163–87.

8.354 **Tilly**, C., 'The historian as editor; Francis Parkman's reconstruction of sources in Montcalm and Wolfe', *J.A.H.*, LIII, 1966, 471–86.

8.355 **Tulloch**, H., *The Debate on the Civil War Era*, 1999. Situates the different interpretations advanced by historians about slavery, abolitionism, the causes and progress of the Civil War, and Reconstruction. Bibliography, 244–6.

8.356 ——*James Bryce's American Commonwealth*, 1988. Examines the background to the writing of this classic late nineteenth-century study of the American constitution and its subsequent reputation. Bibliography, 244–65.

8.357 **Vitzthum**, R. C., *The American Compromise. Theme and Method in the Histories of Bancroft, Parkman and Adams*, Norman, OK, 1974.

OTHER COUNTRIES

8.358 **Crabbs**, J. A., *The Writing of History in Nineteenth-Century Egypt. A Study in National Transformation*, Detroit, MI, 1984.

8.359 **Gagnon**, S., *Quebec and its Historians, 1840–1920*, Montreal, 1982. See also Gagnon (1.747).

8.360 **Guha**, R., *An Indian Historiography of India. Nineteenth-Century Agenda and its Implications*, Calcutta, 1988.

8.361 **Mazour**, A. G., *Modern Russian Historiography*, 1939, 3rd ed. Westport, CT, 1975. Extends up to the second half of the nineteenth century.

8.362 **Sato**, M., 'Historiographical encounters; the Chinese and Western traditions in turn of the century Japan', *Storia de Storiog.*, XIX, 1991, 13–22.

8.363 **Taylor**, M. B., *Promoters, Patriots, and Partisans. Historiography in Nineteenth Century English Canada*, Toronto, 1989.

8.364 **Wang**, Q. E., 'History in late imperial China; a tradition', *Storia de Storiog.*, XXII, 1992, 3–22.

8.365 **Young**, J. D., 'South Australian historians and Wakefield's scheme', *Hist. Studs.*, XIV, 1969, 32–53.

9

THE TWENTIETH CENTURY

GENERAL

9.1 **Abelove**, H. *et al.* (eds), *Visions of History*, 1983. Published under the auspices of the (US) Radical Historians Organization. Includes interviews with E. P. Thompson, Eric Hobsbawm, Sheila Rowbotham, Natalie Zemon Davis and Herbert Gutman.

9.2 **Achenbaum**, W. A., 'Public history's past, present, and prospects', *A.H.R.*, XCII, 1987, 1162–74.

9.3 **Adelson**, R. (ed.), *Speaking on History. Conversations with Historians*, East Lansing, MI, 1997. Reprints the texts of fourteen interviews with American historians conducted between 1990 and 1995. Included are Natalie Zemon Davis, John Demos, W. H. McNeill and C. vann Woodward.

9.3a **Alter**, P. (ed.), *Out of the Third Reich. Refugee Historians in Postwar Britain*, 1998. A collection of autobiographies by Sidney Pollard, G. R. Elton, Walter Ullman, E. P. Hennock and H. G. Koenigsberger. See also Lehman and Sheehan (9.70).

9.4 **Armytage**, W. H. G., *Civic Universities. Aspects of a British Tradition*, 1955.

9.5 **Arnstein**, W. L. (ed.), *Recent Historians of Great Britain. Essays on the post-1945 Generation*, Ames, IA, 1990. Essays on Elton, Gash, Hill, Hurstfield, Lyons, Plumb, Stone and E. P. Thompson.

9.6 **Ashplant**, T. G. and **Wilson**, A., 'Present-centred history and the problem of historical knowledge', *Hist. J.*, XXXI, 1988, 253–74.

9.7 ——'Whig history and present-centred history', *Hist. J.*, XXXI, 1988, 1–16.

9.8 **Bailyn**, B., 'The challenge of modern historiography', *A.H.R.*, LXXXVII, 1982, 1–24.

9.9 **Ballard**, M. (ed.), *New Movements in the Study and Teaching of History*, 1970. Essays concerned with the broadening scope of historical studies – both geographically and socially – and with changing methods and cross-disciplinary connections.

9.10 **Barraclough**, G., *History and the Common Man*, 1967. Pamphlet.

9.11 ——*History in a Changing World*, 1956. Includes a number of general historiographical essays from a historian renowned for his opposition to old-style specialisation.

9.12 ——*An Introduction to Contemporary History*, 1964. Though principally concerned with the subject matter of contemporary history the first chapter attempts a definition of the nature of the enterprise.

9.13 **Barraclough**, S. and **Samuel**, R., 'History and television', *Hist. Workshop J.*, XII, 1981, 172–76.

9.14 **Beales**, A. C. F., 'Fifty years of historical teaching', *Historical Ass. Jubilee Addresses*, 1956.

9.15 **Beaver**, D. R. (ed.), *Some Pathways in Twentieth-Century History. Essays in*

Honour of Reginald Charles McGrane, Detroit, MI, 1969. A *festschrift* which includes an essay on the history and historiography of American peace efforts before Munich, 177–220.

9.16 **Ben-Ghiat**, Ruth, 'Fascism, writing and memory; the realistic aesthetic in Italy, 1930–50', *J.M.H.*, LXVII, 1995, 627–65.

9.17 **Birn**, Ruth B., 'Revising the Holocaust', *Hist. J.*, XL, 1997, 195–216.

9.18 **Booth**, A. and **Hyland**, P. (eds), *History in Higher Education*, 1996. Sixteen essays and an introduction dealing with innovative practice in history curricula and teaching. Race, gender, distance learning, work placements and new styles of assessment are among the issues explored.

9.19 **Bosworth**, R. J. B., *Explaining Auschwitz and Hiroshima. History Writing and the Second World War*, New York, 1993.

9.20 **Brinton**, C., 'Many mansions', *A.H.R.*, LXIX, 1964, 306–26. An American Historical Association presidential address concerning the burgeoning varieties of history.

9.21 **Brown**, H., 'History and the learned journal', *J. Hist. Ideas*, XXXIII, 1972, 365–78. See also Hay (9.49) and Stieg (9.96).

9.22 **Burke**, P. (ed.), *New Perspectives on Historical Writing*, 1991. A collection of essays dealing with the strengths and weaknesses of new approaches to the subject. Chapters on the history of images, the body and reading are particularly successful.

9.23 **Butterfield**, H., 'History in the Twentieth Century', *Historical Ass. Jubilee Addresses*, 1956.

9.24 —— 'Official history; its pitfalls and criteria', *Studs.*, XXXVIII, 1949, 129–44.

9.25 **Cantor**, N. F. (ed.), *Perspectives on the European Past*, 2 vols, New York, 1971. Interviews with historians arranged chronologically according to their specialism. The historians include Kitto, Syme, Jones, Southern, Elton, Dickens, Hartwell and Briggs.

9.26 **Carrard**, P., *Poetics of the New History. French Historical Discourse from Braudel to Chartier*, Baltimore, MD, 1992.

9.27 **Clark**, G. K., 'A hundred years of the teaching of history at Cambridge, 1873–1973', *Hist. J.*, XVI, 1973, 535–53.

9.28 **Clarke**, P., *Liberals and Social Democrats*, 1978. Includes some discussion of the Hammonds.

9.29 **Cochrane**, T. C., 'History and cultural crisis', *A.H.R.*, LXXVIII, 1973, 1–10.

9.30 **Collier**, C., 'History, culture and communication', *Hist. and Theory*, XX, 1981, 150–67.

9.31 **Cooper**, F., 'Race, ideology and the perils of comparative history', *A.H.R.*, CI, 1996, 1122–38.

9.32 **Delzell**, C. (ed.), *The Future of History*, Nashville, TN, 1977. A symposium which includes essays on 'The new urban history' and on 'History and the social sciences in the twentieth century'.

9.33 **Fieldhouse**, D. K., 'Can Humpty Dumpty be put together again? Imperial history in the 1980s', *J. Imp. and Comm. Hist.*, XII, 1984, 9–23.

9.34 **Finberg**, H. P. R. (ed.), *Approaches to History. A Symposium*, 1962. Includes essays on political, economic, social and local history.

9.35 **Foner**, E. (ed.), *The New American History*, Philadelphia, PA, 1990.

9.36 **Fredrickson**, G., 'From exceptionalism to variability; recent developments in cross-national comparative history', *J.A.H.*, LXXXII, 1995, 587–604.

9.37 **Furber**, Elizabeth C., *Changing Views on British History. Essays on Historical Writing since 1939*, Cambridge, MA, 1966.

9.38 **Gifford**, B. R., *History in the Schools. What shall we Teach?*, New York, 1988. A sane appraisal of values, curriculum and teaching strategies in the place of history in US schools.

9.39 **Gilb**, Corinne L., 'Time and change in twentieth-century thought', *J. World Hist.*, IX, 1966, 867–83.

9.40 **Gilbert**, F. and **Graubard**, S. R. (eds), *Historical Studies Today*, New York, 1972. A rich collection reprinted from the journal *Daedalus* which includes essays on 'Archaeology and history',

'Intellectual history; its aims and method', 'The relations between history and history of science' and 'Prosopography'.

9.41 **Goldstein**, Doris S., 'The organisational development of the British historical profession, 1884–1921', *B.I.H.R.*, LV, 1982, 180–93.

9.42 —— 'The professionalisation of history in the late nineteenth and early twentieth centuries', *Storia de Storiog.*, I, 1983, 3–26.

9.43 **Green**, J. J. D., 'The Tawney–Strauss connection; on historicism and values in the history of political ideas', *J.M.H.*, LXVII, 1995, 255–77.

9.44 **Halperin**, S. W. (ed.), *Some Twentieth-Century Historians*, Chicago, IL, 1961. Includes essays on British historians such as Trevelyan, Butterfield, Webster and Gooch. The European historians dealt with here include Pirenne, Lefebvre and Febvre.

9.45 **Halsey**, A. H. and **Trow**, M. A., *The British Academics*, 1971.

9.46 **Hamerow**, T. S., *Reflections on History and Historians*, Madison, WL, 1987. Concerned with the present position of the discipline in the United States. Comparisons are made with the state of the subject in the nineteenth century, with other countries and with other academic specialisms.

9.47 **Hancock**, W. K., *The History of our Times*. 1950. Lecture. A plea for the study of contemporary history.

9.48 **Handlin**, O., 'History; a discipline in crisis?', *Am. Scholar*, XL, 1971, 447–65.

9.48a **Hay**, D., 'British historians and the beginning of the civil history of the Second World War' in M. R. D. Foot (ed.), *War and Society. Historical Essays in Honour and Memory of J. R. Western*, 1973, 39–55.

9.49 —— 'The historical periodical; some problems', *Hist.*, LIV, 1969, 165–77.

9.50 **Hexter**, J. H., 'The historian and his society; a sociological enquiry – perhaps' in G. Smith (ed.), *The Professor and the Public. The Role of the Scholar in the Modern World*, Detroit, ML, 1972.

9.51 —— *On Historians*, 1979. Includes studies of Becker, Braudel, Hill, Stone and Pocock.

9.52 **Hill**, C. *et al.*, '*Past and Present*; origins and early years', *P.P.*, 100, 1983, 3–14. See also Le Goff (9.69).

9.53 —— 'History and the present' in Hill, *A Nation of Change and Novelty. Radical Politics, Religion and Literature in Seventeenth-Century England*, 1990, 244–57.

9.54 **Himmelfarb**, Gertrude, *The New History and the Old. Critical Essays and Reappraisals*, 1987. A (distinctly) cool appraisal of current trends in the writing of history (social history, psychohistory, quantitative history, Marxist history, *mentalité* history) and the way in which they have tended to displace older approaches centred on politics and intellectual traditions.

9.55 **Hine**, Darlene C. (ed.), *The State of Afro-American History. Past, Present and Future*, Baton Rouge, LA, 1986.

9.56 **Hobsbawm**, E. J., 'Looking forward; history and the future', *New Left R.*, CXXV, 1981, 3–19.

9.57 **Hogebrom**, W. L., 'The Cold War and revisionist historiography', *Soc. Studs.*, LXI, 1970, 314–18.

9.58 **Holdsworth**, W. S., 'The place of English legal history in the education of English lawyers' in Holdsworth, *Essays in Law and History*, 1946, 20–36.

9.59 **Howe**, Barbara J. and **Kent**, E. L., *Public History. An Introduction*, Malibar, FL, 1986.

9.60 **Iggers**, G. C., *New Directions in European Historiography*, 1975, rev. ed. 1985. There are four sections which deal with the crisis of the conventional conception of 'scientific' history, the *Annales* tradition, beyond historicism, and with Marxism and modern social history. Bibliography.

9.61 —— *Historiography in the Twentieth Century. From Scientific Objectivity to the Postmodern Challenge*, Hanover, NH, 1997. Examines the ways in which history's responses to the challenge of the social sciences have themselves been called into question by postmodernism.

9.62 **Jenkins**, K., *On 'What is History?'. From Carr and Elton to Rorty and White*, 1995. The four writers mentioned in the title each receive a separate chapter, with Carr and Elton depicted as museum pieces in today's academic world.

9.63 **Jones**, G. S., 'History; the poverty of empiricism' in R. Blackburn (ed.), *Ideology in Social Science*, 1972, 96–118.

9.64 —— 'The pathology of English history', *New Left R.*, XLVI, 1967, 29–43. A Marxist critique of the liberal/positivist legacy which Blackburn considers still encumbers modern historians.

9.65 **Karamanski**, T. J. (ed.), *Ethics and Public History. An Anthology*, Malibar, FL, 1990.

9.66 **Karlman**, R., *Evidencing Historical Classifications in British and American Historiography*, Stockholm, 1976.

9.67 **Kennedy**, P. M., 'The decline of nationalistic history in the West, 1900–70', *J. Contemp. Hist.*, VIII, 1973, 77–100.

9.68 **Lefkowitz**, Mary, *Not out of Africa. How Afrocentrism became an Excuse to teach Myth as History*, New York, 1996.

9.69 **Le Goff**, G. J., '*Past and Present*; later history', *P.P.*, 100, 1983, 14–28. See also Hill (9.52).

9.70 **Lehmann**, H. and **Sheehan**, J. J. (eds), *An Interrupted Past. German-speaking Refugee Historians in the United States after 1933*, 1991. See also Alter (9.3a).

9.71 **McGerr**, M., 'The price of the "new transnational history"', *A.H.R.*, XCVI, 1991, 1056–67.

9.72 **Marwick**, A., 'Two approaches to historical study; the metaphysical (including "postmodernism") and the historical', *J. Contemp. Hist.*, XXX, 1995, 5–31.

9.73 **Mehta**, V., *The Fly and the Flybottle. Encounters with British Intellectuals*, 1963. Includes E. H. Carr, Hill, Tawney and Namier.

9.74 **Milne**, A. T., 'Twenty-five years at the Institute, 1946–71', *B.I.H.R.*, XLIV, 1971, 284–92.

9.75 —— 'History at the universities; then and now', *Hist.*, LIX, 1974, 33–46.

9.76 **Morton**, Marian J., *The Terrors of Ideological Politics. Liberal Historians in a Conservative Mood*, Cleveland, OH, 1972.

9.77 **Myres**, J. L., *The Provision for Historical Studies at Oxford*, 1915.

9.78 **Neale**, J. E., 'The biographical approach to history' in Neale, *Essays in Elizabethan History*, 1963, 240–52.

9.79 **Oliver**, W. H., *Towards a New History*, Dunedin, 1971.

9.80 **Osborne**, J. W., 'The endurance of "literary" history in Britain; Charles Oman, G. M. Trevelyan and the genteel tradition', *Clio*, II, 1972, 7–17.

9.81 **Parsloe**, G., 'Recollections of the Institute, 1922–43', *B.I.H.R.*, XLIV, 1971, 270–83.

9.82 **Plumb**, J. H., *The Making of an Historian*, 1988. Includes a very long section on Namier, Namierism and its critics. Other essays include brief studies of Macaulay, Toynbee, Trevelyan and Braudel.

9.83 **Pollard**, A. F., 'Historical criticism', *Hist.*, V, 1920, 21–9.

9.84 —— 'The University of London and the study of history' in Pollard, *Factors in Modern History*, 3rd ed. 1932, 234–320.

9.85 **Porter**, R. and **Wear**, A., *Problems and Methods in the History of Medicine*, 1987.

9.86 **Powicke**, F. M., *Modern Historians and the Study of History*, 1955. Includes a variety of memoirs of individual historians – Vinogradoff, Pirenne, Firth and Poole – and an extended study of the Manchester School of History. Part Two collects together some general essays, such as 'Historical study in Oxford' and 'Modern methods of medieval research'.

9.87 **Rabb**, T. K., 'Toward the future; coherence, synthesis and quality in history', *J. Interdis. Hist.*, XII, 1981, 315–32.

9.88 **Robbins**, K., 'History, the Historical Association and the national past', *Hist.*, LXVI, 1981, 413–25.

9.89 **Robinson**, J. H., *The New History*, New York, 1912, reprinted with a new introduction by H. Wish, New York, 1965. A vigorous plea for a wider, more inclusive study.

9.90 **Rowse**, A. L., *Historians I have Known*, 1995. Twenty-seven brief, and often barbed, pen-portraits of leading historians.

9.91 **Schlesinger**, A. M., 'Nationalism and history', *J. Negro Hist.*, LIV, 19–31.

9.92 **Schmitt**, B. E. (ed.), *Some Historians of Modern Europe. Essays in*

Historiography, Port Washington, NY, 1942.

9.93 **Scott**, W., 'François Furet and democracy in France', *Hist. J.*, XXXIV, 1991, 147–72.

9.94 **Shafer**, B. C. *et al.* (eds), *Historical Study in the West*, New York, 1968. Deals principally with modern trends in France, Germany, Britain and America.

9.95 **Stevenson**, J., 'Writing Scotland's history in the twentieth century; thoughts from across the border', *Scot. H.R.*, LXXVI, 1997, 103–14.

9.96 **Stieg**, Margaret F., *The Origin and Development of Scholarly Historical Periodicals*, University, AL, 1986. See also Brown (9.21) and Hay (9.49).

9.97 **Sutherland**, Gillian, 'The study of the history of education', *Hist.*, LIV, 1969, 49–59.

9.98 **Taylor**, A. J., 'History at Leeds, 1877–1974; the evolution of a discipline', *Northern Hist.*, X, 1975, 141–64.

9.99 **Thomson**, D., 'The writing of contemporary history', *J. Contemp. Hist.*, II, 1967, 25–34.

9.100 **Toews**, J. E., 'Perspectives on *The Old History and the New*; a comment', *A.H.R.*, XCIV, 1989, 693–8.

9.101 **Trevelyan**, G. M., *The Recreations of an Historian*, 1919. Includes the famous rebuke to the new breed of scientific historians, 'The muse of history'.

9.102 ——*An Autobiography and other Essays*, 1949. As well as the brief autobiography this volume collects together fifteen essays. They include 'History and the reader', 'Bias in history' and 'The influence of Sir Walter Scott on history'.

9.103 **Tyrrell**, I. R., *The Absent Marx. Class Analysis and Liberal History in Twentieth-Century America*, New York, 1986.

9.104 **Vincent**, J., *An Intelligent Person's Guide to History*, 1995. Forthright, epigrammatic, highly conservative, and at times jaundiced, observations on the current practice of history and on the evolution of the subject.

9.105 **Watt**, D. C. (ed.), *Contemporary History in Europe. Problems and Perspectives*, 1969. A wide-ranging collection on post-war historiography.

9.106 **Webster**, C. K., 'Fifty years of change in historical teaching and research' in *Historical Ass. Jubilee Addresses*, 1956.

9.107 **Wiener**, J. M., 'Radical historians and the crisis in American history, 1959–80', *J.A.H.*, LXXVI, 1989, 399–434.

9.108 **Wilson**, N. J., *History in Crisis. Recent Directions in Historiography*, Upper Saddle River, NJ, 1999. A lively introduction to current opportunities and predicaments.

9.109 **Wolfe**, P., 'Imperialism and history; a century of theory from Marx to postcolonialism', *A.H.R.*, CII, 1997, 388–420.

9.110 **Woodward**, E. L., 'Modern historical studies in England since 1939', *B.I.H.R.*, XXI, 1946–48, 131–6.

9.111 ——'Some considerations on the present state of historical studies', *Proc. Brit. Acad.*, XXXVI, 1950, 91–112.

HISTORY AND OTHER DISCIPLINES

9.112 **Abbott**, A., 'History and sociology; the lost synthesis', *Soc. Sci. Hist.*, XV, 1991, 201–38.

9.113 **Abrams**, P., *Historical Sociology*, Ithaca, NY, 1982.

9.114 ——'History, sociology, historical sociology', *P.P.*, 87, 1980, 3–16.

9.115 **Amselle**, J. L., 'Anthropology and historicity', *Hist. and Theory*, XXXII, 1993, 12–31.

9.116 **Appignanesi**, Lisa (ed.), *Ideas from France. The Legacy of French Theory*. ICA Documents, 1989. Has sections on 'The pleasures and pitfalls of theory', 'The rise and fall of structural Marxism', 'The uses of history' and 'The archaeology of Michel Foucault'.

9.117 **Attridge**, D. *et al.* (eds), *Poststructuralism and the Question of History*, 1987. Examines the relations between poststructural and historical literary theory and criticism.

9.118 **Baker**, A. R. H. and **Gregory**, D. (eds), *Explorations in Historical Geography. Interpretative Essays*, 1984. Includes chapters on the relations of historical geography, the *Annales* school and *terrae incognitae* in historical geography.

9.119 **Banks**, J. O., 'Historical sociology and the study of population', *Daedalus*, XCVII, 1968, 397–414.

9.120 **Barnes**, H. E., *The New History and the Social Studies*, New York, 1925.

9.121 **Barthes**, R., 'Historical discourse' in M. Lane (ed.), *An Introduction to Structuralism*, New York, 1970, 145–55.

9.122 **Beidelman**, T. O., 'Lévi-Strauss and history', *J. Interdis. Hist.*, I, 1971, 511–25.

9.123 **Bell**, J. H. and **Sturmer**, J. R. von, 'Claude Lévi-Strauss; social anthropology and history', *Aust. J. Pol. and Hist.*, XVI, 1970, 218–26.

9.124 **Berkhofer**, R. F., *A Behavioral Approach to Historical Analysis*, New York, 1969. Combines sociological and historical perspectives in its analysis of issues in the study of human behaviour, culture and society.

9.125 ——*Beyond the Great Story. History as Text and Discourse*, Cambridge, MA, 1995. Looks at the claims of history as a subject in the light of challenges from literary, multiculturalist and feminist theorising.

9.126 **Bertaux**, D. (ed.), *Biography and Society. The Life History Approach in the Social Sciences*, 1982.

9.127 **Biersack**, Aletta (ed.), *Clio in Oceana. Toward a Historical Anthropology*, Washington, DC, 1991.

9.128 **Bock**, K. E., *The Acceptance of Histories. Toward a Perspective for Social Science*, Berkeley, CA, 1956.

9.129 **Bremen**, Teresa, *History after Lacan*, 1993.

9.130 **Bremmer**, R. H. (ed.), *Essays on History and Literature*, Columbus, OH, 1966. Includes 'American scholarship; a subjective interpretation of nineteenth-century cultural history' and 'History and literature; branches of the same tree'.

9.131 **Brooks**, T., *The New Historicism and other Old-fashioned Topics*, Princeton, NJ, 1991.

9.132 **Brown**, R. H., *Explanation in Social Science*, 1963.

9.133 ——and **Lyman**, S. M. (eds), *Structure, Consciousness and History*, 1978. Exam-

ines aspects of the conflicts between positivism and romanticism, objectivity and subjectivity, and the different kinds of sociological method. There are chapters on 'History and hermeneutics' and on 'The history of *mentalités*'.

9.134 **Bullock**, A., *Is History becoming a Social Science? The Case of Contemporary History*, 1977. An attempt to vindicate political history.

9.135 **Burke**, P., *Sociology and History*, 1980. Bibliography, 106–12.

9.136 ——*History and Social Theory*, 1992.

9.137 **Cadenhead**, I. E. (ed.), *Literature and History*, Tulsa, OK, 1970.

9.138 **Cahnman**, W. J. and **Boskoff**, A. (eds), *Sociology and History. Theory and Research*, New York, 1964. Includes 'Durkheim and history', 'Weber and the methodological controversy in the social sciences' and 'Recent theories of social change'.

9.139 **Caplan**, J., 'Postmodernism, poststructuralism and deconstruction; notes for historians', *Central European Hist.*, XXII, 1989, 260–78.

9.140 **Chaunu**, P., *Histoire science sociale. La durée, l'espace et l'homme à l'époque moderne*, Paris, 1974.

9.141 **Checkland**, S. G., 'The historian as model builder', *Philos. J.*, VI, 1969, 36–49.

9.142 **Clubb**, J., 'History as a social science', *Internat. Soc. Sci. J.*, XXXIII, 1981, 596–610.

9.143 **Cohen**, S., 'Structuralism and the writing of intellectual history', *Hist. and Theory*, XVII, 1978, 175–206.

9.144 **Cohn**, B., *An Anthropologist among the Historians and other Essays*, 1988.

9.145 **Crozier**, D., 'History and anthropology', *Internat. Soc. Sci. J.*, XVII, 1965, 561–70.

9.146 **Damon**, P. (ed.), *Literary Criticism and Historical Understanding*, New York, 1967. Includes 'History and idea in Renaissance criticism' and 'Historical interpretation and the history of criticism'.

9.147 **Darby**, H. C., 'History and geography in England 1928–80; continuity and change', *Trans. I.B.G.*, VIII, 1983, 421–28.

9.148 **Davis**, Natalie Zemon, 'Anthropology and history in the 1980s; the possibilities of the past', *J. Interdis. Hist.*, XII, 1981, 267–75.

9.149 **Dean**, Carolyn J., 'The productive hypothesis; Foucault, gender, and the theory of sexuality', *Hist. and Theory*, XXXIII, 1994, 271–96.

9.150 **Dean**, M., *Critical and Effective Histories. Foucault's Methods and Historical Sociology*, 1994.

9.151 **Deluz-Chiva**, A., 'Anthropology, history and historiography', *Internat. Soc. Sci. J.*, XVII, 1965, 571–81.

9.152 **De Man**, P., 'Literary history and literary modernity', *Daedalus*, 99, 1970, 383–404.

9.153 **Dovring**, F., *History as a Social Science. An Essay on the Nature and Purpose of Historical Study*, The Hague, 1960.

9.154 **Drake**, M. (ed.), *Applied Historical Studies*, 1973. Reprinted articles which illustrate ways in which the methodologies of history and the social sciences could be mutually enriching.

9.155 **Dymond**, D. P., *Archaeology and History. A Plea for Reconciliation*, 1974. Advocates and illustrates the benefits of a co-ordinated approach.

9.156 **Erikson**, K. T., 'Sociology and the historical perspective', *American Sociologist*, V, 1970, 331–8.

9.157 **Ermath**, Elizabeth D., *Sequel to History. Postmodernism and the Crisis of Representational Time*, Princeton, NJ, 1992.

9.158 **Fabian**, J., 'Language, history and anthropology', *Philos. Soc. Sci.*, I, 1971, 19–47.

9.159 **Fisher**, F. M., 'On the analysis of history and the interdependence of the social sciences', *Philos. Sci.*, XXVII, 1960, 147–58.

9.160 **Flenley**, R., 'History and its neighbours today', *Canadian Hist. R.*, XXXIV, 1953, 324–35.

9.161 **Frader**, Laura L., 'Dissent over discourse; labor history, gender, and the linguistic turn', *Hist. and Theory*, XXXIV, 1996, 213–30.

9.162 **Francis**, E. K., 'History and the social sciences; some reflections on the reintegration of social science', *R. Politics*, XIII, 1951, 354–74.

9.163 **Gaunt**, D., *Memoir on History and Anthropology*, Stockholm, 1982. A brief analysis of the distinctive and shared characteristics of the two disciplines.

9.164 **Goldthorpe**, J. H., 'The uses of history in sociology; reflections on some recent tendencies', *Brit. J. Sociol*, XLII, 1991, 211–30 and, XLV, 1994, 55–77.

9.165 **Gottschalk**, L., **Kluckhohn**, C., and **Angell**, R., 'The use of personal documents in history, anthropology, and sociology', *Soc. Sci. Research Council*, LIII, 1945.

9.166 **Green**, R. W. (ed.), *Protestantism and Capitalism. The Weber Thesis and its Critics*, Boston, MA, 1959. A collection of readings.

9.167 **Guelke**, L., 'The relations between geography and history reconsidered', *Hist. and Theory*, XXXVI, 1997, 216–34.

9.168 **Gulliver**, P. H. and **Silverman**, Marilyn (eds), *Approaching the Past*, New York, 1992. Includes N. Rogers, 'The anthropological turn in social history', 325–68.

9.169 **Hall**, J. R., 'Where history and sociology meet; forms of discourse and socio-historical enquiry', *Social Theory*, X, 1992, 164–93.

9.170 **Haskell**, F., *History and its Images. Art and the Interpretation of the Past*, New Haven, CT, 1993.

9.171 **Hawke**, G. R., *Economics for Historians*, 1980.

9.172 **Hawthorn**, G., *Enlightenment and Despair. A History of Sociology*, 1976. Shows clearly the relationship between social thought and social context and the overlap between history and sociology.

9.173 **Higham**, J., 'Intellectual history and its neighbours', *J. Hist. Ideas*, XV, 1954, 339–47.

9.174 **Hobsbawm**, E. J., 'The contribution of history to social science', *Internat. Soc. Sci. J.*, XXXIII, 1981, 624–40.

9.175 **Hodder**, I., *Reading the Past. Current Approaches to Interpretation in Archaeology*, 1986. Considers the relations between history and archaeology and the ways in which they have been affected by Marxism, Structuralism and systems theory.

9.176 **Hofstadter**, R., 'History and sociology in the United States' in S. M. Lipset and R. Hofstadter, (eds), *Sociology and History*, New York, 1968, 3–18.

9.177 **Holborn**, H., *History and the Humanities*, New York, 1972.

9.178 **Holloway**, S. J. F., 'Sociology and history', *Hist.*, XLVIII, 1963, 154–80.

9.179 **Hughes**, H. S., 'The historian and the social scientist' in A. V. Riasanovsky and B. Riznik (ed.), *Generalizations in Historical Writing*, Philadelphia, PA, 1963, 18–59.

9.180 ——*History as an Art and as Science. Twin Vistas on the Past*, New York, 1964. A compact volume that includes discussion of historical narrative and of the links between history, anthropology and psychoanalysis.

9.181 **Jenkins**, K. (ed.), *The Postmodern History Reader*, 1997. Thirty-seven readings – including a lengthy series of debates from journals – with editorial introduction and bibliography (434–8).

9.182 ——*Why History? Ethics and Postmodernity*, 1999. An extended polemic about the position of historical studies after the impact of postmodernism. An introduction discussing 'Living in time but outside history; living in morality but outside ethics' is followed by eight chapters devoted to key figures such as Derrida, Lyotard and Hayden White.

9.183 **Johnson**, B., 'Missionaries, tourists and traders; sociologists in the domain of history', *Studies in Symbolic Interaction*, 1982, 115–50.

9.184 **Jones**, G. S., 'Linguistic approach to history in the 1990s', *Hist. Workshop J.*, XLII, 19–36.

9.185 ——'From historical sociology to theoretical history', *Brit. J. Sociol*, XXVII, 1976, 295–305.

9.186 **Jones**, Greta, 'Science, social science and history; a review article', *Comp. Studs. Soc. and Hist.*, XXIV, 1982, 467–80.

9.187 **Kalberg**, S., *Max Weber's Comparative Historical Sociology*, Chicago, IL, 1994.

9.188 **Kanseiner**, W., 'Hayden White's critique of the writing of history', *Hist. and Theory*, XXXII, 1993, 273–95.

9.189 **Kaufman**, F., *Methodology of the Social Sciences*, Glencoe, IL, 1949.

9.190 **Klein**, K. L., 'In search of narrative mastery; postmodernism and the peoples without history', *Hist. and Theory*, XXXIV, 1995, 275–98.

9.191 **Kilminster**, R., *Praxis and Method. A Sociological Dialogue with Lukács, Gramsci and the early Frankfurt School*, 1979.

9.192 **Konstan**, D., 'The function of narrative in Hayden White's *Metahistory*', *Clio*, XI, 1981, 65–78.

9.193 **Kousser**, J. M., 'The state of social science history in the late 1980s', *Hist. Methods*, XXII, 1989, 13–20.

9.194 **Kroeber**, A. L., *An Anthropologist looks at History*, Berkeley, CA, 1963.

9.195 **Krug**, M. M., *History and the Social Sciences*, Waltham, MA, 1967.

9.196 **Kussmaul**, A., 'Agrarian change in seventeenth-century England; the economic historian as palaeontologist', *J.Ec.H.*, XLV, 1985, 1–30.

9.197 **La Capra**, D., *History and Criticism*, 1985. Advocates the value of historical study in the various modes of modern criticism, such as structuralism, reader-response theory, Marxist and feminist criticism.

9.198 **Landes**, D. S. and **Tilly**, C. (eds), *History as Social Science*, Englewood Cliffs, N. J., 1971.

9.199 **Lee**, C. H., *Social Change and History. An Investigation into the Application of Theory and Quantification in British Economic and Social History*, 1983.

9.200 **Lipset**, S. M. and **Hofstadter**, R. (eds), *Sociology and History*, New York, 1968.

9.201 **McEwen**, W. P., *The Problem of Social Scientific Knowledge*, Totowa, NJ, 1963.

9.202 **McGann**, J. (ed.), *Historical Studies and Literary Criticism*, Madison, WI, 1985. The essays by Marilyn Butler ('Against tradition; the case for a particularised historical method') and Terry Eagleton ('Ideology and scholarship') are particularly useful.

9.203 **Marshall**, G., *In Search of the Spirit of Capitalism. An Essay on Max Weber's Protestant Ethic Thesis*, 1982. A well organised guide to the seemingly unending controversies which have surrounded Weber's work. Excellent bibliography.

9.204 **Means**, R. L., 'Sociology and history; a new look at their relationships', *Am. J. Ec. and Sociol.*, XXI, 1962, 285–98.

9.205 **Megill**, A., 'Foucault, structuralism and the ends of history', *J.M.H.*, LI, 1979, 451–503.

9.206 **Mink**, L. O., 'History and fiction as modes of comprehension', *New Lit. Hist.*, I, 1970, 541–58.

9.207 **Mommsen**, W., 'Max Weber's political sociology and his philosophy of world history', *Internat. Soc. Sci. J.*, XVII, 1965, 23–45.

9.208 **Morazé**, C., 'The application of the social sciences to history', *J. Contemp. Hist.*, III, 1968, 207–16.

9.209 **Morera**, Esteve, *Gramsci's Historicism*, 1990.

9.210 **Moxey**, K., *The Practice of Theory. Poststructuralism, Cultural Politics and Art History*, Ithaca, NY, 1994.

9.211 **Mullings**, Christine, *New Technologies for the Humanities*, 1996.

9.212 **Multhauf**, R. P. and **Stevenson**, L. G. (eds), *Medicine, Science and Culture* Baltimore, MD, 1968.

9.213 **Munslow**, A., *Deconstructing History*, 1997. An examination of the theory and practice of history in the postmodern age. Foucault and Hayden White each get chapters to themselves. Bibliography, 191–6.

9.214 **Natanson**, M., *Literature, Philosophy and the Social Sciences*, The Hague, 1962, esp. part 3 on 'History and the social sciences'.

9.215 **Nathan**, N. M. L., 'History, literature and the classification of knowledge', *Aust. J. Philos.*, XLVIII, 1970, 213–33.

9.216 **Nichols**, R. F., 'History and the Social Science Research Council', *A.H.R.*, L, 1945, 491–9.

9.217 **Noiriel**, G., 'Foucault and history; the lessons of a disillusion', *J.M.H.*, LXVI, 1994, 547–68.

9.218 **O'Brien**, J. and **Roseberry**, W., *Golden Ages, Dark Ages. Imagining the Past in Anthropology and History*, Berkeley, CA, 1991.

9.219 **O'Farrell**, Clare, *Foucault. Historian or Philosopher?*, 1989.

9.220 **Ohnuki-Tierney**, E., *Culture through Time. Anthropological Approaches*, Stanford, CA, 1990.

9.221 **Ostrowski**, D., 'A metahistorical analysis; Hayden White and four narratives of Russian history', *Clio*, XIX, 1990, 215–36.

9.222 **Pitt**, D. C., *Using Historical Sources in Anthropology and Sociology*, New York, 1972. Deals with the main kinds of documentary material available and with methods of reaching, recording and analysing data. There is a case study chapter on social context and economic development in Samoa.

9.223 **Postan**, M. M., *Fact and Relevance. Essays on Historical Method*, 1971. Includes 'History and the social sciences', 'The historical method in social science' and 'Fact and relevance in historical study'.

9.224 **Prescott**, O. (ed.), *History as Literature*, New York, 1970.

9.225 **Rabb**, T. K. and **Rotberg**, R. I. (eds), *The New History. The 1980s and Beyond. Studies in Interdisciplinary History*, 1982. Has sections on political history, family history, economic history, demographic history, anthropology, intellectual history and history of science in the 1980s.

9.226 **Rapp**, F., 'Structural models in historical writing; the determinants of technological development during the industrial revolution', *Hist. and Theory*, XXI, 1982, 327–46.

9.227 **Rashevsky**, N., *Looking at History through Mathematics*, Cambridge, MA, 1968. Applies mathematical models to problems of social formation and development over long periods of time.

9.228 **Raychaudhuri**, T., 'The social sciences and the study of Indian economic history', *Internat. Soc. Sci. J.*, XVII, 1965, 635–43.

9.229 **Raymond**, P., *L'Histoire et les Sciences*, Paris, 1975.

9.230 **Roseberry**, W., *Anthropologies and Histories*, New Brunswick, NJ, 1989.

9.231 **Rosenam**, Pauline M., *Postmodernism and the Social Sciences. Insights, Inroads and Intrusions*, Princeton, NJ, 1992.

9.232 **Rotenstreich**, N., *Between Past and Present*, New Haven, CT, 1958. Analyses the nature of historical time and the relations between historical and sociological explanation.

9.233 **Roth**, G., 'History and sociology in the work of Max Weber', *Brit. J. Sociol.*, XXVII, 1976, 306–16.

9.234 **Roth**, M. S., 'Foucault's "history of the present"', *Hist. and Theory*, XX, 1981, 32–46.

9.235 **Roth**, P. A., 'Hayden White and the aesthetics of historiography', *History* *of the Human Sciences*, V, 1992, 17–35.

9.236 **Rothman**, D. J., 'Sociology and history', *P.P.*, 52, 1971, 126–34.

9.237 **Rudner**, R. S., *Philosophy of Social Science*, Englewood Cliffs, NJ, 1966. Deals with the construction of social theory, with objectivity and with functionalism.

9.238 **Ryan**, A., *The Philosophy of the Social Sciences*, 1970.

9.239 **Samuelson**, P. A., 'Economists and the history of ideas', *Am. Econ. R.*, LII, 1962, 1–18.

9.240 **Saveth**, E. N. (ed.), *American History and the Social Sciences*, New York, 1964. The editor's introduction deals with the conceptualisation of American history. The book is then divided into sections on 'history and the disciplines', 'the concepts', 'quantification and machine processes', and 'beyond social science'.

9.241 **Saunders**, P. M., 'History; pure and applied', *Canadian Hist. R.*, XLIII, 1962, 315–27.

9.242 **Schulzem**, L. and **Wetzels**, W., *Literature and History*, Lanham, MD, 1983. A collection of essays weighted towards Germany.

9.243 **Sherif**, M. and **Carolyn**, E. (eds), *Interdisciplinary Relationships in the Social Sciences*, Chicago, IL, 1969. Includes an essay on 'obstacles to a *rapprochement* between history and sociology'.

9.244 **Small**, M. (ed.), *Public Opinion and Historians. Interdisciplinary Perspectives*, Detroit, MI, 1970.

9.245 **Smith**, D., *The Rise of Historical Sociology*, 1991.

9.246 **Spring**, D., 'History and sociology; a plea for humanity', *Canadian Hist. R.*, XXX, 1949, 211–26.

9.247 **Sprinzack**, E., 'Weber's thesis as an historical explanation', *Hist. and Theory*, XI, 1972, 294–320.

9.248 **Stock**, B., *Listening for the Past. On the Uses of the Past*, Philadelphia, PA, 1990. A genuinely interdisciplinary collection of essays concerned with the Middle Ages and, more generally, with the creation of the past as text.

9.249 **Stone**, L., *The Past and the Present*, 1981, 2nd ed. 1987. Part One consists of three general essays of a methodological kind: 'History and the social sciences in the twentieth century', 'Prosopgraphy' and 'The revival of narrative; reflections on a new old history'.

9.250 **Stretton**, H., *The Political Sciences. General Principles of Selection in Social Science and History*, 1969. Explores the conjunction of knowledge, imagination and persuasion in the work of historians and social scientists.

9.251 **Sturtevant**, W. C., 'Anthropology, history, and ethnohistory', *Ethnohistory*, XIII, 1966, 1–51.

9.252 **Szreter**, R., 'History and the sociological perspective in educational studies', *U. Birm. J.*, XII, 1969, 1–19.

9.253 **Tawney**, R. H., *Social History and Literature*, 1949, rev. ed. 1958.

9.254 **Thomas**, K., 'History and anthropology', *P.P.*, 24, 1963, 3–24.

9.255 **Thomas**, N., *Out of Time. History and Evolution in Anthropological Discourse*, 1989.

9.256 **Thompson**, E. P., 'On history, sociology and historical relevance', *Brit. J. Sociol.*, XXVII, 1976, 387–402.

9.257 **Thrupp**, Sylvia L., 'Comparative studies in society and history; a working alliance among specialists', *Internat. Soc. Sci. J.*, XVII, 1965, 644–54.

9.258 **Tilly**, C., *As Sociology meets History. Studies in Social Discontinuity*, New York, 1981.

9.259 **Todd**, W. L., *History as Applied Science. A Philosophical Study*, Detroit, MI, 1972. Divided into two sections dealing with types of history and with historical methodology.

9.260 **Toews**, J. E., 'Intellectual history after the linguistic turn; the anatomy of meaning and the irreducibility of experience', *A.H.R.*, XCII, 1987, 879–907.

9.261 **Topolski**, J., 'Lévi-Strauss and Marx on history', *Hist. and Theory*, XII, 1973, 192–207.

9.262 **Trevor-Roper**, H. R., 'The past and the present; history and sociology', *P.P.*, 42, 1969, 3–17.

9.263 **Turner**, C. M., 'Sociological approaches to the history of education', *Brit. J. Ed. Studs.*, XVII, 1969, 146–55.

9.264 **Usher**, A. P., 'The significance of modern empiricism for history and economics', *J.Ec.H.*, IX, 1949, 137–55.

9.265 **Vann**, R. T., 'History and demography', *Hist. and Theory*, supplement 9, 1969, 64–78.

9.266 **Veeser**, A. H., *The New Historicism*, New York, 1989.

9.267 **Viet**, J., *Les Méthodes structuralistes dans les sciences sociales*, Paris, 1965.

9.268 ——*Les Sciences de l'homme en France. Tendances et organisation de la recherche*, Paris, 1966.

9.269 **Weeks**, J., 'Foucault for historians', *Hist. Workshop J.*, XIV, 1982, 106–19.

9.270 **White**, H. V., 'Foucault decoded; notes from underground', *Hist. and Theory*, XII, 1973, 23–54.

9.271 **Wilderson**, P., 'Archaeology and the American historian; an interdisciplinary challenge', *Am. Q.*, XXVII, 1975, 115–32.

9.272 **Wilson**, B. R., 'Sociological methods in the study of history', *T.R.H.S.*, 5th ser., XXI, 1971, 101–18.

9.273 **Windschuttle**, K., *The Killing of History*, New York, 1966? An attack on what are perceived as the destructive implications of postmodernism and the erosion of the possibility of truth.

9.274 **Winn**, J. A., 'An old historian looks at the new historicism', *Comp. Studs. Soc. and Hist.*, XXV, 1993, 859–70.

9.275 **Zagorin**, P., 'Historiography and postmodernism; reconsiderations', *Hist. and Theory*, XXIX, 1990, 263–74.

THE *ANNALES* SCHOOL

9.276 **Aymard**, M., 'The *Annales* and French historiography', *J. Europ. Ec. Hist.*, I, 1972, 491–511.

9.277 **Braudel**, F., *On History*, 1980. Includes 'History and the social sciences; the *longue durée*', 'Unity and diversity in the human sciences', 'History and sociology', 'Towards a historical economics', 'On a concept of social history' and 'Demography and the scope of the human sciences'.

9.278 **Burguiere**, A., 'The fate of the history of *mentalités* in the *Annales*', *Comp. Studs. Soc. and Hist.*, XXIV, 1982, 424–37.

9.279 ——'Histoire d'une histoire; la naissance des *Annales*', *Annales*, XXXIV, 1979, 1344–59.

9.280 **Burke**, P. (ed.), *A New Kind of History from the Writings of Lucien Febvre*, 1973. Essays by one of the founders of the *Annales* school on history and psychology, sensibility and on 'a new kind of history'.

9.281 ——*The French Historical Revolution. The Annales School, 1929–89*, 1990.

9.282 ——'Strengths and weaknesses of the history of mentalities', *Hist. European Ideas*, VII, 1986, 439–51.

9.283 **Couthau-Begarie**, H., *Le Phénomène 'nouvelle historie'*, Paris, 1983. Deals with the *Annales* historians Braudel, Chaunu and Le Roy Ladurie.

9.284 **Davies**, R. R., 'Marc Bloch', *Hist.*, LII, 1967, 265–82.

9.285 **Dosse**, F., *New History in France. The Triumph of the Annales*, Urbana, IL, 1994.

9.286 **Fink**, Carole, *Marc Bloch. A Life in History*, 1991. See also Friedman (9.287).

9.287 **Friedman**, Susan W., *Marc Bloch. Sociology and Geography. Encountering Changing Disciplines*, 1996. Examines Bloch's contribution to the changing frontiers of history and adjacent academic disciplines. See also Fink (9.286).

9.288 **Furet**, F., 'Beyond the *Annales*', *J.M.H.*, LV, 1983, 389–410.

9.289 **Harggor**, M., 'Total history: the *Annales* school', *J. Contemp. Hist.*, XIII, 1978, 1–13.

9.290 **Hexter**, J. H., 'Fernand Braudel and the *monde braudellien*', *J.M.H.*, XLIV, 1972, 480–539.

9.291 **Hufton**, Olwen, 'Fernand Braudel', *P.P.*, 112, 1986, 208–13.

9.292 **Hunt**, Lynn, 'French history in the last twenty years: the rise and fall of the *Annales* paradigm', *J. Contemp. Hist.*, XXI, 1986, 209–24.

9.293 **Hutton**, P. H., 'The history of *mentalités*; the new map of cultural history', *Hist. and Theory*, XX, 1981, 237–59.

9.294 **Kinser**, S., 'Annaliste paradigm? The geohistorical structure of Fernand Braudel', *A.H.R.*, LXXXVI, 1981, 63–105.

9.295 **Le Goff**, J. and **Nora**, P. (eds), *Constructing the Past. Essays in Historical Methodology*, 1985. A collection of *Annales*-style essays. The coverage embraces quantitative history, the history of climate, the history of ideology and *mentalité*, demographic history, and the history of books and learning.

9.296 **Le Roy Ladurie**, E., *The Mind and Method of the Historian*, 1981. Case studies exploring a quantitative approach to history. Opens with a general chapter on 'history that stands still'.

9.297 —— *The Territory of the Historian*, 1979. Essays – all methodological – dealing with aspects of the new, outward-reaching history pioneered by the *Annales* historians.

9.298 **Lyon**, B. and Mary, *The Birth of Annales History. The Letters of Lucien Febvre and Marc Bloch to Henri Pirenne*, Brussels, 1991.

9.299 **Olabarri**, I., ' "New" new history: a *longue durée* structure', *Hist. and Theory*, XXXIV, 1995, 1–29.

9.300 **Raphael**, L., 'The present as challenge for the historian. The contemporary world in the *Annales* ESC, 1929–49', *Storia de Storiog.*, XXI, 1992, 25–44.

9.301 **Renouvin**, R., 'Research in modern and contemporary history; present trends in France', *J.M.H.*, XXXVIII, 1966, 1–12.

9.302 **Ricoeur**, P., *The Contribution of French Historiography to the Theory of History*, 1980. Considers Aron, the *Annales* school, Marrou, Veyne and others.

9.303 **Santamaria**, U. and **Bailey**, A., 'A note on Braudel's structure as duration', *Hist and Theory*, XXIII, 1984, 78–83.

9.304 **Sewell**, W. H., 'Marc Bloch and the logic of comparative history', *Hist. and Theory*, VI, 1967, 208–18.

9.305 **Stoianovich**, T., *French Historical Method. The Annales Paradigm*, 1976. Provides both a history of the *Annales* school and an analysis of its underlying

conceptions and flexible uses. There is a foreword by Braudel.

9.306 **Trevor-Roper**, H. R., 'Fernand Braudel, the *Annales* and the Mediterranean', *J.M.H.*, XLIV, 1972, 468–79.

9.307 **Walker**, L. D., 'Historical linguistics and the comparative method of Marc Bloch', *Hist. and Theory*, XIX, 1980, 154–64.

MARXIST HISTORY

9.308 **Adamson**, W. L., *Marx and the Disillusionment of Marxism*, 1985. A non-orthodox defence of Marxist methodology though it suffers from a failure to consider Marxist historiography directly.

9.309 **Anderson**, P., *Arguments within English Marxism*, 1980. A critical appraisal of E. P. Thompson.

9.310 —— *In the Tracks of Historical Materialism*, 1983. Considers some of the paradoxes in the evolution of Marxist thought since the 1970s.

9.311 **Aronowitz**, S., *The Crisis in Historical Materialism. Class, Politics and Culture in Marxist Theory*, New York, 1981. Bibliographical essay.

9.312 **Bernstein**, H. R., 'Marxist historiography and the methodology of research programs', *Hist. and Theory*, XX, 1981, 424–49.

9.313 **Bertrand**, L., *Le Marxisme et l'histoire*, Paris, 1970.

9.314 **Carlin**, Norah, 'Marxism and the English civil war', *International Socialism*, X, 1980, 113–28.

9.315 —— and **Birchall**, I., 'Kinnock's favourite Marxist; Eric Hobsbawm and the working class', *Internat. Socialism*, XXI, 1983, 88–117.

9.316 **Childs**, D., *Marx and the Marxists*, 1973. A wide-ranging study of the individuals and movements influenced by Karl Marx.

9.317 **Cohen**, J. S., 'The achievements of economic history; the Marxist school', *J. Ec. Hist.*, XXXVIII, 1978, 29–57.

9.318 **Cornforth**, M., 'A. L. Morton; portrait of a Marxist historian' in Cornforth (ed.), *Rebels and their Causes. Essays in Honour of A. L. Morton*, 1978, 7–19.

9.319 **Cronin**, J., 'Creating a Marxist historiography; the contribution of Hobsbawm', *Radical Hist. R.*, IX, 1979, 87–109.

9.320 **Dickson**, T., 'Marxism, nationalism and Scottish history', *J. Contemp. Hist.*, XX, 1985, 323–36.

9.321 **Dirlik**, A., *Revolution and History. Origins of Marxist Historiography in China, 1919–37*, Berkeley, CA, 1978. Bibliography, 269–86.

9.322 **Duncan**, C. A. M., 'Under the cloud of *Capital*; history *v*. theory', *Science and Soc.*, XLVII, 1983, 300–22.

9.323 **Dworkin**, D., *Cultural Marxism in Postwar Britain. History of the New Left and the Origins of Cultural Studies*, Durham, NC, 1997.

9.324 **Feenberg**, A., *Lukács, Marx and the Sources of Critical Theory*, 1981. A comparative evaluation of Marx's *Economic and Philosophical Manuscripts* and Lukács's *History and Class Consciousness*.

9.325 **Fine**, R., 'The rule of law and Muggletonian Marxism; the perplexities of Edward Thompson', *J. Law and Soc.*, XXI, 1994, 193–213.

9.326 **Fleischer**, H., *Marxism and History*, 1973. A valuable survey of the implications of Marxism for the theory and practice of history.

9.327 **Genovese**, E. D., 'The politics of class struggle in the history of society; an appreciation of the work of Eric Hobsbawm' in Pat Thane *et al.* (eds), *The Power of the Past. Essays for Eric Hobsbawm*, 1984, 13–36.

9.328 —— and **Fox-Genovese**, Elizabeth, 'The political crisis of social history; a Marxian perspective', *J. Soc. Hist.*, X, 1976, 205–20.

9.329 **Gorman**, R. A., 'Empirical Marxism', *Hist. and Theory*, XX, 1981, 403–23.

9.330 **Harrison**, R., 'Marxism as nineteenth-century critique and twentieth-century ideology', *Hist.*, LXVI, 1981, 208–20.

9.331 **Hill**, C., 'Premature obsequies' in Hill, *England's Turning Point*, 1998, 291–6.

9.332 **Hirst**, P. Q., *Marxism and Historical Writing*, 1984. Critiques of G. A.
Cohen, E. P. Thompson and Perry Anderson.

9.333 **Hobsbawm**, E. J., 'The Historians' Group of the Communist Party' in Cornforth (9.318), 21–48.

9.334 **Howard**, D., *The Marxian Legacy*, 1977. Looks at the heirs and critics of Marx's ideas and the changing stance of twentieth-century Marxism.

9.335 **Iggers**, G. G. (ed.), *Marxist Historiography in Transformation. East German Social History in the 1980s*, New York, 1991. The editor's historiographical introduction sets the scene for the context-based essays which follow.

9.336 **Johnson**, R. *et al.* (eds), *Making Histories. Studies in History Writing and Politics*, 1982. Eight essays by radical historians which include 'Radical liberalism, Fabianism and social history', 'The Communist Party historians, 1946–56' and 'E. P. Thompson and the discipline of historical context'.

9.337 **Kaye**, H. J., *The British Marxist Historians*, 1984. Explores the 'tradition' of Marxist historiography in England and concentrates on Dodd, Hilton, Hill, Hobsbawm and Thompson as its leading exponents.

9.338 —— *The Education of Desire. Marxists and the Writing of History*, 1992. A continuation of (9.337). Chapters on Gramsci and British Marxist historians, Rudé, Kiernan, E. P. Thompson, A. L. Morton, Leo Huberman and John Berger.

9.339 **Kiernan**, V. G., *History, Classes, and Nation States. Selected Writings of Victor Kiernan*, 1988. Essays by a veteran Marxist historian with a contextualising introduction by H. J. Kaye.

9.340 **Kolanowski**, L., *Marxism and Beyond. On Historical Understanding and Individual Responsibility*, 1969. The gauntlet thrown down by a Polish dissident.

9.341 **Leff**, G., *The Tyranny of Concepts. A Critique of Marxism*, 1961, 2nd ed. 1969. Attacks the assumptions and stifling intellectual consequences of Marxism.

9.342 **Lichtheim**, G. (ed.), *George Lukács*, 1970. Includes essays on 'Lukács's views on how history moulds literature' and on 'Lukács's concept of dialectic'.

9.343 **Locke**, R. R., 'What Marxism means to an American historian', *Pacific H.R.*, XLIV, 1975, 147–70.

9.344 **McInness**, N., *The Western Marxists*, 1972. A popular introduction to the work of Sorel, Gramsci, Lukács and others.

9.345 **McLennan**, G., *Marxism and the Methodologies of History*, 1981. A lively and argumentative study organised around three main divisions: philosophy, methodology and historiography. There are case studies of the debates on the French Revolution and on the labour aristocracy in nineteenth-century Britain.

9.346 **Mah**, H., 'Marxism's "truth"; recent interpretations of Marxist theory', *J.M.H.*, LXI, 1989, 110–27.

9.347 **Meszaros**, I. (ed.), *Aspects of History and Class Consciousness*, 1971. Includes essays on class consciousness in history and on the historical setting of Lukács's *History and Class Consciousness*.

9.348 **Neale**, R. S. (ed.), *History and Class. Essential Readings in Theory and Interpretation*, 1983.

9.349 —— *Writing Marxist History. British Society, Economy and Culture since 1700*, 1985. A miscellaneous collection of essays in which Marxist theory and methodology provide the keys.

9.350 **Nield**, K., 'A symptomatic dispute? Notes on the relation between Marxian theory and historical practice in Britain', *Soc. Research*, XLVII, 1980, 479–506.

9.351 —— and **Seed**, J., 'Versions of historiography. Marxism and the methodologies of history; review article', *Econ. and Soc.*, XII, 1983, 276–84.

9.352 **Nolte**, E., 'The relationship between "bourgeois" and "Marxist" historiography', *Hist. and Theory*, XIV, 1975, 57–73.

9.353 **Novack**, G. E., *Understanding History. Marxist Essays*, New York, 1972. Has chapters on 'Major theories of history from the Greeks to Marxism', 'The role of the individual in history making' and 'The uneven development of the world revolutionary process'.

9.354 **O'Malley**, Pat, 'Social bandits, modern capitalism, and the traditional peasantry; a critique of Hobsbawm', *J. Peasant Studs.*, VI, 1978–79, 489–501.

9.355 **Petrovic**, G., *Marx in the Mid-twentieth Century*, New York, 1967.

9.356 **Plekhanov**, G. V., *Fundamental Problems of Marxism*, 1969. Includes chapters on 'The materialist conception of history' and 'The role of the individual in history'.

9.357 **Poster**, M., *Foucault, Marxism and History. Mode of Production versus Mode of Information*, 1994.

9.358 **Rattansi**, A., 'End of an orthodoxy? The critique of sociology's view of Marx on class', *Sociol. R.*, XXXIII, 1985, 641–69.

9.359 **Resnick**, S. and **Wolff**, R., 'A reformulation of Marxian theory of historical analysis', *J.Ec.H.*, XLII, 1982, 53–59.

9.360 **Samuel**, R., 'British Marxist historians, 1880–1980,' I, *New Left R.*, 120, 1980, 21–96.

9.361 **Saville**, J., *Marxism and History*, 1974. Inaugural lecture.

9.362 **Sawer**, Marian, *Marxism and the Question of the Asiatic Mode of Production*, The Hague, 1977.

9.363 **Seigel**, J., 'Consciousness and practice in the history of Marxism', *Comp. Studs. Soc. and Hist.*, XXIV, 1982, 164–77.

9.364 **Thane**, Pat and **Lunbeck**, Liz, 'An interview with Eric Hobsbawm', *Radical Hist. R.*, XIX, 1978–79, 111–31.

9.365 **Willigan**, J. D., 'Marxist methodologies of history', *Hist. Methods*, XVII, 1984, 219–228.

POLITICAL HISTORY

9.366 **Acton**, E., *Rethinking the Russian Revolution*, 1990.

9.367 **Ashley**, M., *Churchill as a Historian*, 1968. Written by Churchill's former research assistant.

9.368 **Azzi**, S. C., 'The historiography of fascist foreign policy', *Hist. J.*, XXXVI, 1993, 187–204.

9.369 **Boyer**, J. W., 'A. J. P. Taylor and the art of modern history, *J.M.H.*, XLIX, 1977, 40–72.

9.370 **Bridge**, C. (ed.), *Manning Clark. Essays on his Place in History*, Carlton, Australia, 1994. The leading Australian nationalist historian of his generation.

9.371 **Brock**, M., *'The Strange Death of Liberal England'*, *Albion*, XVII, 1985, 409–23.

9.372 **Cole**, C. R., '"Hope without illusion"; A. J. P. Taylor's dissent, 1955–61' in C. R. Cole and M. E. Moody (eds), *The Dissenting Tradition. Essays for Leland H. Carlson*, Athens, OH, 1975, 226–61.

9.373 ——'A. J. P. Taylor and the origins of the Second World War' in H. T. Parker (ed.), *Problems in European History*, Durham, NC, 1979, 267–82.

9.374 **Dray**, W. H., 'Concepts and causation in A. J. P. Taylor's account of the origins of the Second World War', *Hist. and Theory*, XVII, 1978, 149–74. See also Williams (9.402).

9.375 **Ellison**, H. J., 'Soviet historians and the Russian Revolution' in L. H. Legters (ed.), *Russia. Essays in History and Literature*, Leiden, 1972.

9.376 **Elton**, G. R., *Political History. Principles and Practice*, 1970. A vigorous defence of the threatened pre-eminence of political history by one of the grand masters of the discipline.

9.377 **Evans**, R. J., *In Hitler's Shadow. West German Historians and the Attempt to Escape from the Nazi Past*, 1989. Bibliographical essay, 186–9.

9.378 **Fagg**, J. E., 'Sir Charles Webster' in Halperin (9.44), 171–99.

9.379 **Galbraith**, V. H., 'Albert Frederick Pollard, 1869–1948', *Proc. Brit. Acad.*, XXXV, 1949, 257–74.

9.380 **Hurstfield**, J., 'John Ernest Neale, 1890–1975', *Proc. Brit. Acad.*, LXIII, 1977, 403–21.

9.381 **Lodge**, Margaret, *Sir Richard Lodge. A Biography*, 1946. Written by his daughter, the biography offers some account of his academic career at the University of Edinburgh.

9.382 **Lodge**, R., 'Thomas Frederick Tout; a retrospect of twin academic careers', *Cornhill Mag.*, LXVIII, 1930, 114–26.

9.383 **Morgan**, K. O., 'Lloyd George and the historians', *Trans. Hon. Soc. Cymmrodorion*, 1971, 65–85.

Sir Lewis Namier

9.384 **Brooke**, J., 'Namier and Namierism', *Hist. and Theory*, III, 1963–64, 331–47. A disciple's analysis.

9.385 **Colley**, Linda, *Namier*, 1989. A short study of Namier's significance, stressing the importance of his own non-British background and his distinctive fusion of political and social history.

9.386 **Gaines**, D. I., 'Namier on eighteenth-century England', *Historian*, XXV, 1962–3, 213–25.

9.387 **Mansfield**, H. C., 'Sir Lewis Namier considered', *J. Brit. Studs.*, II, 1962, 28–55.

9.388 ——'Sir Lewis Namier again considered', *J. Brit. Studs.*, III, 1964, 109–19. A critique of the deficiencies of Namier's eighteenth-century studies.

9.389 **Namier**, Julia, *Lewis Namier. A Biography*, 1971. Written by his wife.

9.390 **O'Gorman**, F., 'Fifty years after Namier; the eighteenth century in British historical writing', *Eighteenth Century. Theory and Interpretation*, XX, 1979, 99–120.

9.391 **Price**, J. M., 'Party, purpose and pattern; Sir Lewis Namier and his critics', *J. Brit. Studs.*, I, 1961, 71–93.

9.392 **Sutherland**, Lucy S., 'Sir Lewis Namier, 1888–1960', *Proc. Brit. Acad.*, XLVIII, 1962, 371–85.

9.393 **Walcott**, R., '"Sir Lewis Namier considered" considered', *J. Brit. Studs.*, III, 1964, 85–108.

9.394 **Watt**, D. C., 'Sir Lewis Namier and contemporary European history', *Camb. Hist. J.*, VII, 1953–54, 579–600.

9.395 **Payne**, S. G., 'Recent historiography on the Spanish Republic and Civil War', *J.M.H.*, LX, 1988, 540–56.

9.396 **Shapiro**, Ann-Louise, 'Fixing history; narratives of World War I in France', *Hist. and Theory*, XXXVI, 21997, 111–30.

9.397 **Simmons**, J., 'Sir Reginald Coupland, 1884–1952', *Proc. Brit. Acad.*, XLV, 1959, 287–95.

9.398 **Smith**, S., 'Writing the history of the

Russian Revolution after the fall of Communism', *Europe and Asia Studs.*, XLVI, 1994, 563–78.

9.399 **Stansky**, P., '*The Strange Death of Liberal England* fifty years after', *Albion*, XVII, 1985, 401–3. See also Brock (9.371) and White (9.401a).

9.400 **Taylor**, M., 'Patriotism, history and the left in twentieth-century Britain', *Hist. J.*, XXXIII, 1990, 971–88.

9.401 **Walston**, J., 'History and memory of the Italian concentration camps', *Hist. J.*, XL, 1997, 169–83.

9.401a **White**, C. M., '*The Strange Death of Liberal England* in its time', *Albion*, XVII, 1985, 425–47. See also Brock (9.371) and Stansky (9.399).

9.402 **Williams**, H. R., 'A. J. P. Taylor' in H. A. Schmitt (ed.), *Historians of Modern Europe*, Baton Rouge, LA, 1971, 78–94.

9.403 **Zapponi**, N., 'Fascism in Italian historiography, 1986–93; a fading national identity', *J. Contemp. Hist.*, XXIX, 1994, 547–68.

ECONOMIC HISTORY

9.404 **Abu-Lughod**, Janet, 'The world-system perspective in the construction of economic history', *Hist. and Theory*, XXXIV, 1995, 86–98.

9.405 **Andreano**, R. (ed.), *The New Economic History. Recent Papers on Methodology*, New York, 1970. Collects together a variety of contributions originating mainly in the United States, the home of the 'new economic history'.

9.406 **Barker**, T. C., 'The beginnings of the Economic History Society', *Ec.H.R.*, 2nd ser., XXX, 1977, 1–19.

9.407 **Basman**, R. L., 'The role of the economic historian in the productive testing of proffered "economic" laws', *Ex. Entrep. Hist.*, 2nd ser., II, 1965, 159–86.

9.408 **Bergier**, J. F., 'New tendencies in economic history', *Diogenes*, LVIII, 1967, 104–22.

9.409 **But**, J., 'Achievement and prospect; transport history in the 1970s and 1980s', *J. Trans. Hist.*, 3rd ser., II, 1981, 1–24.

9.410 **Cairncross**, A. K., 'In praise of economic history', *Ec.H.R.*, 2nd ser., XLII, 1989, 173–85.

9.411 **Cameron**, R., 'Economic history; pure and applied', *J. Ec. Hist.*, XXXVI, 1976, 3–27.

9.412 **Chambers**, J. D., 'The Tawney tradition', *Ec.H.R.*, 2nd ser., XXIV, 1971, 355–69.

9.413 **Chandler**, J. D. and **Galambos**, L. (eds), *Economic History. Retrospect and Prospect. Papers presented to the Thirtieth Annual Meeting of the Economic History Association*, 1971. (A special issue of *J. Ec. Hist.*, XXXI, 1971). Contains papers by W. N. Parker, A. Fishlow, R. W. Fogel, J. Swanson, J. Williamson, P. Temin and D. C. North.

9.414 **Clark**, G. N., 'Sir John Harold Clapham, 1873–1946', *Proc. Brit. Acad.*, XXXII, 1946, 339–52.

9.415 **Coats**, A. W., 'The historical context of the "new economic history"', *J. Europ. Ec. H.*, IX, 1980, 185–207.

9.416 **Cole**, A. H. 'Economic history in the United States; formative years of a discipline', *J. Ec. Hist.*, XXVIII, 1968, 556–89.

9.417 **Cole**, W. A., *Economic History as a Social Science*, 1967. Inaugural lecture.

9.418 **Coleman**, D. C., *History and the Economic Past. An Account of the Rise and and Decline of Economic History in Britain*, 1987. Considers the nineteenth-century emergence of economic history as a separate subject in its own right distinct from both orthodox history and orthodox political economy and proceeds to analyse the twentieth-century vicissitudes of post-war boom and later decline.

9.419 —— 'History, economic history, and the numbers game', *Hist. J.*, XXXVIII, 1995, 635–46.

9.420 —— *What has Happened to Economic History?*, 1972. Inaugural lecture.

9.421 —— 'What is economic history?', *Hist. Today*, XXXV, 1985, 35–43.

9.422 **Conrad**, A. H., 'Economic theory, statistical inference and economic history', *J. Ec. Hist.*, XVII, 1957, 524–44.

9.423 ——and **Meyer**, J. R., *Studies in Econometric History*, 1965. A collection of essays, all heavily methodological, some generalised discussions, others specific (on *ante bellum* south slavery and on nineteenth-century US income growth).

9.424 **Crafts**, N. F. R., 'Cliometrics, 1971–86: a survey', *J. Applied Econometrics*, II, 1987, 171–92.

9.425 **Cruise**, H. F., 'The economic historian and the growth debate', *Aust. Ec.H.R.* XV, 1975, 83–106.

9.426 **Davis**, L. E., '"And it will never be literature". The new economic history; a critique', *Ex. Entrep. Hist.*, 2nd ser., VI, 1969, 75–92.

9.427 ——*et al.*, 'Aspects of quantitative research in economic history', *J. Ec. Hist.*, XX, 1960, 539–47.

9.428 **Desai**, M., 'Some issues in econometric history', *Ec.H.R.*, 2nd ser., XXI, 1968, 1–16.

9.429 **Federn**, K., *The Materialist Conception of History. A Critical Analysis*, 1939. A refutation of Marx's dialectical materialism.

9.430 **Field**, A. J. (ed.), *The Future of Economic History*, Boston, MA, 1987.

9.431 **Fishlow**, A. and **Fogel**, R. W., 'Quantitative economic history; an interim evaluation of past trends and present tendencies', *J. Ec. Hist.*, XXXI, 1971, 15–42.

9.432 **Fogel**, R. W., 'The "new economic history"; its findings and methods', *Ec.H.R.*, 2nd ser., XIX, 1966, 642–57.

9.433 ——and **Elton**, G. R., *Which Road to the Past? Two Views of History*, 1983. An unlikely combination of defences of the new scientific history and of the traditional values.

9.434 **Gallman**, R. E. (ed.), *Recent Developments in the Study of Business and Economic History*, Greenwich, CT, 1977.

9.435 **Gould**, J. D., 'Hypothetical history', *Ec.H.R.*, 2nd ser., XXII, 1969, 195–207.

9.436 **Gras**, N. S. B., 'The rise and development of economic history', *Ec.H.R.*, I, 1927–28, 12–34.

9.437 **Habakkuk**, H. J., 'Economic history and economic theory', *Daedalus*, C, 1971, 305–22.

9.438 **Harte**, N. B. (ed.), *The Study of Economic History*, 1971. An invaluable collection of inaugural lectures – by Ashton, Tawney, Clapham, Postan, Pollard and others – with a useful introduction.

9.439 ——'Trends in publications on the economic and social history of Great Britain and Ireland', *Ec.H.R.*, 2nd ser., XXX, 1977, 20–41.

9.440 **Hicks**, J., *A Theory of Economic Hisotry*, 1969. A general discussion of the market economy. The book opens with a section on theory and history.

9.441 **Hill**, C., 'Historians and the rise of British capitalism', *Science and Soc.*, XIV, 1950, 307–21.

9.442 **Hughes**, J. R. T., 'Fact and theory in economic history', *Ex. Entrep. Hist.*, III, 1966, 75–100.

9.443 ——*et al.*, 'The future of the new economic history in Britain', in D. McCloskey (ed.), *Essays on a Mature Economy. Britain after 1840*, Princeton, NJ, 1971, 401–39.

9.444 **Hunt**, E. H., 'The new economic history', *Hist.*, LIII, 1968, 3–18.

9.445 **James**, J. A., 'The use of general equilibrium analysis in economic history', *Ex. Entrep. Hist.*, 2nd ser., XXI, 1984, 231–53.

9.446 **Kidd**, A. J., 'Historians or polemicists? How the Webbs wrote their *History of the Poor Laws*', *Ec.H.R.*, 2nd ser., XL, 1989, 400–17.

9.447 **Lee**, C. H., *The Quantitative Approach to Economic History*, 1977. Includes a discussion of the new economic history. Bibliography.

9.448 **Lindert**, P. H., 'Remodelling British economic history; a review article', *J. Ec. Hist.*, XLIII, 1983, 986–92.

9.449 **McClelland**, P. D., *Causal Explanation and Model Building in History, Economics and the New Economic History*, 1975. Examines the philosophical assumptions.

9.450 **McCloskey**, D. N., 'The problem of audience in historical economics; rhetorical thoughts on a text by Robert Fogel', *Hist. and Theory*, XXIV, 1985, 1–22.

9.451 **Marriner**, Sheila, 'Francis Edward Hyde' in Sheila Marriner (ed.), *Business and Businessmen. Studies in Business*,

Economics and Accounting History, 1978, 1–10. A study of one of the leading figures in the development of business history in England.

9.452 **Morineau**, M., 'Old, new but true economic history', *Rev. Hist. Moderne et Contemp.*, XXXII, 1985, 451–80.

9.453 **Murphy**, G. G. S., 'The "new" history', *Ex. Entrep. Hist.*, 2nd ser., II, 1965, 132–46.

9.454 **North**, D. C., 'Structure and performance; the task of economic history', *J. Ec. Lit.*, XVI, 1978, 963–78.

9.455 **Parker**, W. N. (ed.), *Economic History and the Modern Economist*, 1986.

9.456 **Ransom**, R. L. *et al.* (eds), *Explorations in the New Economic History. Essays in Honour of Douglass C. North*, 1982.

9.457 **Redlich**, F., 'New and traditional approaches to economic history and their interdependence', *J. Ec. Hist.*, XXV, 1965, 480–95.

9.458 —— 'Potentialities and pitfalls in economic history', *Ex. Entrep. Hist.*, 2nd ser., VI, 1969, 93–108.

9.459 **Rostow**, W. W., 'The interrelation of theory and economic history', *J. Ec. Hist.*, XVII, 1957, 509–23.

9.460 **Sayers**, R. S., 'Thomas Southcliffe Ashton, 1889–1968', *Proc. Brit. Acad.*, LVI, 1970, 263–81.

9.461 **Schweitzer**, A., 'Economic systems and economic history', *J. Ec. Hist.*, XXV, 1965, 660–79.

9.462 **Supple**, B. E., 'Economic history and economic growth', *J. Ec. Hist.*, XX, 1960, 548–68.

9.463 —— 'Economic history in the 1980s; old problems and new directions', *J. Interdis. Hist.*, XII, 1981–82, 199–215.

9.464 **Swanson**, J. and **Williamson**, J., 'Explanations and issues; a prospectus for quantitative economic history', *J. Ec. Hist.*, XXXI, 1971, 43–57.

9.465 **Tawney**, R. H., 'J. L. Hammond, 1872–1949', *Proc. Brit. Acad.*, XLVI, 1960, 267–94. See also Winkler (9.481).

R. H. Tawney

9.466 **Ashton**, T. S., 'Richard Henry Tawney, 1880–1962', *Proc. Brit. Acad.*, XLVIII, 1962, 461–82.

9.467 **Court**, W. H. B., 'R. H. Tawney' in Court, *Scarcity and Choice in History*, 1970, 127–40.

9.468 **Martin**, D. A., 'R. H. Tawney's normative economic history of capitalism', *R. Soc. Ec.*, XLIII, 1985, 85–102.

9.469 **Ormrod**, D. O., 'R. H. Tawney and the origins of English capitalism', *Hist. Workshop J.*, XVIII, 1984, 138–59.

9.470 **Stone**, L., 'R. H. Tawney', *P.P.*, 21, 1962, 73–77.

9.471 **Terrill**, R., *R. H. Tawney and his Times. Socialism as Fellowship*, 1973. A biographical study of Tawney which analyses the centrality of his socialism in his activity as a historian and assesses his continuing importance. Bibliography of Tawney's writings, 287–313.

9.472 **Winter**, J. M., 'R. H. Tawney's early political thought', *P.P.*, 47, 1970, 71–96.

9.473 —— (ed.), *History and Society. Essays by R. H. Tawney*, 1978. The substantial introduction (1–40) places Tawney in perspective.

9.474 **Temin**, P., 'The future of "new economic history"', *J. Interdis. Hist.*, XII, 1981–82, 179–97.

9.475 —— (ed.), *New Economic History*, 1973. Fourteen reprinted essays dating from 1958 to 1971. The six sections include 'The measurement of economic growth', 'Railroads and their social savings' and 'The economic effects of slavery'. Fogel and Engerman are among the historians represented in the collection. Bibliography, 429–34.

9.476 **Topolski**, J., 'The model method in economic history', *J. Europ. Ec. H.*, I, 1972, 713–26.

9.477 **Tuma**, E. H., *Economic History and the Social Sciences*, Berkeley, CA, 1971. Offers a consideration of themes for the study of economic history and an evaluative framework. The relations and tensions between traditional and 'new' economic history are considered. Bibliography, 293–310.

9.478 **Tunzelmann**, G. N. von, 'The new economic history; an econometric appraisal', *Ex. Entrep. Hist.*, 2nd ser., V, 1968, 175–200.

9.479 **Walters**, W. R., 'Methods of explanation in economic history', *Econ, and Hist.*, XV, 1972, 3–18.

THE STUDY OF HISTORY

9.480 **Williamson**, S. H., 'The history of cliometrics' in J. Mokyr (ed.), *The Vital One. Essays in Honor of Jonathan R. T. Hughes*, Greenwich, CT, 1991.

9.481 **Winkler**, H. R., 'J. L. Hammond' in Schmitt (9.92), 95–119.

and his sources', *Am. Archivist*, XXX, 1967, 19–31.

9.495 **Williamson**, H. F., 'Business history and economic history', *J. Ec. Hist.*, XXVI, 1966, 407–17.

9.496 **Wilson**, J. F., *British Business History, 1720–1994*, 1995.

BUSINESS HISTORY

9.482 **Church**, R. A., 'Business history in England', *J. Europ. Ec.H.*, V, 1976, 209–28.

9.483 **Cole**, A. H., 'Aggregrative business history', *Bus. H.R.*, XXXIX, 1965, 287–300.

9.484 —— 'What is business history?', *Bus. H.R.*, XXXVI, 1962, 98–109.

9.485 **Duboff**, R. B. and **Herman**, E. S., 'Alfred Chandler's new business history; a review', *Politics and Society*, X, 1980, 87–110.

9.486 **Fohlen**, C., 'The present state of business history in France', *Bus. H.R.*, XLI, 1967, 94–103.

9.487 **Hannah**, L., 'New issues in British business history', *Bus. H.R.*, LVII, 1983, 165–74.

9.488 **John**, R. R., 'Elaborations, revisions, dissents; Alfred D. Chandler's *The Visible Hand* after twenty years'. *Bus. H.R.*, LXXI, 1997, 151–200.

9.489 **Johnson**, A. M., 'Where does business history go from here?', *Bus. H.R.*, XXXVI, 1962, 11–21.

9.490 **Klompmaker**, H., 'Business history in Holland', *Bus. H.R.*, XXXVIII, 1964, 501–10.

9.491 **Redlich**, F., 'Approaches to business history', *Bus. H.R.*, XXXVI, 1962, 61–9. Followed by comments from other practitioners (69–86).

9.492 **Tucker**, K. A. (ed.), *Business History*, 1977. A collection of twenty reprinted essays which includes a section on aims and methods in business history.

9.493 **Walton**, C. C., 'Business history; some major challenges', *Bus. H.R.*, XXXVI, 1962, 21–34.

9.494 **White**, G. T., 'The business historian

LOCAL HISTORY

9.497 **Benas**, B. B. B., 'A centenary retrospect of the Historic Society of Lancashire and Cheshire', *Trans. Hist. Soc. Lancs. and Ches.*, supplement to vol. C. 1948.

9.498 **Beresford**, M. W., *History on the Ground. Six Studies in Maps and Landscapes*, 1957, 2nd ed. 1971.

9.499 *Blake Report. Report of the Committee to Review Local History*, 1979.

9.500 **Bruce-Mitford**, R., *The Society of Antiquaries of London*, 1951. A brief history to celebrate the Society's centenary. See also Evans (9.505).

9.501 **Buchanan-Dunlop**, W. R., 'A hundred years, 1854–1954; the story of the Worcestershire Archaeological Society', *Trans. Worcs. Arch. Soc.*, n.s., XXX, 1953, 2–15.

9.502 **Clark**, E. K., *The History of a Hundred Years of the Life of the Leeds Philosophical and Literary Society*, 1924.

9.503 **Cunnington**, B. H., 'The origin and history of the Wiltshire Archaeological and Natural History Society', *Wilts. Arch. and Nat. Hist. Soc.*, XLV, 1930, 1–9.

9.504 **Currie**, C. R. J. and **Lewis**, C. P. (eds), *English County Histories. A Guide*, 1994. An invaluable county-by-county survey of the published histories.

9.505 **Evans**, Joan, *A History of the Society of Antiquaries*, 1956. A survey extending from the Society's Renaissance origins to the 1950s. Bibliography.

9.506 **Everitt**, A. M., *New Avenues in English Local History*, 1970. Inaugural lecture.

9.507 **Finberg**, H. P. R., *Local History in the University*, 1964. Inaugural lecture.

9.508 **Fite**, G. C., 'The rising place of local and state history in American historiography', *Locus*, I, 1988, 1–10.

9.509 **Goss**, C. W. F., 'An account of the London and Middlesex Archaeological Society, 1855–1930', *Trans. London and Middx Arch. Soc.*, n.s., VI, 1933, 405–35.

9.510 **Goubert**, P., 'Local history' in F. Gilbert and S. R. Graubard (eds), *Historical Studies Today*, New York, 1972, 300–14.

9.511 **Greenslade**, M. W., 'The Staffordshire historians', *N. Staffs. J. Field Studs.*, XVI, 1976, 23–41.

9.512 **Hey**, D. (ed.), *The Oxford Companion to Local and Family History*, 1996. Partly historiographical in its coverage. As well as Hey the contributors include Charles Phythian-Adams and Joan Thirsk.

9.513 **Hoskins**, W. G., *English Local History. The Past and the Future*, 1965. Inaugural lecture.

9.514 ——*Local History in England*, 1959, 3rd ed. 1984. A standard work which includes a historiographical introduction.

9.515 **Iredale**, D., *Local History Research and Writing*, 1974.

9.516 **Jackson**, J. W., 'The genesis and progress of the Lancashire and Cheshire Antiquarian Society', *Trans. Lancs. and Ches. Antiquarian Soc.*, XLIX, 1933, 104–12.

9.517 **Kammen**, Carol, *On Doing Local History. Reflections on what Local Historians do, why, and what it means*, Walnut Creek, CA, 1986, 2nd ed., 1995. A primer – aimed at the American market – offering practical advice on the pursuit of local history.

9.518 ——(ed.), *The Pursuit of Local History. Readings on Theory and Practice*, Walnut Creek, CA, 1996. An edited collection of general statements (mainly American) about the concept and practice of local history. They range in date from 1832 to 1982. Bibliography.

9.519 **Kammen**, M., *Challenges and Opportunities in Writing State and Local History*, Indianapolis, IN, 1983.

9.520 **Kyvig**, D. E. and **Marty**, M. A., *Nearby History. Exploring the Past around You*, Nashville, TN, 1982.

9.521 **Lowther**, A. W. G., 'A brief history of the society', *Trans. Surrey Arch. Soc.*, LIII, 1954, 1–34.

9.522 **Marshall**, J. D., *The Tyranny of the Discrete. A Discussion of the Problems of Local History in England*, 1997. A vigorous plea for the final abandonment of the antiquarian outlook in local history and a stern warning against the dangers of the 'heritage' approach to the subject.

9.523 **Meinig**, D. W., 'Reading the landscape; an appreciation of W. G. Hoskins and J. B. Jackson' in Meinig (ed.), *The Interpretation of Ordinary Landscapes*, New York, 1979, 195–244. A comparison of two influential landscape historians.

9.524 **Michell**, A. R., 'Regional history or local history? The contribution of *Midland History* and *Northern History* to the writing of English economic history at a local level', *J. Europ. Ec.H.*, II, 1973, 481–93. Looks at the ways in which these journals have raised the standards of local history.

9.525 **Moir**, Esther A. L., 'The historians of Gloucestershire' in H. P. R. Finberg (ed.), *Gloucestershire Studies*, 1957, 267–90.

9.526 **Phythian-Adams**, C., *Local History and Folklore. A New Framework*, 1975.

9.527 ——*Rethinking English Local History*, 1987.

9.528 **Pollard**, J. G., 'The history of the Society', *Camb. Antiq. Soc. Proc.*, LXVIII, 1978, 105–16.

9.529 **Pugh**, R. B., 'The Victoria County History', *Brit. Studs. Monitor*, II, 1971, 15–23.

9.530 **Ralph**, Elizabeth, 'The Society, 1876–1976' in P. McGrath and J. Cannon (eds), *Essays in Bristol and Gloucestershire History*, 1976, 1–49.

9.531 **Rath**, F. L. *et al.*, *Local History, National Heritage*, Nashville, TN, 1991. Essays on the work of the American Association for State and Local History to mark its fiftieth anniversary.

9.532 **Rogers**, A. (ed.), *Approaches to Local History*, 1977.

9.533 **Royle**, E. (ed.), *Issues of Regional Identity in Honour of John Marshall*, 1998. Includes a general introduction by the editor on the historical representation of regions (1–13), and affectionate assessment of John Marshall (226–39) and a bibliography of his writings (240–7).

9.534 **Rubinstein**, S., *Historians of London*, 1968. Discusses the various topographers and historians of London from Stow onwards. Bibliography, 219–26.

9.535 **Simmons**, J. (ed.), *English County Historians*, 1978. Eight chapters on individual historians with an introduction.

9.536 ——*Parish and Empire. Studies and Sketches*, 1952. Includes Simmons's inaugural lecture on 'Local, national and imperial history' and an essay on parish history.

9.537 **Skipp**, V., 'Local history; a new definition', *Loc. Hist.*, XIV, 1981, 325–31.

9.538 **Smith**, T. H., 'The renascence of local history', *Historian*, XXXV, 1972, 1–17.

9.539 **Tait**, J., 'The Chetham Society; a retrospect', *Miscellany* VII, Chetham Society, n.s., 100, 1939, 1–26.

9.540 **Tiller**, Kate, *English Local History. An Introduction*, 1992. Chiefly a practical handbook; the opening chapter is historiographical. Bibliography, 237–40.

9.41 **Williams**, G., 'Local and national history in Wales', *Welsh H.R.*, V, 1970–71, 45–66.

CHURCH HISTORY AND THE HISTORY OF RELIGION

9.542 **Bezzant**, J. S., 'The Very Reverend Norman Sykes, 1897–1961', *Proc. Brit. Acad.*, XLVII, 1961, 417–28.

9.543 **Bowden**, H. W., 'Ends and means in Church history', *Church Hist.*, LIV, 1985, 74–8.

9.544 **Brooke**, C. N. L., 'David Knowles, 1896–1974', *Proc. Brit. Acad.*, LXI, 1975, 439–77. See also Morey (9.550).

9.545 ——'Problems of the Church historian', *Studs. in Church Hist.*, I, 1964, 1–19.

9.546 ——'What is religious history?', *Hist. Today*, XXXV, 1985, 43–52.

9.547 **Ellis**, J. T., 'The ecclesiastical historian in the service of Clio', *Church Hist.*, XXXVIII, 1969, 106–20.

9.548 **Frend**, W. H. C., 'Ecclesiastical history; its growth and relevance', *Philos. J.*, VIII, 1970, 38–51.

9.549 **Mallard**, W., 'Method and perspective in Church history; a reconsideration', *J. Am. Acad. of Religion*, XXXVI, 1968, 345–65.

9.550 **Morey**, A., *David Knowles. A Memoir*, 1979. A biography of the Benedictine monk turned regius professor at Cambridge.

9.551 **Morrissey**, T. E., 'A. G. Dickens and the men of the sixteenth century', *A.H.R.*, LXXVII, 1972, 453–62.

9.552 **Trinterud**, L. J., 'William Haller, historian of Puritanism', *J. Brit. Studs.*, V, 1966, 33–55.

URBAN HISTORY

9.553 **Blumen**, S. M., 'City limits: two decades of urban history in the *Journal of Urban History*', *J. Urban Hist.*, XXI, 1994, 7–30

9.554 **Callow**, A. B. (ed.), *American Urban History. An interpretative reader with commentaries*, New York, 1969. Includes an essay on the dangers as well as the advantages of an urban approach to history.

9.555 **Corfield**, Penelope, 'Urban history and the computer', *Soc. Hist.*, VIII, 1983, 95–6.

9.556 **Daly**, Mary E., 'Irish urban history: a survey', *Urb. Hist. Year.*, 1986, 61–72.

9.557 **Davison**, G., 'Australian urban history: a progress report', *Urb. Hist. Year.*, 1979, 100–9.

9.558 **Dyos**, H. J. (ed.), *The Study of Urban History*, 1968. The proceedings of a conference held in 1966. The general chapters include 'Agenda for urban historians', 'Problems in the quantitative study of urban history' and 'Toward a definition of urban history'.

9.559 ——Urbanity and Suburbanity, 1973. Inaugural lecture. On Dyos see Fraser (9.561), Mandlebaum (9.569) and Thompson (9.576).

9.560 **Engeli**, C. and **Matzerath**, H. (eds), *Modern Urban History Research in Europe*, USA *and Japan. A. Handbook*, New York, 1989.

9.561 **Fraser**, D. and **Sutcliffe**, A. (eds), *The Pursuit of Urban History*, 1983. Twenty-three chapters – international in their range – concerned with the present state of urban history. Chapters 17–23 deal with the concepts and methods of urban history and suggest possible lines of development in the future.

9.562 **Goldman**, E. F., *Historiography and Urbanization*, Baltimore, MD, 1941.

9.563 **Hamer**, D. A. and **Kelly**, M., 'Urban history in Australasia', *Urb. Hist. Year.*, 1984, 61–80.

9.564 **Hammerstrom**, Ingrid, 'Urban history in Scandinavia', *Urb. Hist. Year.*, 1978, 46–55.

9.565 **Handlin**, O. and **Burchard**, J. (eds), *The Historian and the City*, Cambridge, MA., 1963. Opens with a valuable essay by Handlin on 'The modern city as a field of historical study' (1–26).

9.566 **Hoover**, D. W., 'The diverging paths in American urban history', *Am. Q.*, XX, 1968, 296–317.

9.567 **Kubinyi**, A., 'L'historiographie hongroise moderne des villes', *Acta Hist. Acad. Sci. Hungaricae*, VIII, 1961, 175–89.

9.568 **Lampard**, E. E., 'American historians and the study of urbanization', *A. H. R.*, LXVII, 1961, 49–61.

9.569 **Mandlebaum**, S. J., 'H. J. Dyos and urban history', *Ec.H.R.*, 2nd ser., XXXVIII, 1985, 437–47. See also Thompson (9.576).

9.570 **Miller**, Z. L. *et al.*, 'Urban history in North America', *Urb. Hist. Year.*, 1977, 6–29.

9.571 **Reulecke**, J. and **Huck**, G., 'Urban history research in Germany: its development and present condition', *Urb. Hist. Year.*, 1981, 39–54.

9.572 **Roche**, D., 'Urban history in France', *Urb. Hist. Year.*, 1980, 12–22.

9.573 **Rodger**, R., *European Urban History. Prospect and Retrospect*, 1993.

9.574 ——*Research in Urban History*, 1994.

9.575 **Spodek**, H., 'Studying the history of urbanisation in India', *Jnl. Urb. Hist.*, VI, 1980, 251–96.

9.576 **Thompson**, F. M. L., 'Dyos and the urban past', *London J.*, IX, 1983, 67–70.

SOCIAL HISTORY

9.577 **Akerman**, S., 'An evaluation of the family reconstitution technique', *Scand. Ec.H.R.*, XXV, 1977, 160–70.

9.578 **Burke**, P. and **Porter**, R. (eds), *The Social History of Language*, 1987. A pathfinding collection of essays which open up this vital dimension of social history. Bibliographical essay, 210–13.

9.579 **Chartier**, R., *Cultural History. Between Practices and Representations*, 1988. A stimulating study which looks at the different approaches to the history of cultural forms taken by the *Annales* school, Foucault, Darnton, Ginzburg and others. Four case studies follow, drawn from French history.

9.580 **Cobban**, A., *The Social Interpretation of the French Revolution*, 1964. The first three chapters are of a general, methodological nature and deal with the present state of history as a discipline, with its relations with sociology, and with the problem of social history.

9.581 **Corfield**, Penelope J., *Language, History and Class*, 1991. A collection of twelve essays, wide-ranging in geography and period, with a searching historiographical introduction by the editor. Bibliography, 298–303.

9.582 **Cox**, J. and **Stromquist**, S. (eds), *Contesting the Master Narrative. Essays in Social History*, Iowa City, IA, 1998. A volume of essays that emphasises the subversiveness of social history as a means of breaking out of the top-down narratives that have dominated historical interpretation. Gender perspectives and non-European contexts figure prominently.

9.583 **Davis**, Natalie Z., 'The shapes of social history', *Storia de Storiog*, XVII, 1990, 28–38.

9.584 **Eley**, G., 'Playing it safe, or How is social history represented? The new *Cambridge Social History of Britain*', *Hist. Workshop J.*, XXXV, 1993, 206–220.

9.585 —— and **Nield**, K., 'Why does social history ignore politics?', *Soc. Hist.*, V, 1980, 249–71.

9.585a **Evans**, R. J. H., 'Social history in the postmodern age', *Storia de Storiog.*, XVIII, 1990, 36–42.

9.585b **Furedi**, F., *Mythical Past, Elusive Future. History and Society in an Anxious Age*, 1992.

9.586 **Gross**, D. L., 'The "new history" and beyond: the view from the 1970s', *Soc. Sci. J.*, XV, 1978, 23–38.

9.587 **Hareven**, Tamara K., 'The history of the family and the complexity of social change', *A.H.R.*, XCVI, 1991, 95–124.

9.588 —— and **Plakans**, A. (eds), *Family History at the Crossroads. A Journal of Family History Reader*, Princeton, NJ, 1987. The contributors include David Herlihy, Peter Laslett and Charles Tilly.

9.589 **Henretta**, J. A., 'Social history as lived and written', *A.H.R.*, LXXXIV, 1979, 1293–322.

9.590 **Henry**, L., 'Historical demography', *Daedalus*, XCVII, 1968, 385–96.

9.591 **Hexter**, J. H., 'A new framework for social history', in Hexter, *Reappraisals in History*, 1961, 14–25.

9.592 **Hobsbawm**, E. J., 'From social history to the history of society' in M. W. Flinn and T. C. Smout (eds), *Essays in Social History*, 1974, 1–22.

9.593 **Hochstadt**, S., 'Social history and politics: a materialist view', *Soc. Hist*, VII, 1982, 75–83.

9.594 **Houston**, R. and **Smith**, R., 'A new approach to family history?', *Hist. Workshop J.*, XIV, 1982, 120–31.

9.595 **Innes**, Joanna and **Styles**, J., 'The crime wave: recent writing on crime and criminal justice in eighteenth-century England', *J. Brit. Studs.*, XXV, 1986, 380–435.

9.596 **Johnson**, R., 'Culture and the historian' in J. Clarke *et al.* (eds), *Working Class Culture. Studies in History and Theory*, 1979, 41–71.

9.597 **Jones**, G. S., 'From historical sociology to theoretic history', *Brit. J. Soc.*, XXVII, 1976, 295–305.

9.598 **Judt**, T., 'A clown in regal purple: social history and the historians', *Hist. Workshop J.*, VII, 1979, 66–94.

9.599 **Knapp**, P., 'Can social theory escape from history? A view of history in social science', *Hist. and Theory*, XXII, 1984, 34–52.

9.600 **Kocka**, J., 'Theory and social history', *Social Research*, XLVII, 1980, 426–57.

9.601 **Landes**, D. S., 'The treatment of population in historical textbooks', *Daedalus*, XCVII, 1968, 363–84.

9.602 **Laslett**, P., 'The wrong way through the telescope', *Brit. J. Sociol.*, XXVII, 1976, 319–42.

9.603 **Levine**, L. W. (ed.), *The Unpredictable Past. Explorations in American Cultural History*, New York, 1993. Concentrates on issues in Afro-American and popular culture.

9.604 **Lloyd**, C., *Explanation in Social History*, 1986. The nature, relationships and explanatory procedures of social history are considered. 45 pp. bibliography.

9.605 —— 'The methodologies of social history: a critical survey and defense of structuralism', *Hist. and Theory*, XXX, 1991, 188–219.

9.606 **McClymer**, J. F., 'The historian and the poverty line', *Hist. Methods*, XVIII, 1985, 105–10.

9.607 **Mayfield**, D. and **Thorne**, Susan, 'Social History and its discontents: Gareth Stedman Jones and the politics of language', *Soc. Hist.*, XVII, 1992, 165–88.

9.608 **Miller**, F. M., 'Social history and archival practice', *Am. Archivist*, XLIV, 1981, 113–24.

9.609 **Newton**, Judith, ' "Family fortunes", "new history" and "new historicism" ', *Radical Hist. R.*, 1989, 5–22.

9.610 **Noonan**, J. T., 'Intellectual and demographic history', *Daedalus*, XCVII, 1968, 463–85.

9.611 **Nugent**, W., *Structures of American Social History*, Bloomington, IN, 1981.

9.612 **Palmer**, B., *Descent into Discourse. The Reification of Language and the Writing of Social History*, Philadelphia, PA, 1990.

9.613 **Pavar**, C. N., 'Restoring cultural history: beyond Gombrich', *Clio*, XX, 1991, 157–67.

9.614 **Perkin**, H. J., *The Structured Crowd. Essays in English Social History*, 1981. A reprint collection of the author's essays which includes 'What is social history?', 'Middle class intellectuals and the history of the working class' and 'Social history in Britain'.

9.615 **Prost**, A., 'What has happened to French social history?', *Hist. J.*, XXXV, 1992, 671–80.

9.616 **Redmond**, G., 'Sport history in academe: reflections on a half-century of peculiar progress', *Brit. J. Sport Hist.*, I, 1984, 24–40.

9.617 **Samuel**, R. *et al.*, 'What is social history?', *Hist. Today*, XXXV, 1985, 34–8.

9.618 **Schofield**, R. S., 'Historical demography: some possibilities and some limitations', *T.R.H.S.*, 5th ser., XXI, 1971, 119–32.

9.619 **Stearns**, P. N., 'Modernization and social history: some suggestions and a muted cheer', *J. Soc. Hist.*, XIV, 1980, 189–211.

9.620 **Stinchcombe**, A. L., *Theoretical Methods in Social History*, New York, 1978. Considers – *inter alia*, – the work of de Tocqueville and Smelser.

9.621 **Stone**, L., 'Family history in the 1980s: past achievements and future trends', *J. Interdis. Hist.*, XII, 1981, 51–87.

9.622 **Suny**, R. G., 'Revision and retreat in the historiography of 1917: social history and its critics', *Russ. Rev.*, LIII, 1994, 165–82. See also *ibid.*, LIV, 1995, 260–4.

9.623 **Thompson**, F. M. L., 'The British approach to social history', *Storia de Storiog.*, X, 1986, 162–9.

9.624 **Tilly**, L. A. and **Cohen**, M., 'Does the family have a history? A review of theory and practice in family history', *Soc. Sci. Hist.*, VI, 1982, 131–80.

9.625 **Toll**, W., 'The "new social history" and recent Jewish historical writing', *Am. Jewish Hist.*, LXIX, 1980, 325–41.

9.626 **Torsendahl**, R., 'Social history at the end of the 1980s', *Storia de Storiog.*, XVIII, 1990, 29–35.

9.627 **Wachter**, K. W. and **Hammer**, E. A., 'The genesis of experimental history' in L. Bonfield *et al.* (eds), *The World we have Gained. The History of Population and Social Structure*, 1986, 388–406. Looks at the pioneering work in computer simulation techniques in demographic studies by Peter Laslett and others.

9.628 **Walker**, D. D., *Clio's Cowboys. Studies in the Historiography of the Cattle Trade*, Lincoln, NE, 1981.

9.629 **Watt**, D. C., *What about the People? Abstraction and Reality in History and the Social Sciences*, 1983. Lecture.

9.630 **Wilson**, A., 'The infancy of the history of childhood: an appraisal of Philippe Ariès', *Hist. and Theory*, XIX, 1981, 132–53.

9.631 ——*Rethinking Social History English Society 1570–1920 and its Interpretation*, 1993. Seeks to explain what is seen as a current malaise of social history in which the expectations of the 1960s and 1970s are still largely unfulfilled. The editor offers two essays – 'A critical portrait of social history' and 'Foundations of an integrated historiography'. Also included are essays by Keith Wrightson ('The enclosure of English social history') and Patrick Curry ('Towards a post-Marxist social history: Thompson, Clark and beyond').

9.632 **Woods**, R. L., 'Individuals in the rioting crowd: a new approach', *J. Interdis. Hist.*, XIV, 1983, 1–24.

9.633 **Wrigley**, E. A., 'The prospects for population history', *J. Interdis. Hist.*, XII, 1981-82, 207–20.

9.634 **Zeldin**, T., 'Personal history and the history of the emotions', *J. Soc. Hist.*, XV, 1982, 439–47.

9.635 **Zunz**, O. (ed.), *Reliving the Past. The Worlds of Social History*, Chapel Hill, NC, 1985.

'HISTORY FROM BELOW'

9.636 **Berlantstein**, L. R. (ed.), *Rethinking Labor History. Essays on Discourse and Class Analysis*, Urbana, IL, 1993.

9.637 **Briggs**, A., 'Trade union history and labour history', *Bus. Hist.*, VIII, 1966, 39–47.

9.638 ——*et al.*, 'What is the history of popular culture?', *Hist. Today*, XXXV, 1985, 39–45.

9.639 **Burke**, P., 'From pioneers to settlers: recent studies in the history of popular culture', *Comp. Studs. Soc. and Hist.*, XXV, 1983, 181–87.

9.640 ——Popular culture reconsidered', *Storia de Storiog.*, XVII, 1990, 41–50.

9.641 **Clarke**, J. *et al.* (eds), *Working Class Culture. Studies in History and Theory*, 1979. Challenges Marxist–Leninist notions of labour history and warns against the dangers of the new 'socialist romantics' such as E. P. Thompson.

9.642 **Edmunds**, R. D., 'Native Americans, new voices. American Indian history, 1895–1995', *A.H.R.*, C, 1995, 717–40.

9.643 **Floud**, R., 'Quantitative history and people's history', *Hist. Workshop J.*, XVII, 1984, 113–24.

9.644 **Harrison**, R., 'The last ten years in British labour historiography', *Canadian Hist. Ass. Papers*, LVIII, 1980, 212–27.

9.645 **Hobsbawm**, E. J., 'Labour history and ideology', *J. Soc. Hist.*, VII, 1974, 371–81.

9.646 **Krantz**, F. (ed.), *History from Below. Studies in Popular Protest and Popular Ideology in Honour of George Rudé*, Montreal, 1985. Includes a general essay by E. J. Hobsbawm on the problems of writing history from below.

9.647 **McNulty**, P. J., 'Labour problems and labour economics: the roots of an academic discipline', *Labor Hist.*, IX, 1968, 239–61.

9.648 **Samuel**, R. (ed.), *People's History and Socialist Theory*, 1981. After substantial, forty-page 'editorial prefaces' on people's history and on history and theory the book moves into its forty-nine chapters. They include studies of 'People's history or total history', 'Worker historians in the 1920s', 'The new oral history in France', 'Feminism and labour history', 'Women's history in the USA', 'The discovery of popular culture' and 'The Webbs as historians of trade unionism'.

9.649 **Selbourne**, D. and **Samuel**, R., 'On the methods of History Workshop', *Hist Workshop J.*, IX, 1980, 150–76.

9.650 **Van der Linden**, M. (ed.), 'The end of labor history', special supplement, *Internat. R. Soc. Hist.*, XXXVIII, 1993.

9.651 **Vicinus**, Martha, 'The study of Victorian popular culture', *Vict. Studs.* XVIII, 1975, 473–83.

9.652 **Winters**, S. B., 'Trends in labour historiography in Czechoslavakia', *Labor Hist.*, X, 1969, 602–28.

9.653 **Zeitlin**, J., 'From labour history to the history of industrial relations', *Ec.H.R.*, 2nd ser., XL, 1987, 159–84.

GENDER STUDIES

9.654 **Alexander**, Sally, 'Women, class and sexual differences in the 1830s and 1840s: some reflections on the writing of a feminist history', *Hist. Workshop J.*, XVII, 1984, 125–49.

9.655 ——'Feminist history and psychoanalysis', *Hist. Workshop J.*, XXXII, 1991, 128–33.

9.656 ——*Becoming a Woman and other Essays in Nineteenth and Twentieth Century Feminist History*, New York, 1995.

9.657 **Allan**, J., 'Evidence and silence: feminism and the limits of history' in C. and E. Cross (eds), *Feminist Challenges*, 1986, 173–89.

9.658 **Angerman**, A. *et al.* (eds), *Current Issues in Women's History*, 1987. Conference papers, some of them expressly historiographical.

9.659 **Anthias**, F. and **Davis**, Y., 'Contextualising feminism – gender, ethnic and class divisions', *Feminist R.*, XV, 1983, 62–75.

9.660 **Armitage**, S., 'Making the personal political: women's history and oral history', *Oral H.R.*, XVII, 1989, 154–64.

9.661 **Banner**, Lois W., 'On writing women's history', *J. Interdis. Hist.*, II, 1971, 347–58.

9.662 **Beard**, Mary R., *Woman as Force in History. A Study in Traditions and*

Realities, 1946. Considers male–female relations in the light of wartime and immediately post-war experience. Brings historical evidence into play in her discussion of subjection and equality. See the appreciation by C. N. Degler, *Daedalus*, CIII, 1974, 67–73.

9.663 **Beddoe**, Deirdrie, *Discovering Women's History. A Practical Manual*, 1983. Looks at the reasons for studying women's history and offers constructive guidance on the means to pursue it.

9.664 —— 'Towards a Welsh women's history', *Llafur*, III, 1981, 32–38.

9.665 **Bell**, Susan G. (ed.), *Women. From the Greeks to the French Revolution*, Belmont, CA, 1973.

9.666 **Bennett**, Judith, 'Feminism and history', *Gender and Hist.*, I, 1989, 251–72.

9.667 **Berg**, Maxine, 'The first women economic historians', *Ec.H.R.*, 2nd ser., XLV, 1992, 308–29.

9.668 **Bock**, M., 'Women's history and gender history: aspects of an international debate', *Gender and Hist.*, I, 1989, 7–30.

9.669 **Boulding**, Elise, *The Underside of History. A View of Women through Time*, Boulder, CO, 1976.

9.670 **Branca**, Patricia, *Women in Europe since 1750*, 1978. Has an introduction justifying women's history and an epilogue which looks beyond it. Bibliography, 221–7.

9.671 **Bridenthal**, Renate and **Koonz**, Claudia (eds), *Becoming Visible. Women in European History*, Boston, MA, 1977. The twenty chapters follow a chronological sequence and deal with women's position in society from the ancient world to the twentieth century. There is a general introduction by the two editors.

9.672 **Bullough**, V. L. and Bonnie, *The Subordinate Sex. A History of Attitudes toward Women*, Urbana, IL, 1973. Highly generalised both geographically and chronologically. Bibliographical essay, 355–66.

9.673 **Burton**, A., ' "History is now": feminist theory and the production of historical feminisms', *Women's H.R.*, I, 1992, 25–38.

9.674 **Carroll**, Bernice A., *Liberating Women's*

History. Theoretical and Critical Essays, Urbana, IL, 1975. Twenty-three essays with an editorial introduction. They are arranged in sections on historiography, ideology, sex and history, class, sex and social change. The final section looks 'toward a future human past'.

9.675 **Colls**, R., *Feminism and Women's History*, 1988.

9.676 **Crawford**, Patricia *et al.* (eds), *Exploring Women's Past*, Carlton, Australia, 1983. There are five main chapters dealing with the position of women in medieval, early modern and Victorian England and in nineteenth-century Australia. There are a general introduction and reading list, 207–210.

9.677 **Daniels**, K., 'Feminism and social history', *Australian Feminist Studs*, I, 1985, 27–40.

9.678 **Davidoff**, Leonora, *Life is Duty, Praise and Prayer*. Some *Contributions of the New Women's History*, 1981. Lecture. Bibliography.

9.679 —— ' "Adam spoke first and named the orders of the world": masculine and feminine domains in history and sociology' in H. Carr and L. Mamieson (eds), *The Politics of Every Day. Continuity and Change in Work, Labour, and the Family*, 1990, 229–55.

9.680 **Davin**, Anna, 'Feminism and labour history' in R. Samuel (ed.), *People's History, Socialist Theory*, 1981, 176–81.

9.681 **Davis**, Natalie Z., ' "Women's history" in transition: the European case', *Feminist Studs.*, III, 1976, 83–103.

9.682 —— 'Women and the world of the *Annales*', *Hist. Workshop J.*, XXXIII, 1992, 121–37.

9.683 —— and Scott, Joan (eds), *Women's History as Women's Education*, Northampton, MA, 1985.

9.684 **Degler**, C. N., *Is there a History of Women?*, 1975. Inaugural lecture. Presents a case for women's history and draws chiefly on American illustrations.

9.685 **D'Emilio**, J., 'Not a simple matter: Gay history and gay historians', *J.A.H.*, LXXVI, 1989, 435–42.

9.686 **Diner**, Helen, *Mothers and Amazons. The First Feminine History of Culture*, 1932. Anthropological perspectives.

9.687 **Duberman**, M. B. *et al.* (eds), *Hidden from History. Reclaiming the Gay and*

Lesbian Past, 1991. A wide-ranging collection.

9.688 **Fox-Genovese**, Elizabeth, 'Placing women's history in history', *New Left R.*, CXXXIII, 1982, 5–29.

9.689 —— 'Socialist-feminist American women's history, *J. Women's Hist.*, I, 1990, 181–210.

9.690 **Geiger**, S., 'What's so feminist about doing women's oral history?', *J. Women's Hist.*, II, 1990, 169–82.

9.691 **Gluck**, Sherna B. and **Patai**, Daphne (eds), *Women's Words. The Feminist Practice of Oral History*, 1991.

9.692 **Goggin**, Jacqueline, 'Challenging sexual discrimination in the historical profession: women historians and the American Historical Association, 1890–1940', *A.H.R.*, XCVII, 1992, 769–802.

9.693 **Hall**, Catherine, *White, Male and Middle Class. Explanations in Feminism and History*, 1992.

9.694 **Harrison**, B. and **McMillan**, J., 'Some feminist betrayals of women's history', *H.J*, 26, 1983, 375–89.

9.695 **Hartman**, Mary S. and **Banner**, Lois (eds), *Clio's Consciousness Raised. New Perspectives on the History of Women*, New York, 1976. A general collection which extends geographically from England and France to America and chronologically from the Middle Ages to the twentieth century. The miscellaneous subject matter embraces puberty, religion, librarianship, prostitution and the social consequences of the washing machine.

9.696 **Helly**, Dorothy O. and **Rekerby**, Susan M. (eds), *Gendered Domains. Rethinking Public and Private in Women's History*, Ithaca, NY, 1992.

9.697 **Hilden**, P., 'Women's history: the second wave', *Hist. J.*, XXV, 1982, 501–12.

9.698 **Hoff**, Joan, 'Gender as a postmodern category of paralysis', *Women's Hist. R.*, 3, 1994, 149–68.

9.699 **Hufton**, Olwen, 'Women in history: early modern period', *P.P.*, 101, 1983, 125–40. Bibliographical essay.

9.700 —— *et al.*, 'What is women's history?', *Hist. Today*, XXXV, 1985, 38–48.

9.701 **Hunt**, Nancy R., 'Placing African women's history and locating gender', Soc. Hist., 14, 1989, 353–79.

9.702 **Johnson-Odim**, Cheryl and **Strobel**, Margaret (eds), *Expanding the Boundaries of Women's History. Essays on Women in the Third World*, Bloomington, IN, 1992. Though chiefly consisting of content-based essays some of the contributions are expressly historiographical.

9.703 **Kanner**, Barbara (ed.), *The Women of England from Anglo-Saxon Times to the Present. Interpretative Bibliographical Essays*, Hamden, CT, 1979.

9.704 **Kelly**, Joan, *Women. History and Theory* Chicago, IL, 1985. Includes general essays on 'The social relation of the sexes: methodological implications of women's history', The doubled vision of feminist theory' and 'Family and society' as well as two which deal more specifically with women in the Renaissance.

9.705 **Kerber**, Linda K., 'Separate spheres, female worlds, women's place: the rhetoric of women's history', *J.A.H.*, 75, 1988, 9–39.

9.706 **Kleinberg**, S. J. (ed.), *Retrieving Women's History*, New York, 1988.

9.707 **Lerner**, Gerda, *The Majority finds its Past. Placing Women in History*, 1979. A collection combining case studies from American history and general essays. The latter include 'New approaches to the study of women in American history', 'Placing women in history: definitions and challenges' and 'The challenge of women's history'.

9.708 **Lerner**, Gerda, 'A view from the women's side', *J.A.H.*, 76, 1989, 446–56.

9.709 **Lewis**, Jane (ed.), *Labour and Love. Women's Experience of Home and Family, 1850–1940*, 1986. Includes a general introduction on the issues and methods involved in the reconstruction of women's history.

9.710 **Liddington**, Jill, 'Rediscovering suffrage history', *Hist. Workshop J.*, IV, 1977, 192–202.

9.711 **MacCurtain**, Margaret and **O'Corrain**, Donncha (eds), *Women in Irish Society. The Historical Dimension*, Dublin, 1979. Ten brief essays, originally broadcast talks.

9.712 **McMillan**, J. F., 'Writing women's history', *Hist. Today*, XXXI, 1981, 58–59.

9.713 **Newman**, Louise, 'Critical theory and the history of women: what's at stake in deconstructing women's history', *J. Women's Hist.*, III, 1991, 58–68.

9.714 **Newton**, Judith *et al.* (eds), *Sex and Class in Women's History. Essays from Feminist Studies*, 1983. The editors' introduction and the final chapter on 'The doubled vision of feminist theory' address the genre of women's history'.

9.715 **Oakley**, Ann, *Sex, Gender and Society*, 1972. A wide survey which is not principally historical. Bibliography, 213–22.

9.716 —— *Woman's Work. The Housewife Past and Present*, New York, 1976.

9.717 **Offen**, Karen, **Pierson**, Ruth R., and **Rendall**, Jane (eds), *Writing Women's History. International Perspectives*, Bloomington, IN, 1991. Twenty-six essays. Though divided into two general sections all but two offer national surveys of the state of the art in women's history in the countries in question.

9.718 **Pollock**, G., *Vision and Difference. Feminity, Feminism and Histories of Art*, 1988.

9.719 **Prior**, Mary (ed.), *Women in English Society, 1500–1800*, 1985. Contains a long historiographical introduction by Joan Thirsk on women's history and women historians in England.

9.720 **Ray**, Bharati (ed.), *From the Seams of History. Essays on Indian Women*, Delhi, 1995.

9.721 **Riley**, Denise, *Am I that Name? Feminism and the Category of 'Women' in History*, Minneapolis, MN, 1988.

9.722 **Roberts**, Helen (ed.), *Doing Feminist Research*, 1981.

9.723 **Rowbotham**, Sheila, *Hidden from History. Rediscovering Women in History from the Seventeenth Century to the Present*, 1973. Feminist perspectives. Useful bibliography.

9.724 **Sarah**, E., 'Towards a reassessment of feminist history', *Women's Studs. Internat. Forum*, V, 1982, 519–24.

9.725 **Scott**, Joan W., 'Women in history: the modern period', *P.P.*, 101, 1983, 141–57.

9.726 —— *'Experience' in Feminists' Theorising the Political*, New York, 1992.

9.727 —— (ed.), *Feminism and History*, 1996.

9.728 —— *Gender and the Politics of History*, New York, 1988.

9.729 **Shapiro**, Anne-Louise (ed.), *Feminists Revision History*, New Brunswick, NJ, 1994. A wide-ranging collection of twelve essays extending from ancient Greece to the present day. All, in different ways, blend feminist theory with historical practice.

9.730 **Smith**, Bonnie, 'The contribution of women to modern historiography in Great Britain, France and the USA, 1750–1940', *A.H.R.*, LXXXIX, 1984, 709–32.

9.731 —— *The Gender of History. Men, Women and Historical Practice*, Cambridge, MA, 1998. Challenges the notion of absolute male dominance in past historiography.

9.732 **Smith**, Judith E., 'Family history and feminist history', *Feminist Studs.*, XVII, 1991, 349–64.

9.733 **Smith-Rosenberg**, Carroll, 'The new woman and the new history', *Feminist Studs.*, III, 1975, 185–98.

9.734 **Spender**, Dale (ed.), *Men's Studies Modified. The Impact of Feminism on the Academic Disciplines*, 1981.

9.735 **Strobel**, Margaret, *Gender, Sex and the Empire*, Washington, DC, 1994.

9.736 **Thirsk**, Joan, 'The history women' in Mary O'Dowd and Sabine Wichert (eds), *Chattel, Servant or Citizen Women's Status in Church, State and Society. Historical Studies* XIX, 1995, 1–11.

9.737 **Tilly**, L. A., 'Gender, women's history and social history', *Soc. Sci. Hist.*, XIII, 1989, 439–62.

9.738 —— 'Women's history and family history: fruitful collaboration or missed connections?', *J. Family Hist.*, XII, 1987, 303–15.

9.739 **Vickery**, Amanda, 'Golden Age to separate spheres? A review of the categories and chronology of English women's history', *Hist. J.*, XXVI, 1993, 383–414.

9.740 **Walkowitz**, Judith, 'Patrolling the borders: feminist historiography and the new historicism', *Radical H.R.*, XLIII, 1989, 23–44.

9.741 **Zinsser**, Judith P., *History and Feminism. A Glass Half Full*, New York, 1993.

BLACK HISTORY

9.742 **Blassingame**, J. W., 'Black studies: an intellectual crisis', *Am. Scholar*, XXXVIII, 1969, 548–61.

9.743 **De Graaf**, L. B., 'Recognition, racism and reflections on the writing of Western black history', *Pacific H.R.*, XLIV, 1975, 22–51.

9.744 **Fogel**, R. and **Engerman**, S. L., *Time on the Cross*, 2 vols, New York, 1974. The most famous attempt to apply the principles and methods of the 'new economic history' to the study of American slavery.

9.745 **Genovese**, E. D., 'Influence of the Black Power movement on historical scholarship: reflections of a white historian', *Daedalus*, XCIX, 1970, 473–94.

9.746 **Goldman**, M. S., 'Black arrival in American history: a historiographical look at the sixties', *Soc, Studs.*, LXII, 1971, 209–19.

9.747 **Hagan**, W. T., 'On writing the history of the American Indian', *J. Interdis. Hist.*, II, 1971, 149–54. Interesting for comparative purposes.

9.748 **Hine**, Darlene C. (ed.), *The State of Afro-American History. Past, Present and Future*, Baton Rouge, LA, 1986. A study of the necessity and politics of negro history.

9.749 **Holt**, T., 'On the cross: the role of quantitative methods in the reconstruction of the Afro-American experience', *J. Negro Hist.*, LXI, 1976, 158–72.

9.750 **Hoover**, D. W. (ed.), *Understanding Negro History*, Chicago, IL, 1986. A collection of reprinted essays. They are divided into sections on 'The uses of negro history', 'Problems in writing negro history' and 'Major trends in negro history'.

9.751 **Meier**, A. and **Rudwick**, E., *Black History and the Historical Profession, 1915–80*, Champaign, IL, 1986.

9.752 **Newby**, I. A., 'Historians and negroes', *J. Negro Hist.*, LIV, 1969, 32–47.

9.753 **Starobin**, R., 'The negro: a central theme in American history', *J. Contemp. Hist.*, III, 1968, 37–53.

9.754 **Thorpe**, E. E., *Black Historians. A Critique*, New York, 1969.

9.755 **Wylie**, K. C., 'The uses and misuses of ethnohistory', *J. Interdis. Hist.*, III, 1973, 707–20.

ORAL HISTORY

9.756 **Cutler**, W., 'Oral history – its nature and uses for educational history', *Hist. Educ. Q.*, XI, 1971, 184–94.

9.757 **Dunaway**, D. K. and **Baum**, Willa K. (eds), *Oral History. An Interdisciplinary Anthology*, Nashville, TN, 1984, 2nd ed., 1996.

9.758 **Evans**, G. E., *Spoken History*, 1987. Reflections and case studies by a pioneer of oral history, dealing *inter alia* with the necessary sensitivities of interview techniques and with the importance of language to the historian.

9.759 **Frisch**, M., *A Shared Authority. Essays on the Craft and Meaning of Oral and Public History*, Albany, NY, 1990.

9.760 **Henige**, D., *Oral Historiography*, 1982. A useful, if uneven, appraisal of the value of oral history and its methods.

9.761 **Howells**, K. and **Jones**, M., 'Oral history and contemporary history', *Oral Hist.*, XI, 1983, 15–20.

9.762 **Humphries**, S., *The Handbook of Oral History*, 1984.

9.763 **Mullins**, S. and **Stockdale**, D., *Talking Shop. An Oral History of Retailing in the Harborough Area during the Twentieth Century*, 1994.

9.764 **Portelli**, A., 'The peculiarities of oral history', *Hist. Workshop J.*, XII, 1981, 96–107.

9.765 **Seldon**, A. and **Pappworth**, Joanna, *By Word of Mouth. 'Elite' Oral History*, 1983. A four-part study concerned with the role of oral history, its methodology and evaluation, case studies of the implementation of the genre, and oral archives. The endnotes provide a useful fund of bibiographical information.

9.766 **Stave**, B. M., *The Making of Urban History. Historiography through Oral History*, Beverly Hills, CA, 1977.

9.767 **Thompson**, P., 'Oral history and the historian', *Hist. Today*, XXXIII, 1983, 24–8.

9.768 —— *The Voice of the Past. Oral History*, 1978, 2nd ed. 1988. Strong advocacy of the value of oral history with guidelines for its successful practice.

9.769 **Tonkin**, Elizabeth, *Narrating our Pasts. The Social Construction of Oral History*, 1992. Anthropological perspectives.

9.770 **Vansina**, J., *Oral Tradition as History*, 1985. An updated and substantially revised edition of *Oral History*, first published in 1981.

PSYCHOHISTORY

9.771 **Albin**, M. (ed.), *New Directions in Psychohistory. The Adelphi Papers in Honor of Erik H. Erikson*, Lexington, MA, 1980.

9.772 **Barzun**, J., *Clio and the Doctors. Psycho History, Quanto History and History*, Chicago, IL 1974. A sceptical account of the new trends and the assumptions on which they rest.

9.773 **Bronson**, F. A., *The Unconscious in History*, New York, 1959.

9.774 **Capps**, D. *et al.* (eds), *Encounter with Erikson. Historical Interpretation and Religious Biography*, Missoula, MT, 1977.

9.775 **Cocks**, G. and **Crosby**, T. (eds), *Psychohistory. Readings in the Method of Psychology, Psychoanalysis and History*, New Haven, CT, 1987. Eighteen reprinted essays arranged in three sections: 'Psychology, psychoanalysis, and history', 'The psychology of the individual in history', 'The psychology of the group in history'.

9.776 **Crews**, F., 'The Freudian way of knowledge', *New Criterion*, II: 10, 1984, 7–25.

9.777 **Crunden**, R. M., 'Freud, Erikson and the historian; a bibliographical survey', *Canadian Rev. American Studs.*, IV, 1973, 48–64.

9.778 **Dilthey**, W., *Descriptive Psychology and Historical Understanding*, The Hague, 1977. English translations from originals in German (dating from 1894 and 1910) of pioneering explorations of the dividing line between humane studies and the natural sciences.

9.779 **Eisser**, K. R., 'Freud and the psychoanalysis of history', *J. American Psychoanalytic Ass.*, XI, 1963, 675–703.

9.780 **Erikson**, E., *The Young Man Luther*, New York, 1958. A provocative, much debated psychoanalytical study of Luther and the Reformation. See Johnson (9.785).

9.781 **Freeman**, R., *Repentance and Revolt. A Psychological Approach to History*, Rutherford, NJ, 1970.

9.782 **Friedlander**, S., *History and Psychoanalysis. An Inquiry into the Possibilities and Limits of Psychohistory*, New York, 1978.

9.783 **Gay**, P., *Freud for Historians*, 1985. A sequel in some ways to the same author's earlier *Style in History* (1975). Looks at the nature of Freudian psychology and its implications for the historian's analysis of human nature, reason and the relations between the individual and society. Bibliography, 213–39.

9.784 —— 'Sigmund Freud; a German and his discontents' in Gay, *Freud, Jews and other Germans. Masters and Victims in Modernist Culture*, 1978, 29–92.

9.785 **Johnson**, R. A. (ed.), *Psychohistory and Religion. The Case of Young Man Luther*, Philadelphia, PA, 1977. Seven responses – from historians, psychoanalysts and theologians – to Erikson's study. (See 9.780.)

9.786 **Lifton**, R. J. and **Olsen**, E., *Explorations in Psychohistory*, New York, 1974.

9.787 **Loewenberg**, P., *Decoding the Past. The Psychohistorical Approach*, Berkeley, CA, 1985.

9.788 **Mandle**, W. F., 'Psychohistory and history', *N.Z. J. Hist.*, II, 1968, 1–17.

9.789 **Manuel**, F. E., 'The use and abuse of psychology in history', *Daedalus*, C., 1971, 187–213.

9.790 **Mazlish**, B., 'Group psychology and problems of contemporary History', *J. Contemp. Hist.*, III, 1968, 163–77.

9.791 —— 'What is psychohistory?', *T.R.H.S.*, 5th ser., XXI, 1971, 79–99.

9.792 —— (ed.), *Psychoanalysis and History*, Englewood Cliffs, NJ, 1963. A collection of essays which explore the links and disharmonies between the two disciplines.

9.793 **Pomper**, P., 'Problems of a naturalistic psychohistory', *Hist. and Theory*, XII, 1973, 367–88.

9.794 **Puitenbeek**, H. M. (ed.), *Psychoanalysis and Social Science*, New York, 1962.

9.795 **Saussure**, R. de, 'Psychology and history' in G. Roheim (ed.), *Psychoanalysis and the Social Sciences*, II, 1950, 7–64.

9.796 **Smith**, J. H. and **Morris**, H. (eds), *Telling Facts. History and Narration in Psychoanalysis*, Baltimore, MD, 1992. A wide-ranging collection which embraces art and fiction as historical evidence.

9.797 **Stannard**, D. E., *Shrinking History. On Freud and the Failure of Psychohistory*, 1980.

9.798 **Strout**, C., 'Ego psychology and the historian', *Hist. and Theory*, XII, 1968, 281–97.

9.799 **Toews**, J. E., 'Historicizing psychoanalysis; Freud in his time and for our time', *J.M.H.*, LXIII, 1991, 504–45.

9.800 **Wallace**, E. R., *Historiography and Causation in Psychoanalysis. An Essay in Psychoanalytic and Historical Epistemology*, 1985.

9.801 **Weinstein**, F., 'Psychohistory and the crisis of the social sciences', *Hist. and Theory*, XXXIV, 1995, 299–319.

9.802 —— and **Platt**, G. M., 'The coming crisis in psychohistory', J.M.H., XLVII, 1975, 202–28.

9.803 —— 'History and theory; the question of psychoanalysis', *J. Interdis. Hist.*, II, 1972, 419–34.

9.804 ——*Psychoanalytic Sociology. An Essay on the Interpretation of Historical Data and the Phenomenon of Collective Behaviour*, Baltimore, MD, 1973.

9.805 **Wohlman**, B. B. (ed.), *The Psychoanalytic Interpretation of History*, New York, 1971.

HISTORIANS AND FILM

9.806 **Abrash**, Barbara and **Walkowitz**, D. J., 'Sub/versions of history; a meditation on film and historical narrative', *Hist. Workshop J.*, XXXVIII, 1994, 203–14.

9.807 **Barsom**, R. M., *Nonfiction Films and Critical History*, 1974.

9.808 **Buscombe**, E., 'America on screen? Hollywood feature film as social and political evidence' in M. J. Clark (ed.), *Politics and the Media*, 1979.

9.809 **Carnes**, M. C. (ed.), *Past Imperfect. History according to the Movies*, New York, 1995. Reviews a wide variety of films, chronologically arranged according to their subject matter, and their depictions of history.

9.810 **Godmilow**, Jill and **Shapiro**, Anne-Louise, 'How real is the reality in documentary film?', *Hist. and Theory*, XXIV, 1997, 80–101.

9.811 **Grenville**, J. A. S., *Film as History. The Nature of Film Evidence*, 1971.

9.812 **Smith**, P., *The Historian and Film*, 1976.

9.813 **Sorlin**, P., *The Film as History. Restaging the Past*, 1980. Taking examples drawn from the French Revolution, the American Civil War, the Italian *Risorgimento*, the Russian Revolution, the coming of war in 1939 and the Italian Resistance in World War II, the author examines the film-makers' depictions of the events and issues.

INDIVIDUAL BRITISH AND EUROPEAN HISTORIANS

Arranged alphabetically according to the subject—not the author—of the study

9.814 **Hutton**, P. H., 'The problem of memory in the historical writings of Philippe Aries', *Hist. and Memory*, IV, 1992, 95–122.

9.815 ——and **Wiener**, R. I., 'Philippe Aries; traditionalism as a vision of history', *Proc. Annual Meeting Western Soc. for French Hist.*, XV, 1988, 388–97.

9.816 **Fubini**, R., 'Renaissance historian; the career of Hans Baron', *J.M.H.*, LXIV, 1992, 541–74.

9.817 **Hankins**, J., 'The "Baron thesis" after forty years', *J. Hist. Ideas*, LVI, 1995, 309–38. See also 'Forum; Hans Baron's Renaissance humanism', *A.H.R.*, CI, 1996, 107–44.

9.818 **Dewar**, K. C., 'Geoffrey Barraclough; from historicism to historical science', *Historian*, LVI, 1994, 449–64.

9.819 **Leventhal**, F. M., *The Last Dissenter. H. N. Brailsford and his World*, 1985. A biography of the journalist/historian, author of *Shelley, Godwin and their Circle* (1913) and of the posthumously published *The Levellers and the English Revolution* (1961).

9.820 **Fraser**, D. (ed.), *Cities, Class and Communication. Essays in Honour of Asa Briggs*, 1990. Includes a profile of Briggs's varied contributions to social history.

9.821 **Huxley**, G., 'The historical scholarship of John Bagnell Bury', *Greek, Roman, and Byzantine Studs.*, XVII, 1976, 81–104.

Herbert Butterfield

9.822 **Brogan**, D. W., 'Sir Herbert Butterfield as a historian; an appreciation' in J. H. Elliott amd H. G. Koenigsberger (eds), *The Diversity of History*, 1970, 1–16.

9.823 **Chadwick**, O., 'Acton and Butterfield', *J. Ecc. Hist.*, XXXVIII, 1987, 386–405.

9.824 **Elton**, G. R., 'Herbert Butterfield and the study of history', *Hist. J.*, XXVII, 1984, 729–43.

9.825 **Hobart**, M., 'History and religion in the thought of Herbert Butterfield'. *J. Hist. Ideas*, XXXII, 1971, 543–54.

9.826 **Parker**, H. T., 'Herbert Butterfield' in S. W. Halperin (ed.), *Some Twentieth-Century Historians. Essays on Eminent Europeans*, Chicago, IL, 1961, 75–101.

9.827 **Thompson**, K. W. (ed.), *Herbert Butterfield. The Ethics of History and Politics*, Washington, DC, 1980.

9.828 **Cheney**, C. R., 'Helen Maud Cam, 1885–1968', *Proc. Brit. Acad.*, LV, 1969, 293–310.

E. H. Carr

9.829 **Davies**, R. W., 'Edward Hallett Carr, 1892–1982'. *Proc. Brit. Acad.*, LXIX, 1983, 473–511.

9.830 **Deutscher**, I., 'E. H. Carr as historian of Soviet Russia', *Soviet Studs.*, VI, 1954–55, 337–50.

9.831 **Howe**, P., The utopian realism of E. H. Carr', *Rev. Internat. Studs.*, XX, 1994, 277–97.

9.832 **Brooke**, C. N. L., 'Christopher Robert Cheney, 1906–87', *Proc. Brit. Acad.*, LXXIII, 1987, 425–46.

9.833 **Floud**, R., 'Words not numbers; John Harold Clapham', *Hist. Today*, XXXIX, 1989, 42–7.

9.834 **Lyons**, M., 'Cobb and the historians' in G. Lewis and C. Lucas (eds), *Beyond the Terror. Essays in French Regional and Local History, 1794–1815*, 1983.

9.835 **Bosher**, J. F., 'Alfred Cobban's view of the Enlightenment', *Studs. in Eighteenth Century Culture*, I, 1971, 37–53.

9.836 **Carpenter**, L. P., *G. D. H. Cole. An Intellectual Biography*, 1973. Looks in particular at his publications and ideas on social theory.

9.837 **Cole**, Margaret, *The Life of G. D. H. Cole*, 1971. A first-hand biography by his widow.

9.838 **Smith**, D. M., 'Benedetto Croce; history and politics'. *J. Contemp. Hist.*, VIII, 1973, 41–61.

9.839 **Weaver**, J. R. H. and **Poole**, A. L.

(eds), *Henry William C. Davis, 1874–1928. A Memoir*, 1933.

Isaac Deutscher

9.840 **Beilharz**, P., 'Isaac Deutscher; history and necessity', *Hist. Political Theory*, VII, 1982, 375–92.

9.841 **Horowitz**, D. (ed.), *Isaac Deutscher. The Man and his Work*, 1971. Part Two deals with Deutscher as historian and theoretician.

9.842 **Labedz**, L., 'Isaac Deutscher; historian, prophet, biographer', *Survey*, XXX, 1988, 33–93.

9.843 **Kirk**, J., *Her Majesty's Historiographer. Gordon Donaldson, 1913–93*, 1996. Includes a bibliography of his writings.

9.844 **Roskell**, J. S., 'John Geronwy Edwards, 1891–1976', *Proc. Brit. Acad.*, LXIV, 1978, 359–96.

G. R. Elton

9.845 **Beer**, B. L., 'G. R. Elton; Tudor champion' in W. L. Arnstein (ed.), *Recent Historians of Great Britain. Essays on the post-1945 Generation*, Ames, IA, 1990, 13–35.

9.846 **Holmes**, C., 'G. R. Elton as a legal historian', *T.R.H.S.*, *6th* ser., VII, 1997, 267–80.

9.847 **Skinner**, Q., 'Sir Geoffrey Elton and the practice of history', *T.R.H.S.*, 6th ser., VII, 1997, 301–16.

9.848 **Wormald**, P., **Gillingham**, J., and **Richmond**, C., 'Elton on the English; a discussion', *T.R.H.S.*, 6th ser., VII, 1997, 317–36.

9.849 **Ashley**, M., 'Sir Charles Firth; a tribute and a reassessment', *History Today*, VII, 1957, 251–6.

9.850 **Kenyon**, J. P., 'Sir Charles Firth and the Oxford school of modern history, 1892–1925' in A. C. Duke and C. A. Tamse (eds), *Clio's Mirror. Historiography in Britain and the Netherlands*, Zutphen, 1985, 163–84.

9.851 **Ogg**, D., *Herbert Fisher, 1865–1940. A Short Biography*, 1947.

9.852 **Southern**, R. W., 'Vivian Hunter Galbraith, 1889–1976', *Proc. Brit. Acad.*, LXIV, 1978, 397–525.

9.853 **Dunk**, H. W. von der, 'Pieter Geyl; history as a form of self expression' in Duke and Tamse (9.850), 185–214.

9.854 **Rowen**, H. H., 'The historical work of Pieter Geyl', *J.M.H.*, XXXVII, 1965, 35–49.

Carlo Ginzberg

9.855 **Cohen**, S., 'Desire for history; historiography, scholarship and the vicarious (on Carlo Ginzberg)', *Storia de Storiog.*, XXX, 1996, 57–76.

9.856 **Martin**, J., 'Journeys to the world of the dead; the work of Carlo Ginzberg', *J. Soc. Hist.*, XXV, 1992, 613–26.

9.857 **Wria**, K., 'The paradoxical Carlo Ginzberg', *Radical Hist. R.*, XXXV, 1986, 80–111.

9.858 **Eyck**, E., *G. P. Gooch. A Study in History and Politics*, 1982. A biographical study of this unashamedly old-fashioned British historian.

9.859 **McDowell**, R. B., *Alice Stopford Green. A Passionate Historian*, 1967. Concentrates on her contributions to Irish history and nationalism.

9.860 **Boughey**, J., *Charles Hadfield. Canal Man and More*, 1998. A two-part book, the first being a short autobiography and the other an assessment of Hadfield's contribution to canal history.

Christopher Hill

9.861 **Dray**, W. H., 'Causes, individuals and ideas in Christopher Hill's interpretation of the English Revolution' in B. Y. Kunze and D. D. Brautigam (eds), *Court, Country and Culture. Essays on Early Modern British History*, Rochester, NY, 1992.

9.862 **Eley**, G. and **Hunt**, W. (eds), *Reviving the English Revolution. Reflections and Elaborations on the Work of Christopher Hill*, 1988. Ten of the essays in this collection are expressly historiographical and consider different facets of Hill's work and its significance.

9.863 **Palmer**, W. G., 'The burden of proof; J. H. Hexter and C. Hill', *J. Brit. Studs.*, XIX, 1979, 122–9.

9.864 **Roberts**, M., 'A nation of prophets; England and Christopher Hill', *Hist. Workshop J.*, XXVII, 1989, 164–73.

9.865 **Phythian-Adams**, C., 'Hoskins's England; a local historian of genius and his theme', *Leics. Arch. and Hist. Soc. Trans.*, LXVI, 1992, 143–59.

9.866 **Thirsk**, Joan, 'W. G. Hoskins, 1908–92', *Proc. Brit. Acad.*, LXXXVII, 1995, 339–54.

9.867 **Colie**, R. L., 'Johann Huizinga and the task of cultural history', *A.H.R.*, LXIX, 1964, 607–30.

9.868 **Pantin**, W. A., 'Ernest Fraser Jacob, 1894–1971', *Proc. Brit. Acad.*, LVIII, 1972, 447–74.

9.869 **Shapiro**, G., 'The many lives of Georges Lefebvre', *A.H.R.*, LXXII, 1967, 502–14.

9.870 **Boureau**, A., *Histoires d'un historien. Kantorwicz*, Paris, 1990. A study of the German Jewish medievalist.

9.871 **Brooke**, C. N. L. (ed.), *David Knowles Remembered*, 1991.

9.872 **Mayr-Harting**, H., 'Karl Leyser, 1920–92', *Proc. Brit. Acad.*, XCIV, 1996.

9.873 **Powicke**, F. M., 'Andrew George Little, 1863–1945', *Proc. Brit. Acad.*, XXXI, 1945, 1–23.

9.874 **Samuel**, R. *et al.*, 'Tim Mason; a memorial', *Hist. Workshop J.*, XXX, 1990, 129–88. A collective tribute to the major British historian of Nazi Germany. Includes a bibliography of Mason's writings.

9.875 **Friguglietti**, J., *Albert Mattiez, historien revolutionnaire, 1874–1932*, Paris, 1974.

A. D. Momigliano

9.876 **Bowersock**, G. W. and **Cornell**, T. J. (eds), *A. D. Momigliano. Studies on Modern Scholarship*, Berkeley, CA, 1994.

9.877 **Brown**, P., 'Arnaldo Dante Momigliano', *Proc. Brit. Acad.*, LXXIV, 1988, 405–42.

9.878 **Christ**, K., 'Arnaldo Momigliano and the history of historiography', *Hist. and Theory*, XXX, 1991, 5–12.

9.879 **Goldsmith**, M., *John Needham, Twentieth-Century Renaissance Man*, Paris, 1995.

9.880 **Robertson**, C. G., 'Sir Charles Oman, 1860–1946', *Proc. Brit. Acad.*, XXXII, 1946, 299–306.

9.881 **Rowse**, A. L., 'Richard Pares, 1902–58', *Proc. Brit. Acad.*, XLVIII, 1962, 345–56.

9.882 **Milsom**, S. F. C., 'Theodore Frank Thomas Plucknett, 1897–1965', *Proc. Brit. Acad.*, LI, 1965, 504–19.

9.883 **Galbraith**, V. H., 'Austin Lane Poole, 1889–1963', *Proc. Brit. Acad.*, XLIX, 1963, 431–40.

9.884 **Berg**, Maxine, *A Woman in History. Eileen Power, 1889–1940*, 1996. A sympathetic study of a pioneer in medieval English social history and one of the first women to occupy a leading position in the historical profession.

9.885 **Melman**, Billie, 'Under the Western historian's eyes. Eileen Power and the early feminist encounter with colonialism', *Hist. Workshop J.*, XLII, 1996, 147–68.

9.886 **Southern**, R. W., 'Sir Maurice Powicke, 1879–1963', *Proc. Brit. Acad.*, L, 1964, 275–304.

9.887 **Powicke**, F. M., 'Three Cambridge scholars; C. W. Previte-Orton, Z. N. Brooke and G. G. Coulton', *Camb. Hist. J.*, IX, 1947–49, 106–16.

9.888 **Birley**, E., 'Sir Ian Archibald Richmond, 1902–65', *Proc. Brit. Acad.*, LII, 1966, 293–302.

9.889 **Winslow**, Barbara *et al.*, 'Women's revolutions; the work of Sheila Rowbotham. A twenty-year assessment', *Radical Hist. R.*, LXIII, 1995, 141–65.

9.890 **Thompson**, P., 'Raphael Samuel, 1934–96; an appreciation', *Oral Hist.*, XXV, 1997, 30–7.

9.891 **Spitzer**, A. B., 'Narrative problems; the case of Simon Schama', *J.M.H.*, LXV, 1993, 176–92.

9.892 **Dyos**, H. J., 'Jack Simmons; an appreciation', *J. Transport Hist.*, n.s., III, 1975–6, 133–44.

9.893 **Bosworth**, R. J. B., 'Dennis Mack Smith and the third Italy', *Internat. Hist. R.*, XII, 1990, 782–92.

9.894 'Hommage à A. Soboul', *Annales Historiques de la Révolution Française*, LIV, 1982, 513–53.

9.895 **Major**, Kathleen, 'Doris Mary Stenton, 1894–1971', *Proc. Brit. Acad.*, LVIII, 1972, 525–35.

9.896 **Stenton**, Doris M., 'Frank Merry Stenton, 1880–1967', *Proc. Brit. Acad.*, LIV, 1968, 315–423.

9.897 **Whitelock**, Dorothy, 'Frank Merry

Stenton', *E.H.R.*, LXXXIV, 1969, 1–11.

9.898 **Mitchell**, J. *et al.*, 'Lawrence Stone as seen by others' in A. L. Beier *et al.* (eds), *The First Modern Society. Essays in English History in Honour of Lawrence Stone*, 1989, 1–30. See also, in the same volume, 'Epilogue; Lawrence Stone as seen by himself', 575–95.

9.899 **Sanders**, C. R., *Lytton Strachey. His Mind and Art*, New Haven, CT, 1957. One of the leading popularisers of history.

9.900 **Powicke**, F. M., 'James Tait, 1863–1944', *Proc. Brit. Acad.*, XXX, 1944, 1–32.

9.901 **Cole**, R., *A. J. P. Taylor. The Traitor within the Gates*, 1993. An intellectual biography of the controversial dissenting historian, with its eight chapters concentrating on the writer's principal publications.

9.902 **Fair**, J. D., *Harold Temperley. A Scholar and Romantic in the Public Realm*, Newark, DE, 1992.

9.903 **Chartres**, J. and **Hey**, D. (eds), *English Rural Society, 1500–1800. Essays in Honour of Joan Thirsk*, 1990. In their introduction the editors take stock of Joan Thirsk's distinctive blending of the influences of the 'Leicester school' and the 'Tawney tradition'. Alan Everitt offers a personal appreciation.

9.904 **Douglas**, D. C., 'Alexander Hamilton Thompson, 1873–1952', *Proc. Brit. Acad.*, XXXVIII, 1952, 317–31.

E. P. Thompson

9.905 **Kaye**, H. J. and **McLelland**, K. (eds), *E. P. Thompson. Critical Perspectives*, 1990. A collection of essays from literary specialists, philosophers and sociologists as well as historians which attempts an overall assessment of Thompson's significance.

9.906 **Koditschek**, T., 'A tale of two Thompsons', *Radical Hist. R.*, LVI, 1993, 69–84. E.P. and F.M.L.

9.907 **McCann**, G., *Theory and History. The Political Thought of E. P. Thompson*, 1997. Examines Thompson's placing in British communism and historical materialism and the socialist humanism of his writings.

9.908 **Palmer**, B. D., *Objections and Oppositions. The Histories and Politics of E. P. Thompson*, 1994. A lively, committed study of Thompson as a creatively dissenting voice.

9.909 **McNeill**, W. H., *Arnold Toynbee. A Life*, 1989. One renowned generalist surveys another.

G. M. Trevelyan

9.910 **Cannadine**, D., *G. M. Trevelyan. A Life in History*, 1992. A full-length study of the career of this latter-day Whig historian and of the poetics of his approach to, and practice of, his subject.

9.911 **Clark**, G. N., 'George Macaulay Trevelyan, 1876–1962', *Proc. Brit. Acad.*, XLIX, 1963, 375–86.

9.912 **Hernon**, J. M., 'The last Whig historian and consensus history; George Macaulay Trevelyan, 1876–1962', *A.H.R.*, LXXXI, 1976, 66–97.

9.913 **Moorman**, Mary, *George Macaulay Trevelyan*, 1980. Written by Trevelyan's daughter, this book is best on his patriotism and romantic imagination.

9.914 **Winkler**, H. R., 'George Macaulay Trevelyan' in S. W. Halperin (ed.), *Some Twentieth-Century Historians*, Chicago, IL, 1961, 31–55.

9.915 **Cole**, Margaret (ed.), *The Webbs and their Work*, 1949. Includes a consideration of the husband and wife team as historians.

9.916 **Johnson**, Elizabeth, 'C. V. Wedgwood and her historiography', *Contemporary Rev.*, CCI, 1962, 208–14.

9.917 **Mathias**, P., 'Charles Wilson, 1914–91. A retrospect for a historian', *J. European Ec.H.*, XXII, 1993, 143–54.

9.918 **Rothblatt**, S., 'G. M. Young; England's historian of culture', *Vict. Studs.*, XXII, 1978–79, 413–29.

INDIVIDUAL NORTH AMERICAN HISTORIANS

9.919 **Fullbrook**, Mary and **Skocpol**, Theda, 'Destined pathways; the historical sociology of Perry Anderson' in Theda Skocpol (ed.), *Vision and Method in Historical Sociology*, 1984.

9.920 **Goodard**, L. (ed.), *Harry Elmer Barnes, Learned Crusader. The New History in Action*, Colorado Springs, CO, 1968.

Charles Beard

9.921 **Beale**, H. K. (ed.), *Charles A. Beard*, Lexington, KY, 1954. Includes essays by Harold Laski, Richard Hofstadter and Merle Curti.

9.922 **Benson**, L., *Turner and Beard. American Historical Writing Reconsidered*, Glencoe, IL, 1960. Inconsistencies in the marrying of economic interpretation and economic determinism are explored.

9.923 **Berg**, E., *The Historical Thinking of Charles Beard*, Stockholm, 1957. A brief study of Beard's relativism. Bibliography.

9.924 **Kennedy**, T. C., 'Charles A. Beard and the "court historians"', *Historian*, XXV, 1963, 439–50.

9.925 **Marcell**, D. W., 'Charles Beard; civilisation and the revolt against empiricism', *Am. Q.*, XXI, 1969, 65–86.

9.926 **Mieland**, J. W., 'The historical relativism of Charles A. Beard', *Hist. and Theory*, XII, 1973, 405–13.

Mary Beard

9.927 **Cott**, Nancy F. (ed.), *A Woman Making History. Mary Beard through her Letters*, New Haven, CT, 1991.

9.928 **Lebsock**, Suzanne, 'Reading Mary Beard', *Reviews in Am. Hist.*, XVII, 1989, 324–39.

9.929 **Turoff**, Barbara K., *Mary Beard as a Force in History*, Dayton, OH, 1979.

Carl Becker

9.930 **Brown**, R. E., *Carl Becker on History and the American Revolution*, East Lansing, MI, 1970.

9.931 **Snyder**, R. L. (ed.), *Detachment and the Writing of history. Essays and Letters of Carl L. Becker*, Ithaca, NY, 1967.

9.932 **Strout**, C., *The Pragmatic Revolt in American History. Carl Becker and Charles Beard*, New Haven, CT, 1958.

Explores the revolt against formalism in the 1930s and 1940s.

9.933 **Wilkins**, B. T., *Carl Becker. A Biographical Study in American Intellectual History*, Boston, MA, 1961. Bibliography, 231–42.

9.934 **Diggins**, J. P., 'The perils of naturalism; some reflections on Daniel J. Boorstin's approach to American history', *Am. Q.*, XXIII, 1971, 153–80.

9.935 ——'Consciousness and ideology in American history; the burden of Daniel J. Boorstin', *A.H.R.*, LXXVI, 1971, 99–118.

9.936 **Dawidoff**, R., 'Commager's *The American Mind*; a reconsideration', *Reviews in Am. Hist.*, XII, 1984, 449–62.

9.937 **Andrews**, W. L. (ed.), *Critical Essays on W. E. B. Du Bois*, Boston, MA, 1985. One of the leading Afro-American historians of the twentieth century.

9.938 **Marable**, M., *W. E. B. Du Bois. Black Radical Democrat*, Boston, MA, 1986.

9.939 **Zock**, Hetty, *A Psychology of Ultimate Concern. Erik H. Erikson's Contribution to the Psychology of Religion*, Amsterdam, 1990.

9.940 **Lehmann**, H. (ed.), *Felix Gilbert as Scholar and Teacher*, Washington, DC, 1992.

9.941 **Baker**, Susan S., *Radical Beginnings. Richard Hoftstadter and the 1930s*, Westport, CT, 1985. Concentrates on his early career as a key to understanding his contribution to American historiography. Bibliography, 253–60.

9.942 **Singal**, D. J., 'Beyond consensus; Richard Hofstadter and American historiography', *A.H.R.*, LXXXIX, 1984, 976–1004.

9.943 **Cudjoe**, S. and **Cain**, W. (eds), *C. L. James. His Intellectual Legacies*, Amherst, MA, 1995. One of the founding fathers of modern black history.

9.944 **Hacohen**, M. H., 'Leonard Krieger; historicization and political engagement in intellectual history', *Hist. and Theory*, XXV, 1996, 80–129.

9.945 **Levine**, M., 'A Marxist critique; Leonard Krieger', *Storia de Storiog.*, XII, 1987, 44–71.

9.946 **Costello**, P., 'William McNeill's

ecological mythistory. Toward an ambiguous future', *Hist. Reflections*, XVIII, 1992, 99–119.

Perry Miller

9.947 **Hollinger**, D. A., 'Perry Miller and philosophical history', *Hist. and Theory*, VII, 1968, 189–202.

9.948 **Reinitz**, R., 'Perry Miller and recent American historiography', *Bull. Brit. Ass. Am. Studs.*, VIII, 1964, 27–35.

9.949 **Marsden**, G. M., 'Perry Miller's rehabilitation of the Puritans; a critique', *Church Hist.*, XXXIX, 1970, 91–105.

9.950 **Pfitzer**, G. M., *Samuel Eliot Morison's Historical World. In Quest of a New Parkman*, Boston, MA, 1991.

9.951 **Hughes**, T. P. and Agatha C. (eds), *Lewis Mumford. Public Intellectual*, New York, 1990.

9.952 **Hall**, H. L., *V. L. Parrington. Through the Avenue of Art*, Kent, OH, 1994. A full-length portrait of Parrington (1871–1929), historian of American culture.

9.953 **Hampher-Monk**, I., 'Review article; political languages in time – the work of J. G. A. Pocock', *Brit. J. Pol. Sci.*, XIV, 1984, 89–116.

9.954 **Wes**, M. A., *Michael Rostovtzeff. Historian in Exile. Russian Roots in an American Context*, Stuttgart, 1990.

9.955 **Depoe**, S. P., *Arthur M. Schlesinger Jr and the Ideological History of American Liberalism*, Tuscaloosa, AL, 1994.

9.956 **Roper**, J. H., *Coner vann Woodward, Southerner*, Athens, GA, 1987.

INDEX
AUTHORS, EDITORS, AND COMPILERS

The first number refers to the section, the second to the item within it